序 言

　　「**高中英語聽力測驗**」是「繁星推薦入學」、「個人申請入學」及「考試入學」之招生檢定項目或納爲「個人申請入學」審查資料之一，許多大學也已經把測驗成績列爲入學標準，其重要性可見一斑。考試成績分爲四個等級：A（幾乎完全聽懂）、B（大致聽懂）、C（約略聽懂）、F（僅能聽懂少部分），一年有兩次機會報考，成績有效期限爲3年。5成以上的校系，要求學生至少要有B級的成績。

　　「**高中英語聽力測驗**」，包括「**看圖辨義**」、「**對答**」、「**簡短對話**」及「**短文聽解**」四種題型，詞彙範圍以高中英文常用 4,500 字詞爲主，可參考大考中心高中英文參考詞彙表第一至第四級。測驗內容涵蓋生活化、實用性之主題，情境包括家庭、校園、公共場所、社交場合等。

　　103 學年度在「**看圖辨義**」上，有了新的改變：① 單圖變成四張圖 ② 複選題，難度也因此提高。爲了使各高中生能提早適應新的考題，學習出版公司率先推出最新題型的「**高中英語聽力測驗題本①**」，並搭配「**高中英文聽力測驗詳解①**」一起使用。

　　「**高中英語聽力測驗題本①**」共十回，取材內容生活化，符合大考中心出題方向，題目眾多，提供莘莘學子練習聽力的機會。建議同學在做每一回測驗時，訓練自

己在四十分鐘內作答完畢，因為實際考試時間約六十分鐘（含說明時間），讓自己習慣在較短的時間內寫完，考試時會更得心應手。寫完題目，要看「**高中英語聽力測驗詳解①**」，把錯的題目，不會的單字片語完全搞懂，再聽一次。每題都有詳細的中文說明和註釋，方便同學複習常考的單字和片語。複習時，將不會的題目朗讀一遍，到真正考試時就輕鬆了。本書第十回是附贈的「**103 年高中英語聽力測驗參考試卷**」，讓同學清楚了解英聽考試的方向，並仔細研讀本書詳解，必能在英聽測驗獲得高分。

　　要在「聽力測驗」得高分，就是要不斷地練習，培養出語感，平時聽 MP3 練習時，**一定要養成「先看選項，再聽題目」的習慣**。看選項的速度一定要超前，如果哪一道題目聽不懂，就必須放棄，立刻看下一題的選項，這樣才能掌握答題的重點，及縮短做答的時間。千萬不要等聽完題目，再看選項，否則整個聽力考試，都會失敗。

　　編輯好書是「學習」一貫的宗旨。本書在編審及校對的每一階段，均力求完善，但恐有疏漏之處，誠盼各界先進不吝批評指正。

編者　謹識

高中英聽測驗模擬試題 ① 詳解

一、看圖辨義：第一部分

For question number 1, please look at picture 1.

1. (**B**) Kitty is soaking in the bathtub.　She's also listening to
music and reading a book.

　　凱蒂正在浴缸裡泡澡。她同時也正聽著音樂和看一本書。

　　　＊soak〔sok〕*v.* 浸泡　　　bathtub〔'bæθ,tʌb〕*n.* 浴缸

For question number 2, please look at picture 2.

2. (**B**) A boy is in a pet store.　He just bought two goldfish.

　　一位男孩在寵物店裡。他剛剛買了兩隻金魚。

　　　＊pet〔pɛt〕*n.* 寵物　　　goldfish〔'gold,fɪʃ〕*n.* 金魚

For question number 3, please look at picture 3.

3. (**B**) A rabbit is running though an open field. An eagle is about to snatch the rabbit in its claws. 一隻兔子正跑過一個空曠的田野。一隻老鷹正準備用牠的爪子抓那隻兔子。

　　* *be about to V*. 正要~　　snatch〔snætʃ〕*v.* 抓住
　　claw〔klɔ〕*n.* 爪子

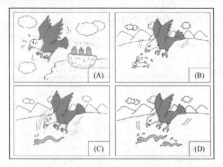

For question number 4, please look at picture 4.

4. (**A**) A couple is seated on an airplane. A flight attendant has just offered them something to drink.

　　一對男女正坐在飛機上。一位空服員剛剛提供了他們一些飲料。

　　* couple〔'kʌpl̩〕*n.* 一對男女　　*be seated* 坐 (= *sit*)
　　flight attendant 空服員　　offer〔'ɔfɚ〕*v.* 提供

一、看圖辨義：第二部分

For question number 5, please look at picture 5.

5. (**B 、 C**) Which TWO of the following are true about the
people in the picture?
關於圖片中的人，下列哪兩項敘述為眞？

   A. Both boys are laughing at the girl.
兩個男孩都在嘲笑那個女孩。

   B. The girl has fallen down. 那個女孩跌倒了。

   C. One boy is laughing at the girl.
有一個男孩正在嘲笑那個女孩。

   D. The girl is pointing at the boy.
那個女孩正指著那個男孩。

   * *laugh at* 嘲笑　　*fall down* 跌倒
point〔pɔɪnt〕v. 指　　*point at* 指著

For question number 6, please look at picture 6.

6. (**C 、 D**) Which TWO of the following are true about the
people in the picture?
關於圖片中的人，下列哪兩項敘述為眞？

   A. There are three boys in the
picture. 圖片裡有三個男孩。

   B. There are three girls in the
picture. 圖片裡有三個女孩。

   C. There is one girl in the picture.
圖片裡有一個女孩。

   D. There are two boys in the picture.
圖片裡有兩個男孩。

For question number 7, please look at picture 7.

7. (**A**、**B**) Which TWO of the following are true about the woman? 關於這位女士，下列哪兩項敘述為眞？

    A. She is applying cosmetics.
       她正在化妝。
    B. She is styling her hair.
       她正在設計頭髮造型。
    C. She is watching television. 她正在看電視。
    D. She is talking on the phone. 她正在講電話。

  * apply ﹝ ə'plaɪ ﹞ v. 塗；抹
    cosmetics ﹝ kɔs'mɛtɪks ﹞ n. pl. 化妝品
    style ﹝ staɪl ﹞ v. 設計；把…製成某種樣式

For question number 8, please look at picture 8.

8. (**C**、**D**) Which TWO of the following are true about the children? 關於這些小孩，下列哪兩項敘述為眞？

    A. They are playing a game.
       他們正在玩遊戲。
    B. They are studying for an
       exam. 他們正在準備考試。
    C. They are wearing costumes.
       他們正穿著造型服裝。
    D. They are celebrating Halloween.
       他們正在慶祝萬聖節。

  * costume ﹝'kɑstjum ﹞ n. 服裝；戲服
    Halloween ﹝,hælo'in ﹞ n. 萬聖節前夕

For question number 9, please look at picture 9.

9. (**A** 、 **D**) Which TWO of the following are true about the people in the picture?

關於圖片中的人，下列哪兩項敘述為眞？

　　A. The girl is crying. 這女孩在哭泣。

　　B. The parents are happy. 這對父母很開心。

　　C. The mother is hitting the girl.
　　　 這位媽媽正在打這位女孩。

　　D. The father is yelling at the girl.
　　　 這位爸爸正對著女孩吼叫。

　* yell〔'jɛl〕v. 吼叫

For question number 10, please look at picture 10.

10. (**A** 、 **C**) Which TWO of the following are true about the car?

關於這輛汽車，下列哪兩項敘述為眞？

　　A. It doesn't have a roof.
　　　 它沒有車頂。

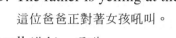

　　B. It has only two seats.
　　　 它只有兩個座位。

　　C. It has four seats. 它有四個座位。

　　D. It is missing a tire. 它少了一個輪胎。

　* roof〔ruf〕n. 車頂　　　seat〔sit〕n. 座位
　　 be missed~ 缺少~　　　tire〔taɪr〕n. 輪胎

二、對答

11. (**C**) Does your mother have a career? 你的媽媽有工作嗎？

　　A. Yes, she will be here. 是的，她會來這裡。

B. He has worked for three years. 他已經工作三年了。
C. No, she is a housewife. 不，她是一位家庭主婦。
D. She is 40 years old. 她今年四十歲。

* career〔kə'rɪr〕*n.* 職業；工作
   housewife〔'haʊs,waɪf〕*n.* 家庭主婦

12. (**B**) Where is William from? 威廉是從哪裡來的？

A. I think he is in the bathroom. 我想他在浴室裡。
B. He is from Canada. 他來自加拿大。
C. That's him over there. 在那裡的就是他。
D. William will be here tomorrow.
   威廉明天會到這裡來。

* bathroom〔'bæθ,rum〕*n.* 浴室
   Canada〔'kænədə〕*n.* 加拿大　　***over there*** 在那裡

13. (**C**) Do you have any pets? 你有養寵物嗎？

A. I love animals. 我超愛動物。
B. No, I have a rabbit. 沒有，我有一隻兔子。
C. Yes, I have a dog and two cats.
   有，我有一隻狗和兩隻貓。
D. I am a vegetarian. 我是素食主義者。

* vegetarian〔,vɛdʒə'tɛrɪən〕*n.* 素食主義者

14. (**B**) Did you enjoy the meal? 你喜歡這頓飯嗎？

A. We will have dinner together. 我們將一起吃晚餐。
B. Yes, it was delicious. 是的，很好吃。
C. Where would you like to go? 你想要去哪裡？
D. I am hungry. 我餓了。

* enjoy〔ɪn'dʒɔɪ〕*v.* 享受；喜歡　　meal〔mil〕*n.* 一餐

15. (**A**) Have you seen any good movies lately?

你最近有看什麼好電影嗎？

A. Not lately. 最近沒有。

B. They are at the movies. 他們在看電影。

C. I can afford it. 我可以負擔得起。

D. Thanks but maybe next time. 謝謝，也許下次吧。

* lately〔'letlɪ〕*adv.* 最近　　*the movies* 電影的放映；一場電影
be at the movies 在看電影　　afford〔ə'ford〕*v.* 負擔得起

16. (**D**) How many students are in your class?

你們班上有多少個學生？

A. He is the best teacher of all time.

他是有史以來最棒的老師。

B. I was sleeping. 我當時正在睡覺。

C. Several students were absent today.

今天有好幾個學生缺席。

D. Thirty-six, including me. 36個，包括我。

* *of all time* 有史以來　　absent〔'æbsn̩t〕*adj.* 缺席的
including〔ɪn'kludɪŋ〕*prep.* 包括

17. (**C**) Is that your sister over there? 在那裡的那位是你的姊姊嗎？

A. No, I have two sisters. 不，我有兩個姊妹。

B. My cousin will be here soon. 我表哥很快就會到這裡。

C. Yes, that's her. 是的，是她。

D. I am not sure if you can see me.

我不確定你是否能見到我。

* cousin〔'kʌzn̩〕*n.* 表（堂）兄弟姊妹

18. (**B**) How did you do on the test? 你考試考得如何？

A. I took the test last week. 我上週參加了考試。

B. We won't know the results until tomorrow.
   我們要到明天才會知道成績。

C. I'm sure you did fine. 我確定你考得很好。

D. I studied all night. 我讀了整晚的書。

* *not~until*… 直到…才~
   results〔rɪ'zʌlts〕*n. pl.* 結果;成績

19. (**C**) What is your favorite sport? 你最喜歡的運動是什麼?

A. He is a good sport. 他是一個輸得起的人。

B. Mind your manners. 請注意你的禮貌。

C. Basketball. 籃球。

D. Sure, you can play. 當然,你可以打。

* sport〔sport〕*n.* 光明磊落的人
   a good sport 輸得起的人   mind〔maɪnd〕*v.* 注意
   manners〔'mænɚz〕*n. pl.* 禮貌;規矩

20. (**B**) How's the weather? 天氣如何?

A. I am feeling positive. 我覺得很確定。

B. Cloudy and cold. 多雲而且很冷。

C. Don't forget your umbrella. 不要忘了你的傘。

D. I will be there if the weather is nice.
   如果天氣好的話,我會去那裡。

* positive〔'pɑzətɪv〕*adj.* 確信的;有把握的
   cloudy〔'klaʊdɪ〕*adj.* 多雲的

三、簡短對話

For question 21, you will listen to a short conversation.

W:Mr. Chang is going to retire at the end of the year, isn't he? 張先生年底就要退休了,不是嗎?

M : That's what I heard, but you never know. He's a stubborn old man and a workaholic. He might hang on until he kicks the bucket. 聽說是這樣，但很難說。他是個固執的老頭，又是個工作狂。也許他會堅持到死翹翹爲止。

* retire〔rɪˋtaɪr〕*v.* 退休　　*at the end of* 在…結束時
You never know. 世事難料；很難說。
stubborn〔ˋstʌbən〕*adj.* 固執的
workaholic〔͵wɜkəˋhɑlɪk〕*n.* 工作狂
hang on 堅持　　kick〔kɪk〕*v.* 踢
bucket〔ˋbʌkɪt〕*n.* 水桶　　*kick the bucket* 過世；死翹翹

21.（**B**）Q : What does the man mean? 這位男士是什麼意思？
　　　A. Mr. Chang has a drinking problem.
　　　　張先生有酗酒的問題。
　　　B. Mr. Chang may or may not be ready to retire.
　　　　張先生可能，也可能還沒準備好要退休。
　　　C. Mr. Chang likes to kick things. 張先生喜歡踢東西。
　　　D. Mr. Chang will retire next year instead.
　　　　張先生會改在明年退休。

　　* *drinking problem* 飲酒問題；酗酒
　　instead〔ɪnˋstɛd〕*adv.* 反而；卻；改爲

For question 22, you will listen to a short conversation.

W : How's your brother adjusting to life in the Marine Corps?
　　你弟弟在海軍陸戰隊的生活適應得如何？

M : He's doing fine. 他還蠻順利的。

W : Will he be deployed overseas? 他會被部署在海外嗎？

M：Actually, he's in the Middle East right now.　He calls home on weekends and sends an occasional e-mail.

事實上，他現在在中東。他週末會打電話回家，偶爾傳個電子郵件回來。

* adjust〔ə'dʒʌst〕v. 適應 < to >　　marine〔mə'rin〕adj. 海洋的
corps〔kor〕n. 軍團；…隊　　*the Marine Corps* 海軍陸戰隊
do fine 做得好；順利 (= *do well*)
deploy〔dɪ'plɔɪ〕v. 部署　　overseas〔'ovɚ'siz〕adv. 在海外
actually〔'æktʃʊəlɪ〕adv. 實際上　　*the Middle East* 中東
occasional〔ə'keʒənḷ〕adj. 偶爾的
e-mail〔'i,mel〕n. 電子郵件

22. (**C**) Q：Where is the man's brother now?

這位男士的弟弟現在在哪裡？

A. At home. 在家裡。

B. At an Internet café. 在網咖。

C. Overseas. 在海外。

D. At sea. 在海上。

* *Internet café* 網咖　　*at sea* 在海上；在航海中

For question 23, you will listen to a short conversation.

W：That girl looks familiar.　Isn't that your ex-girlfriend?

那個女孩看起來很面熟。那不是你的前女友嗎？

M：No, it isn't.　Actually, Tabitha is a brunette and that girl is a redhead.　But I have to agree, she looks a lot like Tabitha. 不，不是。事實上，泰碧莎是褐髮，而那個女孩是紅髮。不過我也有同感，她看起來真的很像泰碧莎。

　* familiar〔 fə'mɪljɚ 〕*adj.* 熟悉的
　　ex-〔 ɛks 〕*adj.* 前任的；以前的
　　brunette〔 bru'nɛt 〕*n.* 深褐色頭髮的人
　　redhead〔'rɛd,hɛd 〕*n.* 紅髮的人
　　agree〔 ə'gri 〕*v.* 有同感；同意

23.（**D**）Q：Who are the speakers looking at?　說話者正在看誰？
　　　A. Tabitha.　泰碧莎。
　　　B. Tabitha's twin sister.　泰碧莎的雙胞胎妹妹。
　　　C. A girl with brunette hair.　一個褐色頭髮的女孩。
　　　D. A stranger.　一個陌生人。
　　　* twin〔 twɪn 〕*adj.* 雙胞胎的　　　stranger〔'strendʒɚ 〕*n.* 陌生人

For question 24, you will listen to a short conversation.

　　W：What did you think of Harry's comedy routine?
　　　　你覺得哈瑞的喜劇節目如何？
　　M：I laughed so hard I almost couldn't breathe.
　　　　我笑得太用力了，差一點無法呼吸。
　　　* *think of* 認爲；覺得　　comedy〔'kɑmədɪ 〕*n.* 喜劇
　　　routine〔 ru'tin 〕*n.* 固定節目；例行公事
　　　hard〔 hɑrd 〕*adv.* 激烈地　　breathe〔 brið 〕*v.* 呼吸

24.（**A**）Q：What does the man mean?　這位男士是什麼意思？
　　　A. The routine was funny.　這個節目很好笑。
　　　B. Harry made him sick.　哈利使他覺得很噁心。
　　　C. The woman is boring.　這位女士很無聊。
　　　D. He doesn't care for comedy.　他不喜歡喜劇。
　　　* funny〔'fʌnɪ 〕*adj.* 好笑的
　　　sick〔 sɪk 〕*adj.* 生病的；噁心想吐的　　*care for* 喜歡

For questions 25 and 26, you will listen to a short conversation.

M : Hi Linda, it's Bob. We need to discuss the budget for next month.

嗨，琳達，我是鮑伯。我們得討論一下下個月的預算。

W : What's the problem, Bob? 有什麼問題嗎，鮑伯？

M : Some of the numbers don't agree. 有些數字無法吻合。

W : I'm afraid my schedule is pretty full this week, Bob.

我這星期的行程恐怕很滿耶，鮑伯。

M : It won't take long, I promise. 不會太久的，我保證。

W : Give my secretary a call next week and she'll set something up. 你下個星期打電話給我的秘書，她會安排的。

* budget〔'bʌdʒɪt〕*n.* 預算　　number〔'nʌmbɚ〕*n.* 數字
agree〔ə'gri〕*v.* 一致；相符　***I'm afraid***… 恐怕…
schedule〔'skɛdʒul〕*n.* 時間表；行程
take〔tek〕*v.* 花費（時間）　　promise〔'prɑmɪs〕*v.* 保證
give sb. a call 打電話給某人　　secretary〔'sɛkrə,tɛrɪ〕*n.* 秘書
set up 安排；策劃

25. (**B**) Q : What does the woman mean? 這位女士是什麼意思？

　　A. Bob is not very good at math. 鮑伯不太擅長數學。

　　B. Her secretary is in charge of her schedule.

　　　 她的秘書負責她的行程。

　　C. She is afraid of Bob. 她很怕鮑伯。

　　D. The budget is Bob's problem. 預算是鮑伯的問題。

　　　* ***be good at*** 擅長　　***in charge of*** 負責管理
　　　be afraid of 害怕

26. (**B**) Q : What does Bob want to do with Linda?

　　　　鮑伯要和琳達一起做什麼？

A. Revise his schedule. 修改他的行程。

B. Discuss the budget. 討論預算。

C. Fire her secretary. 開除她的秘書。

D. Make his promise. 許下他的承諾。

* revise〔rɪ'vaɪz〕v. 修正；修改　　fire〔faɪr〕v. 開除

make a promise 許下諾言

For questions 27 and 28, you will listen to a short conversation.

M：Are you ready to go? Our reservation is at eight-thirty.

　　妳準備好要走了嗎？我們的預約時間是八點三十分。

W：Well, the babysitter hasn't arrived. We can't leave until she gets here. 嗯，褓姆還沒到。我們要等到她來才能離開。

M：Well, if we're more than 10 minutes late, we'll lose our reservation and have to wait at least another hour.

　　嗯，如果我們遲到超過十分鐘，我們的預約會被取消，那就

　　至少得再等一小時。

W：We still have plenty of time. 我們時間還很多。

M：No, we don't. It's ten after eight now. It's a 20-minute drive into the city if traffic is good, but it's Saturday night, dear. If we leave right now, we might make it in time.

　　不，沒有。現在已經八點十分了。如果交通順暢的話，開車進

　　市區要二十分鐘，但親愛的，現在是星期六晚上。如果我們現

　　在離開，也許可以及時趕到。

W：Oh, I think that's her at the door. 噢，我想在門口的是她。

M：I'll start the car. 我去發動車子。

* reservation〔,rɛzə'veʃən〕 n. 預訂
  babysitter〔'bebɪ,sɪtɚ〕 n. 臨時褓姆　　*at least* 至少
  plenty of 很多　　drive〔draɪv〕 n. 車程
  make it 成功；辦到；到達　　*in time* 及時
  at the door 在門口　　start〔stɑrt〕 v. 使起動；發動

27.（**D**）Q：Where are these people? 這兩個人在哪裡？

　　A. They're in a restaurant. 他們在餐廳裡。
　　B. They're at the bank. 他們在銀行裡。
　　C. They're on a cruise ship. 他們在遊艇上。
　　D. They're at home. 他們在家裡。

　　* cruise〔kruz〕 n. 巡航；漫遊　　*cruise ship* 遊艇

28.（**B**）Q：Who or what are these people waiting for?
　　　　這兩個人在等誰或等待什麼？

　　A. They are waiting for dinner to be served.
　　　　他們在等晚餐上菜。
　　B. They are waiting for the babysitter to arrive.
　　　　他們在等褓姆來。
　　C. They are waiting to make a reservation.
　　　　他們在等著預訂。
　　D. They are waiting for the man to start the car.
　　　　他們在等這位男士發動車子。

　　* *wait for* 等待　　serve〔sɝv〕 v. 供應（飯菜）；端上
　　make a reservation 預訂

For questions 29 and 30, you will listen to a short conversation.

　M：Excuse me, but I missed the announcement. Could you
　　　tell me why the flight has been delayed?
　　　對不起，但是我沒聽見廣播。你可以告訴我班機為什麼延誤嗎？

W : Yes, sir. The flight has been delayed due to weather conditions in Singapore.

好的，先生。飛機是因為新加坡的天氣狀況而延誤。

M : How long do we have to wait? 我們必須等多久？

W : The flight has been delayed for 30 minutes, sir.

飛機已經延誤 30 分鐘了，先生。

M : When can we board the plane? 我們何時可以登機？

W : The new departure time is one-fifteen and boarding time is usually twenty minutes prior to take-off. So, ten more minutes and passengers will be seated on the aircraft.

新的出發時間是一點十五分，而登機時間通常是起飛前 20 分鐘。

所以，再過 10 分鐘，乘客們就可以坐上飛機了。

* miss〔 mɪs 〕*v.* 錯過
announcement〔 ə'naʊnsmənt 〕*n.* 宣布；廣播
flight〔 flaɪt 〕*n.* 班機　　delay〔 dɪ'le 〕*v.* 延誤
due to 因為（ = *because of* ）　　condition〔 kən'dɪʃən 〕*n.* 情況
Singapore〔'sɪŋgə,por 〕*n.* 新加坡
board〔 bord 〕*v.* 登上（飛機、船、火車等）
departure〔 dɪ'partʃ⋄ 〕*n.* 啟程；出發
boarding time 登機時間　　*prior to* 在～之前（ = *before* ）
take-off〔'tek,ɔf 〕*n.* 起飛　　passenger〔'pæsṇdʒ⋄ 〕*n.* 乘客
be seated 坐（ = *sit* ）　　aircraft〔'ɛr,kræft 〕*n.* 飛機

29.（ **C** ）Q : When does this conversation take place?

這段對話發生在何時？

A. From the previous day. 從前一天開始。

B. At one o'clock. 在一點鐘時。

C. At 12:45. 在 12 點 45 分。　D. In Keelung. 在基隆。

* *take place* 發生

30. (**B**) Q : Where does this conversation take place?
　　　　　 這段對話發生在何處？
　　　 A. Singapore. 新加坡。
　　　 B. At an airport departure gate. 機場的出境大門。
　　　 C. On an airplane. 在飛機上。
　　　 D. In a weather balloon. 在觀測氣象用的氣球上。

　　　 * airport〔'ɛr،port〕*n.* 機場　　 gate〔get〕*n.* 大門
　　　　 balloon〔bə'lun〕*n.* 氣球
　　　　 weather balloon 觀測氣象用的氣球

四、短文聽解

Questions 31 and 32 are based on the following report.

　　　 There is much speculation as to the origin of origami.
While Japan seems to have the most extensive tradition,
there is evidence of an independent tradition of
paper-folding in China, as well as in Germany and Spain
among other places. However, because of the problems
associated with preserving origami, there is very little
direct evidence of its age or origins, aside from references
in published material.

　　　 關於摺紙術的來源有許多推測。雖然日本似乎有最廣泛的傳
統，但也有證據顯示，中國有著獨立的摺紙傳統，還有德國、西
班牙等地。然而，因為有保存摺紙術的相關問題，所以除了出版
品中有提到之外，它的年代或起源很少有直接的證據。

** ——————————————————————

　　　 speculation〔،spɛkjə'leʃən〕*n.* 推測
　　　 as to 關於　　 origin〔'ɔrədʒɪn〕*n.* 起源

origami〔‚ɔrə'gɑmɪ〕*n.* 摺紙術；摺紙手工品【日文】

while〔hwaɪl〕*conj.* 雖然　　extensive〔ɪk'stɛnsɪv〕*adj.* 廣泛的

tradition〔trə'dɪʃən〕*n.* 傳統　　evidence〔'ɛvədəns〕*n.* 證據

independent〔‚ɪndɪ'pɛndənt〕*adj.* 獨立的　　fold〔fold〕*v.* 摺

as well as 以及　　Germany〔'dʒɝmənɪ〕*n.* 德國

Spain〔spen〕*n.* 西班牙　　***among other things*** 等等

be associated with 與…有關　　preserve〔prɪ'zɝv〕*v.* 保存

direct〔də'rɛkt〕*adj.* 直接的

reference〔'rɛfərəns〕*n.* 提及；參考；指涉

age〔edʒ〕*n.* 時期；年代　　***aside from*** 除了…之外

publish〔'pʌblɪʃ〕*v.* 出版　　material〔mə'tɪrɪəl〕*n.* 資料

published material 出版物；印刷品

31. (**B**) What is origami? "origami" 是什麼？

    A. A type of speculation. 一種推測。

    B. A form of paper-folding. 一種摺紙的形式。

    C. A tradition of preservation. 一種保存的傳統。

    D. A reference to publishing. 一種出版的指涉。

    * preservation〔‚prɛzə'veʃən〕*n.* 保存
      publishing〔'pʌblɪʃɪŋ〕*n.* 出版業

32. (**D**) Where did origami originate? 摺紙術起源於何處？

    A. Japan. 日本。　　　　B. China. 中國。

    C. Germany. 德國。

    D. There is not enough evidence to say.

      沒有足夠的證據可說。

    * originate〔ə'rɪdʒə‚net〕*v.* 起源於

Questions 33 and 34 are based on the following report.

According to a study of over 300 adults by the

German Society of Ophthalmology (GSO), on average,

men cry once every month; women cry at least five times
per month, especially before and during the menstrual
cycle when crying can increase up to five times the
normal rate, often without obvious reasons (such as
depression or sadness). According to the GSO, which
has collated different scientific studies on crying, women
cry on average between 30 and 64 times a year, and men
cry on average between six and 17 times per year.

　　根據「德國眼科協會」一項針對超過三百名成年人的研究，
男性每月平均哭一次；女性每個月至少哭五次，特別是在經期
前和經期中，哭的次數可能增加爲正常比率的五倍，而且通常
沒有明顯的原因（如沮喪、悲傷等）。「德國眼科協會」比對了
有關哭泣的不同科學研究，根據他們的說法，女性一年平均哭
30 到 64 次，而男性則是每年哭 6 到 17 次。

** ———————————

according to 根據　　　study〔'stʌdɪ〕*n.* 研究
adult〔ə'dʌlt〕*n.* 成人　　　German〔'dʒɝmən〕*adj.* 德國的
society〔sə'saɪətɪ〕*n.* 協會；學會
ophthalmology〔,ɑfθæl'mɑlədʒɪ〕*n.* 眼科學
the German Society of Ophthalmology 德國眼科協會
average〔'ævərɪdʒ〕*n.* 平均　　　***on average*** 平均而言
time〔taɪm〕*n.* 次數　　　per〔pɚ〕*prep.* 每…
especially〔ə'spɛʃəlɪ〕*adv.* 尤其；特別是
menstrual〔'mɛnstruəl〕*adj.* 月經的
cycle〔'saɪkl̩〕*n.* 循環；週期
menstrual cycle 月經週期；經期　　　increase〔ɪn'kris〕*v.* 增加
up to 達到　　　normal〔'nɔrml̩〕*adj.* 正常的；標準的
rate〔ret〕*n.* 比率　　　obvious〔'ɑbvɪəs〕*adj.* 明顯的
reason〔'rizn̩〕*n.* 理由　　　depression〔dɪ'prɛʃən〕*n.* 沮喪
sadness〔'sædnɪs〕*n.* 悲傷　　　collate〔kə'let〕*v.* 對照；比對

33. (**C**) What is the study about?　這篇研究是有關什麼的？

　　 A. Weight loss. 減重。　　 B. Menstrual cycles. 經期。
　　 C. Crying. 哭泣。　　　　　 D. Sadness. 悲傷。

　　 * weight〔wet〕*n.* 重量；體重
　　　 loss〔lɔs〕*n.* 損失；降低；減少　　 ***weight loss*** 減重

34. (**D**) How often do men cry on average?　男性平均多久哭一次？

　　 A. Five times per month. 每個月五次。
　　 B. Five times the normal rate. 正常比率的五倍。
　　 C. Sixty-four times a year. 一年六十四次。
　　 D. Once a month. 一個月一次。

Questions 35 and 36 are based on the following report.

　　 For most native English speakers, the most challenging aspect of learning Chinese is mastering the tonal system. English, Germanic and Romantic languages generally use tones to emphasize certain words rather than change their meanings. For instance, in English, the word "horse" means horse, no matter how you say it or who you're speaking to. In Chinese, the word for horse, ma（馬）, also means mother, scold, dragonfly, number, to name but a few. The meaning of the word changes according to the tone and the character used. Which brings us to the second most challenging aspect of learning Chinese: learning the more than 45,000 characters.

　　 對大部分以英文爲母語的人而言，學習中文最有挑戰性的一個方面，就是精通其聲調系統。英語、日耳曼語系和拉丁語系的語言，通常使用語調來強調某些字，但不會改變它們的意思。例如在

英文中，horse 這個字指的是「馬」，無論你怎麼唸這個字，或是對誰說都一樣。在中文裡，「馬」這個字的發音可以指「媽」、「罵」、「蜻蜓」、「碼」等等。這個字的意思會隨著語調與其使用的國字而改變，這帶領我們面對學習中文第二有挑戰性的方面：要學習超過四萬五千個國字。

** ─────────────────────

native 〔'netɪv 〕 adj. 本地的
native English speaker 以英文爲母語的人
challenging 〔'tʃælɪndʒɪŋ 〕 adj. 有挑戰性的
aspect 〔'æspɛkt 〕 n. 方面　　master 〔'mæstɚ 〕 v. 精通
tonal 〔'tonḷ 〕 adj. 語調的　　system 〔'sɪstəm 〕 n. 系統
Germanic 〔 dʒɚ'mænɪk 〕 adj. 日耳曼語系的【英語、德語、荷蘭語和丹麥語等】
Romantic 〔 ro'mæntɪk 〕 adj. 羅曼語的；拉丁語系的【自拉丁文演變而成的語言，如葡萄牙語、西班牙語、法語、義大利語、羅馬尼亞語等】
generally 〔'dʒɛnərəlɪ 〕 adv. 一般地；通常　　tone 〔 ton 〕 n. 語調
emphasize 〔'ɛmfə,saɪz 〕 v. 強調　　certain 〔'sɝtṇ 〕 adj. 某些
rather than 而不是　　instance 〔'ɪnstəns 〕 n. 例子
for instance 舉例來說　　scold 〔 skold 〕 v. 責罵
dragonfly 〔'drægən,flaɪ 〕 n. 蜻蜓【蜻蜓的幼蟲稱爲水薑】
name 〔 nem 〕 v. 說出；提出；列舉
to name but a few 只列舉一些；諸如此類；等等
　（ = *to name just a few* ）　　character 〔'kærɪktɚ 〕 n. 文字

35. (**C**) Who is talking? 說話的人是誰？

　　A. A mechanic. 一位技工。

　　B. A horse trainer. 一位馬的訓練師。

　　C. A language professor. 一位語言教授。

　　D. A mail carrier. 一位郵差。

　　* mechanic 〔 mə'kænɪk 〕 n. 技工；機械工人
　　trainer 〔'trenɚ 〕 n. 訓練師　　professor 〔 prə'fɛsɚ 〕 n. 教授
　　carrier 〔'kærɪɚ 〕 n. 運送人；郵差　　***mail carrier*** 郵差

36.（**C**）What is true about the word "horse"?

有關「馬」這個字何者正確？

A. It is only used in German. 這個字只使用於德語。

B. There is no way to say it in Chinese.
這個字沒辦法用中文說出來。

C. It means horse in English. 這個字英文的意思是「馬」。

D. The meaning changes if said to a horse.
這個字如果對一匹馬說意思會改變。

Questions 37 and 38 are based on the following report.

Tropical storm Meari, currently in the seas east of the Philippines, strengthened into a typhoon at 2:00 p.m. yesterday and is likely to threaten Taiwan, according to the Central Weather Bureau. Officials say the center of the typhoon was 1,200 kilometers southeast of Ouluanpi in the southern county of Pingtung at 2:00 p.m, moving west-northwest at a speed of 19 kilometers per hour. The radius of the area mostly likely to be affected reached 150 kilometers. The officials forecast that the outer bands of Typhoon Meari may affect Taiwan from June 24-26, and the possibility of the typhoon directly hitting Taiwan has not been ruled out.

中央氣象局的說法，熱帶風暴米爾利目前位於菲律賓東方海域，昨天下午兩點鐘已增強為颱風，而且可能會威脅到台灣。氣象局官員表示，下午兩點鐘時，颱風中心位於台灣南部屏東縣的鵝鑾鼻東南方 1,200 公里處，以每小時 19 公里的速度向西北西移動。最可能受到影響的地區半徑有 150 公里。官員預測，米爾利颱風的外圍環流影響到台灣的時間，可能在 6 月 24 到 26 日，而颱風直接襲台的可能性尚未排除。

**

tropical〔ˈtrɑpɪkḷ〕*adj.* 熱帶的

storm〔stɔrm〕*n.* 風暴;暴風雨

currently〔ˈkɝəntlɪ〕*adv.* 目前;現在　　east〔ist〕*adv.* 在東方

the Philippines 菲律賓群島

strengthen〔ˈstrɛŋ(k)θən〕*v.* 增強　***be likely to V.*** 可能~

threaten〔ˈθrɛtn̩〕*v.* 威脅　　bureau〔ˈbjʊro〕*n.* (政府機關) 局

the Central Weather Bureau 中央氣象局

official〔əˈfɪʃəl〕*n.* 官員　　kilometer〔kɪˈlɑmɪtɚ〕*n.* 公里

southeast〔ˌsaʊθˈist〕*adv.* 在東南方

southern〔ˈsʌðɚn〕*adj.* 南方的　　county〔ˈkaʊntɪ〕*n.* 縣

move〔muv〕*v.* 移動　***west-northwest*** *adv.* 向西北西方

at a speed of 以…的速度　　radius〔ˈredɪəs〕*n.* 半徑

mostly〔ˈmostlɪ〕*adv.* 大概;主要地　　affect〔əˈfɛkt〕*v.* 影響

reach〔ritʃ〕*v.* 到達;達到　　forecast〔forˈkæst〕*v.* 預測

outer〔ˈaʊtɚ〕*adj.* 外面的　　band〔bænd〕*n.* 帶狀部分

outer band (颱風) 外圍環流

possibility〔ˌpɑsəˈbɪlətɪ〕*n.* 可能性

directly〔dəˈrɛktlɪ〕*adv.* 直接地

hit〔hɪt〕*v.* 侵襲　***rule out*** 排除

37.（ **B** ）When did Meari become a typhoon? 米爾利何時成為颱風？

　　A. On Friday. 在星期五。

　　B. At 2:00 p.m. yesterday. 在昨天下午兩點鐘。

　　C. In Pingtung. 在屏東。　　D. June 24. 在 6 月 24 日。

38.（ **D** ）How fast is Typhoon Meari moving?
　　米爾利颱風的移動速度有多快？

　　A. Southeast of Ouluanpi. 在鵝鑾鼻東南方。

　　B. 1,200 kilometers. 1,200 公里。

　　C. West-northwest. 向西北西方向。

　　D. 19 kilometers per hour. 每小時 19 公里。

Questions 39 and 40 are based on the following report.

Islam in its traditional form was a religion of remarkable tolerance for its time, allowing Jews and Christians the right to practice their beliefs in a way we have not seen fit to do in recent generations in the West. It set an example which was not copied for many centuries in the West. The surprise is the extent to which Islam has been a part of Europe for so long, first in Spain, and then in the Balkans, and it has contributed so much towards the civilization which we all too often think of as entirely Western. Islam is part of our past and our present, in all fields of human endeavor.

傳統的伊斯蘭教在當時是個非常寬容的宗教，容許猶太人和基督徒有權利信奉猶太教和基督教，那樣的做法在近代西方是被認為是很不恰當的。他們樹立了一個榜樣，但在西方許多世紀以來都沒有被仿效。令人驚訝的是，伊斯蘭教已經成為歐洲的一部份如此之久，最初在西班牙，然後在巴爾幹半島諸國，它對於歐洲的文明貢獻非常大，但我們太常將這個文明視為是全然西方的。在人類各項努力的領域中，伊斯蘭教是我們過去和現在的一部份。

** ————————————————

Islam〔'ɪsləm〕 *n.* 伊斯蘭教；回教
traditional〔trə'dɪʃənḷ〕 *adj.* 傳統的
form〔fɔrm〕 *n.* 型態　　religion〔rɪ'lɪdʒən〕 *n.* 宗教
remarkable〔rɪ'mɑrkəbḷ〕 *adj.* 令人驚訝的；非凡的
tolerance〔'tɑlərəns〕 *n.* 容忍　　allow〔ə'laʊ〕 *v.* 允許；給予
Jew〔dʒu〕 *n.* 猶太人　　Christian〔'krɪstʃən〕 *n.* 基督徒
right〔raɪt〕 *n.* 權利
practice〔'præktɪs〕 *v.* 實踐；遵循【practice Christianity 信奉基督教】

belief〔bə'lif〕n. 信念；信仰　　fit〔fɪt〕adj. 適當的；合適的
recent〔'risnt〕adj. 最近的　　generation〔,dʒɛnə'reʃən〕n. 世代
set an example 樹立榜樣　　copy〔'kɑpɪ〕v. 效法；模仿
century〔'sɛntʃərɪ〕n. 世紀
surprise〔sə'praɪz〕n. 令人驚訝的事　　extent〔ɪk'stɛnt〕n. 程度
Europe〔'jʊrəp〕n. 歐洲　　Balkan〔'bɔlkən〕adj. 巴爾幹半島的
the Balkans 巴爾幹半島各國
contribute〔kən'trɪbjut〕v. 貢獻 < to/toward >
civilization〔,sɪvlə'zeʃən〕n. 文明　　**all too** 極為；甚為
think of A as B 認為 A 是 B　　entirely〔ɪn'taɪrlɪ〕adv. 完全地
Western〔'wɛstən〕adj. 西方的　　past〔pæst〕n. 過去
present〔'prɛznt〕n. 現在　　field〔fild〕n. 領域
human〔'hjumən〕adj. 人類的　　endeavor〔ɪn'dɛvə〕n. 努力

39. (**C**) What is Islam? 什麼是伊斯蘭教？

　　A. A surprise. 一件令人驚訝的事。

　　B. A law. 一條法律。　　C. A religion. 一種宗教。

　　D. A story. 一個故事。

　　* law〔lɔ〕n. 法律

40. (**A**) What does the speaker say about Islam?

　　說話者提到有關伊斯蘭教的什麼事？

　　A. It is an important part of Western culture.

　　　　它是西方文化很重要的一部份。

　　B. It is entirely Western. 它是全然西方的。

　　C. It is extremely intolerant. 它非常不寬容。

　　D. It is uncooperative. 它很不合作。

　　* culture〔'kʌltʃə〕n. 文化
　　　extremely〔ɪk'strimlɪ〕adv. 極端地；非常
　　　intolerant〔ɪn'tɑlərənt〕adj. 不寬容的
　　　uncooperative〔,ʌnko'ɑpə,retɪv〕adj. 不合作的

高中英聽測驗模擬試題 ② 詳解

一、看圖辨義：第一部分

For question number 1, please look at picture 1.

1. (**D**) A student is in a large classroom. He is taking an exam.

一個學生在一個大教室裡。他正在參加考試。

　　* **take an exam** 參加考試

For question number 2, please look at picture 2.

2. (**B**) A girl is seated in front of a television. She is watching her favorite dance program.

一個女孩正坐在電視機的前方。她正在看他最喜歡的舞蹈節目。

　　* **be seated** 坐（= *sit*）　　program〔'progræm〕*n.* 節目

For question number 3, please look at picture 3.

3. (**B**) Ms. Franklin is a vendor. She sells sandwiches from a cart which she pushes from place to place.

富蘭克林小姐是個小販。她推著她的手推車到處賣三明治。

  * vendor〔'vɛndɚ〕 *n.* 小販　　sandwich〔'sændwɪtʃ〕 *n.* 三明治

  cart〔kɑrt〕 *n.* 手推車　　push〔pʊʃ〕 *v.* 推

  from place to place 到處

For question number 4, please look at picture 4.

4. (**D**) Sandy is walking in the park. She stopped to feed a couple of stray animals.

珊蒂正在公園散步。她停下來餵一些流浪的動物。

  * feed〔fid〕 *v.* 餵　　***a couple of*** 數個

  stray〔ste〕 *adj.* 迷途的；流浪的

一、看圖辨義：第二部分

For question number 5, please look at picture 5.

5.（ **B、C** ）Which TWO of the following are true about the
students? 關於圖片中的學生，下列哪兩項敘述為眞？

  A. They are late for class. 他們上課遲到了。

  B. They are wearing school
   uniforms. 他們正穿著學校制服。

  C. Both boys are carrying bags.
   兩個男孩都背著書包。

  D. The girl isn't wearing shoes. 那個女孩沒穿鞋。

  * uniform〔'junə,fɔrm〕 *n.* 制服 carry〔'kærɪ〕 *v.* 攜帶

For question number 6, please look at picture 6.

6.（ **A、C** ）Which TWO of the following are true about the
woman? 關於這位女士，下列哪兩項敘述為眞？

  A. She is holding a baby.
   她正抱著個寶寶。

  B. She is wearing a hat.
   她正戴著帽子。

  C. She has long hair. 她有著一頭長髮。

  D. She is in a hurry. 她非常趕時間。

  * *in a hurry* 匆忙地

For question number 7, please look at picture 7.

7.（ **A、C** ）Which TWO of the following are true about the
people in the picture?

  關於圖片中的人，下列哪兩項敘述為眞？

A. One woman is wearing sunglasses.
   一位女士正戴著太陽眼鏡。

B. Both women are selling something. 兩位女士都正在賣東西。

C. Only one woman is selling something.
   只有一位女士在賣東西。

D. Both women are shopping. 兩位女士都在購物。

* sunglasses〔'sʌnˌglæsɪz〕*n. pl.* 太陽眼鏡

For question number 8, please look at picture 8.

8. (**C、D**) Which TWO of the following are true about the man and woman?
   關於這位男士和女士，下列哪兩項敘述爲眞？

   A. They are kissing. 他們在接吻。

   B. They are talking.
      他們正在講話。

   C. They have their backs turned to each other. 他們背對彼此。

   D. They have drawn a line down the middle of the room. 他們在房間的中央畫了一條線。

   * **have** one's **back turned to** 轉身背對 (= *turn one's back on*)
   each other 彼此　　down〔daʊn〕*prep.* 沿著

For question number 9, please look at picture 9.

9. (**B、C**) Which TWO of the following are true about the woman? 關於這位女士，下列哪兩項敘述爲眞？

   A. She is carrying a suitcase. 她正提著一個行李箱。

B. She has recently been
shopping. 她最近一直在購物。

C. She is wearing a coat.
她穿著一件大衣。

D. She is making dinner. 她正在準備晚餐。

* suitcase〔'sut͵kes〕*n.* 小型旅行箱；手提箱
recently〔'risn̩tlɪ〕*adv.* 最近

For question number 10, please look at picture 10.

10. (**A**、**D**) Which TWO of the following are true about the man
on the treadmill?

關於跑步機上的男士，下列哪兩項敘述為真？

A. He is fat. 他很胖。
B. He is skinny. 他非常瘦。
C. He is wearing shorts.
他穿著短褲。

D. He is exercising vigorously. 他正激烈地運動。

* treadmill〔'trɛd͵mɪl〕*n.* 跑步機
skinny〔'skɪnɪ〕*adj.* 極瘦的；皮包骨的
shorts〔ʃɔrts〕*n. pl.* 短褲
vigorously〔'vɪgərəslɪ〕*adv.* 激烈地

（二）對答

11. (**C**) Have you installed the program on your computer?
你的電腦安裝好那個程式了嗎？

A. I think I need a computer. 我認為我需要一台電腦。
B. The program starts at seven o'clock. 那節目七點開始。
C. Not yet. 還沒。
D. I paid the installation fee. 我付了安裝費。

> * install〔ɪn'stɔl〕v. 安裝
> program〔'progræm〕n. 程式;節目
> installation〔ˌɪnstə'leʃən〕n. 安裝　　fee〔fi〕n. 費用

12. (**A**) Are you excited about your vacation?
　　　你對你的假期感到興奮嗎?

　　　　　A. Yes, I can't wait. 是的,我等不及了。
　　　　　B. No, I am on vacation. 不,我正在度假。
　　　　　C. I am afraid of flying. 我害怕搭飛機。
　　　　　D. I am afraid it wasn't very exciting.
　　　　　　　我恐怕那不是很令人興奮。

　　　　　* **be on vacation** 度假　　fly〔flaɪ〕v. 搭飛機

13. (**C**) Why do you study at the library? 你為什麼在圖書館讀書?

　　　　　A. Call me later. 晚一點再打電話給我。
　　　　　B. I lost my library card. 我的圖書證遺失了。
　　　　　C. It is quiet and comfortable. 那裡安靜又舒適。
　　　　　D. Return the book. 把書拿去歸還。

　　　　　* quiet〔'kwaɪət〕adj. 安靜的

14. (**A**) When will you graduate from high school?
　　　你什麼時候中學畢業?

　　　　　A. Next June. 明年六月。
　　　　　B. Sundays at three p.m. 每週日下午三點。
　　　　　C. I don't have enough credit. 我沒有足夠的信用。
　　　　　D. I am on my way now. 我現在在路上了。

　　　　　* graduate〔'grædʒu,et〕v. 畢業　　credit〔'krɛdɪt〕n. 信用
　　　　　on one's **way** 在途中

15. (**C**) How long have you been waiting? 你已經等了多久了?

　　　　　A. I am tired of waiting for her. 我已經厭倦等她了。

B. I want to come along. 我想要一起來。

C. About ten minutes. 大約十分鐘。

D. I'll do the best I can. 我會盡全力。

be tired of 厭倦　　along〔əˋlɔŋ〕*adv.* 連同；一起
do the best one can 盡力（= *do one's best*）

16. (**A**) Would you mind if I opened the window?
你介意我打開窗戶嗎？

A. Not at all. It's hot in here. 一點也不。這裡很熱。

B. Lock the door, please. 請鎖門。

C. I can see you through the window.
我可以透過窗戶看見你。

D. I can see my reflection in the window.
我可以看見窗戶裡我的倒影。

lock〔lɑk〕*v.* 鎖　　*reflection*〔rɪˋflɛkʃən〕*n.* 倒影

17. (**D**) What time do you get up in the morning?
你早上幾點鐘起床？

A. I am not a morning person. 我不是早起的人。

B. I need six or seven hours. 我需要六或七個小時。

C. You didn't set the alarm? 你沒有設定鬧鐘嗎？

D. I usually get up around seven. 我通常七點左右起床。

person〔ˋpɝsn〕*n.* 喜歡（或適應）…人
set〔sɛt〕*v.* 設定　　*alarm*〔əˋlɑrm〕*n.* 鬧鐘（= *alarm clock*）

18. (**B**) What is your dog's name? 你的狗叫什麼名字？

A. I am sorry for your loss. 我對於你的損失深感遺憾。

B. His name is Rex. 他的名字是雷克斯。

C. He was sick. 他生病了。

D. I will be at home. 我將會待在家裡。

loss〔lɔs〕*n.* 損失

19. (**A**) Did you finish your homework?　你的功課寫完了嗎？

　　　A. Yes, I did.　是的，我寫完了。

　　　B. No, you can't.　不，你不能。

　　　C. Yes, if I can.　是的，如果我可以的話。

　　　D. No, they should not.　不，它們不應該。

20. (**B**) Are these books suitable for children?

　　　這些書適合小孩閱讀嗎？

　　　A. Sure, they have them.　當然，他們有這些書。

　　　B. No, they are for adults.　不，它們是給成人看的。

　　　C. I read them on the plane.　我在飛機上讀了這些書。

　　　D. Return them for a refund.　把它們還回去，要求退錢。

　　　* suitable〔'sutəbḷ〕 adj. 適合的　　adult〔ə'dʌlt〕 n. 成人
　　　refund〔'ri,fʌnd〕 n. 退錢

（三）簡短對話

For question 21, you will listen to a short conversation.

　　M：We can all go to the riverside to watch the fireworks
　　　　after dinner.　晚餐之後，我們大家可以到河邊看煙火。

　　W：Sure, as long as Mother Nature is cooperative.

　　　　當然，只要大自然肯合作的話。

　　　* riverside〔'rɪvɚ,saɪd〕 n. 河邊；河畔
　　　fireworks〔'faɪr,wɝks〕 n. pl. 煙火　　*as long as* 只要
　　　Mother Nature 大自然
　　　cooperative〔ko'ɑpə,retɪv〕 adj. 合作的

21. (**C**) Q：What does the woman mean?　這位女士是什麼意思？

　　　A. That's a terrible idea.　那是個很糟的主意。

B. Everyone will be tired after dinner.
   晚餐之後每個人都會很累。

C. It depends on the weather. 要視天氣而定。

D. He has to ask his mother for permission.
   他必須徵求他媽媽的許可。

   * terrible〔'tɛrəbḷ〕*adj.* 可怕的；糟糕的
   depend on 視~而定；取決於
   permission〔pɚ'mɪʃən〕*n.* 允許；許可

For question 22, you will listen to a short conversation.

W：I feel like I'm catching a cold. 我覺得我好像要感冒了。

M：Something is going around. Are you running a fever?
   有什麼病在流行吧。妳有發燒嗎？

W：I think so. My throat is sore and I have a headache, too.
   我想有。我喉嚨痛，頭也痛。

M：You should have that checked out by a doctor.
   妳應該找醫生幫妳檢查一下。

   feel like 感覺好像　　***catch a cold*** 感冒
   go around 流行；流傳　　fever〔'fivɚ〕*n.* 發燒
   run a fever 發燒　　throat〔θrot〕*n.* 喉嚨
   sore〔sor, sɔr〕*adj.* 疼痛的　　***check out*** 檢查；查看

22. (**C**) Q：What are the speakers discussing? 說話者在討論什麼？

   A. The weather. 天氣。

   B. The man's business. 這位男士的生意。

   C. The woman's health. 這位女士的健康。

   D. The atmosphere. 大氣層。

   * atmosphere〔'ætməs,fɪr〕*n.* 大氣層；氣氛

For question 23, you will listen to a short conversation.

M : Ricky is trying out for the basketball team next week.

　　瑞奇下週要參加籃球隊的甄選。

W : Won't that take time away from his studies?

　　那不就會佔掉他的讀書時間了嗎？

　　* *try out* 參加甄選　　studies〔ˈstʌdɪz〕*n. pl.* 學業

23. (**B**) Q : What does the woman suggest?　這位女士暗示什麼？

　　A. Ricky is a good basketball player.

　　　　瑞奇的籃球打得很好。

　　B. Ricky needs to spend his time studying.

　　　　瑞奇需要把時間用來讀書。

　　C. Ricky won't make the team.　瑞奇無法成功進入球隊。

　　D. Ricky is too short to play basketball.

　　　　瑞奇太矮了，不能打籃球。

　　* suggest〔sə(g)ˈdʒɛst〕*v.* 暗示　　make〔mek〕*v.* 成功進入

For question 24, you will listen to a short conversation.

M : Hello, I'm calling about the ad in the newspaper. Is the car still for sale?

　　喂，我打來詢問有關報紙上的廣告。那台車還要賣嗎？

W : One moment, please. You want to speak with my husband. 請稍等。你要和我先生說。

　　* *for sale* 出售

24. (**B**) Q : What will the woman most likely do next?

　　　　這位女士接下來最有可能做什麼？

A. Hang up the phone. 掛斷電話。
B. Give the phone to her husband. 把電話交給她的先生。
C. Take a message. 記下留言。
D. Call about the newspaper. 打電話詢問報紙的事情。

* ***hang up*** 掛斷　　***take a message*** 記下留言
call about 打電話詢問（某事）

For questions 25 and 26, you will listen to a short conversation.

M : Hi. Marla. So tell me, how do people in the Philippines celebrate Christmas? Is it considered an important holiday? 嗨，瑪拉。所以告訴我，菲律賓人是如何慶祝耶誕節的呢？它被認為是個重要的節日嗎？

W : Well, Howard, in the Philippines we take it pretty seriously. Filipinos don't just celebrate Christmas Day. We celebrate the whole month of December.
嗯，豪爾德，在菲律賓我們對耶誕節相當認真。菲律賓人不是只慶祝耶誕節當天，我們整個十二月都在慶祝。

M : What do you do during the month? 你們這個月都做什麼？

W : Well, most people go to church every day, or at least several times a week, and then they meet with their families and friends at night. There are also important religious dates leading up to Christmas Day, so people usually celebrate those, too.
嗯，大部分人會每天上教堂做禮拜，或至少一週數次，然後他們晚上會和親戚朋友聚會。也有一些重要的宗教日一直延續到耶誕節當天，所以他們通常也會慶祝。

M : Do people exchange gifts and decorate a tree?

人們會交換禮物和裝飾耶誕樹嗎？

W : Yes and no.　Very few people even have Christmas trees!
Most people exchange gifts only with their closest friends.

是也不是。很少人有耶誕樹！大部分的人只和他們最親密的朋友
交換禮物。

* Philippines〔'fɪlə,pinz〕n. 菲律賓
consider〔kən'sɪdɚ〕v. 認為
take sth. **seriously** 認真看待某事　　pretty〔'prɪtɪ〕adv. 相當地
Filipino〔,fɪlə'pino〕n. 菲律賓人
religious〔rɪ'lɪdʒəs〕adj. 宗教的　　**lead up to** 逐漸進入
exchange〔ɪks'tʃendʒ〕v. 交換　　decorate〔'dɛkə,ret〕v. 裝飾
close〔klos〕adj. 親密的

25. (**B**) Q : When do Filipinos celebrate Christmas?

菲律賓人何時慶祝耶誕節？

A. Several times a week.　一週數次。
B. The whole month of December.　整個十二月。
C. The day before Christmas Day.　耶誕節前一天。
D. Filipinos don't celebrate Christmas.

菲律賓人不慶祝耶誕節。

26. (**C**) Q : What do most people in the Philippines do during
the Christmas season?

在菲律賓的人大部分在耶誕季節時會做什麼事情？

A. Exchange gifts with strangers.　與陌生人交換禮物。
B. Leave presents under a Christmas tree.

在耶誕樹下留下禮物。

C. Go to church.　上教堂。

D. Go to the States. 去美國。

* stranger〔'strendʒɚ〕*n.* 陌生人
   the Sates 美國（ = *the United States* ）

For questions 27 and 28, you will listen to a short conversation.

W : Hi, my name is Judy Smith. I have a ten-fifteen
appointment with Dr. Block. 嗨，我的名字是茱蒂·
史密斯。我和布拉克醫生 10 點 15 分有約。

M : Just a moment. Ms. Smith. Smith… Smith… Yes,
there you are.
請稍等，史密斯小姐。史密斯…史密斯…有了，在這裡。

W : I'm sorry I'm late. The parking situation is a nightmare.
I must have circled the lot for twenty minutes until I
finally found a spot. 很抱歉我遲到了。停車的狀況真是一場
惡夢。我必須在停車場裡繞了 20 分鐘，最後才找到一個位置。

M : Oh, please don't apologize. I'm sorry for the
inconvenience. 噢，請不要道歉。很抱歉造成妳的不便。

W : Why is the parking lot so full these days? It didn't use
to be this bad.
為什麼停車場最近這麼滿呢？以前沒有這麼糟糕啊。

M : Well, more than half of the lot is closed due to
construction. 嗯，停車場一半以上的位置因為施工而封閉。

W : I see. When is it due to be completed?
我了解了。預計何時完工呢？

M : Sometime next month. 下個月某時吧。

* **appointment** (ə'pɔɪntmənt) *n.* 約會；約定
  moment ('momənt) *n.* 片刻；一會兒
  There you are. ①你要的東西在這裡；拿去吧。②原來你在這裡。
  parking ('pɑrkɪŋ) *n.* 停車　　**situation** (,sɪtʃu'eʃən) *n.* 情況
  nightmare ('naɪt,mɛr) *n.* 惡夢　　**circle** ('kɝkḷ) *v.* 繞圈
  lot (lɑt) *n.* 小塊土地【在此指 parking lot (停車場)】
  spot (spɑt) *n.* 地點　　**apologize** (ə'pɑlə,dʒaɪz) *v.* 道歉
  inconvenience (,ɪnkən'vinjəns) *n.* 不便
  these days 最近　　**used to** 以前　　***due to*** 因為
  construction (kən'strʌkʃən) *n.* 建築；施工
  due (dju) *adj.* 到期的；預期的
  complete (kəm'plit) *v.* 完成；完工
  sometime ('sʌm,taɪm) *adv.* 某時

27. (**C**) Q : Where are the speakers? 說話者在哪裡？

    A. They're in a parking lot. 他們在停車場。

    B. They're at a construction site. 他們在建築工地。

    C. They're in a doctor's office. 他們在醫生的診所。

    D. They're on a boat. 他們在船上。

    * **site** (saɪt) *n.* 地點　　**office** ('ɔfɪs) *n.* 診所

28. (**C**) Q : Why is Judy Smith late for her appointment?
    茱蒂·史密斯約會為什麼遲到？

    A. She slept through her alarm. 她鬧鐘響了還繼續睡。

    B. She had car trouble. 她的車子有問題。

    C. She couldn't find a parking spot. 她找不到停車位。

    D. She forgot about it. 她忘了這個約會。

    * ***sleep through*** 不被～吵醒而繼續睡
      trouble ('trʌbḷ) *n.* 問題

For questions 29 and 30, you will listen to a short conversation.

W：How's Paula doing in school these days?

寶拉最近在學校裡表現如何？

M：She's hanging in there. Of course, there's always room for improvement. How's Jimmy doing?

她還在努力中，當然仍有進步的空間。吉米的表現如何呢？

W：He's really having a hard time of it. His grades are consistently getting worse.

他真的挺辛苦的。他的成績持續地退步中。

M：Have you thought about getting him a tutor? That's what we did with Paula and it really seemed to make the difference. 妳有沒有考慮幫他找個家教？我們就是為寶拉找了家教，而似乎好像真的有用。

W：We're thinking about it. Is there someone you can recommend? 我們也在考慮。你有誰可以推薦嗎？

M：Sure! You should call Dennis. He's great.

當然！妳應該打電話找丹尼斯。他很棒。

> *__hang in there__ 堅持；堅忍   room〔rum〕 *n.* 空間
> improvement〔ɪm'prumənt〕 *n.* 改善；進步
> __have a hard time of it__ 很辛苦   grade〔gred〕 *n.* 成績
> consistently〔kən'sɪstəntlɪ〕 *adv.* 持續地   __get worse__ 惡化
> tutor〔'tutɚ〕 *n.* 家教   __make a difference__ 有差別；有影響
> recommend〔ˌrɛkə'mɛnd〕 *v.* 推薦

29. (**A**) Q：What are the speakers discussing?

說話者正在討論什麼？

A. Their children. 他們的小孩。

B. Their jobs. 他們的工作。　　C. Their taxes. 他們的稅。

D. Their neighbors. 他們的鄰居。

* tax〔tæks〕n. 稅　　neighbor〔'nebɚ〕n. 鄰居

30.（**C**）Q：Who is Dennis? 丹尼斯是誰？

A. He is Paula's father. 他是寶拉的父親。

B. He is Jimmy's cousin. 他是吉米的表哥。

C. He is a tutor. 他是一位家教。

D. He is great. 他很棒。

* cousin〔'kʌzn̩〕n. 表（堂）兄弟姊妹

四、短文聽解

Questions 31 and 32 are based on the following report.

Painting is the most beautiful of all arts. In it, all sensations are condensed. One glance can trigger the most profound memories. Everything is summed up in one moment. Painting is a complete art which sums up all the others and completes them. Like music, it acts on the senses; the tones correspond to the harmonies of nature. But in painting, there is a unity which is not found in music, where the listener cannot possibly remember the end and the beginning at the same time. In this sense, the ear is inferior to the eye. The ear can only grasp a single sound at one time, whereas the eye takes in everything and at the same time simplifies it.

繪畫是所有藝術中最美的。在畫中，所有的感覺都被濃縮在一起。只要看一眼，就能引發最深刻的記憶。所有的事物都被概括在一瞬間。繪畫是一種完整的藝術，它概括所有其他藝術，並使它們

完整。就像音樂一樣，繪畫也會影響人的感官；畫中的色調符合大自然中的和諧。但在繪畫中，有一種一致感是音樂找不到的，聆聽者聽音樂時，不可能同時記住開頭和結尾。在這一方面，耳朵就不如眼睛。耳朵只能一次掌握一個單一的聲音，然而眼睛可以看到一切，同時予以簡化。

** ————————————————————

painting (ˈpentɪŋ) n. 繪畫　　sensation (sɛnˈseʃən) n. 感覺

condense (kənˈdɛns) v. 濃縮

glance (glæns) n. 一瞥；看一眼　　trigger (ˈtrɪgɚ) v. 引發

profound (prəˈfaʊnd) adj. 很深的　　memory (ˈmɛmərɪ) n. 記憶

sum up 總計；概括　　moment (ˈmomənt) n. 片刻；瞬間

complete (kəmˈplit) adj. 完整的　 v. 使完整；使完全

act on 對～有影響　　sense (sɛns) n. 感官

tone (ton) n. 色調　　correspond (ˌkɔrəˈspɑnd) v. 符合 < to >

harmony (ˈhɑrmənɪ) n. 和諧　　unity (ˈjunətɪ) n. 一致；和諧

at the same time 同時

in this sense 就這層意義而言；在這一方面

inferior (ɪnˈfɪrɪɚ) adj. 較差的；不如的 < to >

grasp (græsp) v. 抓住；把握　　single (ˈsɪŋgl̩) adj. 單一的

at one/a time 一次；同時　　whereas (ˌhwɛrˈæs) conj. 然而

take in 收進；容納；一眼看出；注意到

simplify (ˈsɪmpləˌfaɪ) v. 使簡化

31. (**B**) What does the speaker think about painting?

說話者對繪畫的看法為何？

A. It is a waste of time. 它浪費時間。

B. It is the most beautiful of all arts.

它是所有藝術中最美的。

C. It is completed by music. 它有了音樂才完整。

D. It is tiring. 它令人疲倦。

* waste (west) n. 浪費　　tiring (ˈtaɪrɪŋ) adj. 令人疲倦的

32. (**A**)　What does the speaker think about music?
　　　　說話者對音樂的看法爲何？
　　　　A.　It is inferior to painting.　它不如繪畫。
　　　　B.　It is sensationally condensed.　它在感覺上是濃縮的。
　　　　C.　It is too complex.　它太複雜了。
　　　　D.　It is the ugliest of all arts.　它是所有藝術中最醜的。
　　　　* complex〔kəm'plɛks〕adj. 複雜的　　ugly〔'ʌglɪ〕adj. 醜陋的

Questions 33 and 34 are based on the following report.

I don't think we should be so determined to preserve the legal right to own firearms. We can't be so determined that we forget about the reality of life for millions of Americans. Handguns are responsible for more deaths in this country than natural causes and drunk driving combined. Our streets are unsafe, under conditions that no other nation has allowed to exist. At some point, I hope the National Rifle Association will go back to putting out valuable information about hunting and the safe use of guns. Knowing the conditions we face today and the growing threat to public safety, firearms no longer belong in our society.

我不認爲，我們應該如此堅決要保有合法擁有武器的權利。我們不能如此堅決，而忘記了數百萬美國人生活的現實面。手槍在這個國家所造成的死亡，比自然死因和酒醉駕車加起來還多。在這種其他國家都不會允許存在的情況之下，我們的街頭很不安全。我希望在某個的時刻，「全國來福槍協會」能恢復公布有關打獵和安全使用槍枝的重要資訊。知道我們今日所面臨的情況，以及對於公共安全日益增加的威脅，武器不該再存在於我們的社會中。

** ────────────────

determined〔dɪˈtɝmɪnd〕adj. 決定的；堅決的
preserve〔prɪˈzɝv〕v. 保存；保護　　legal〔ˈligl〕adj. 合法的
right〔raɪt〕n. 權利　　firearm〔ˈfaɪr͵ɑrm〕n. 火器；武器
reality〔rɪˈælətɪ〕n. 現實　　handgun〔ˈhænd͵gʌn〕n. 手槍
be responsible for　為～負責；是～的原因
natural〔ˈnætʃərəl〕adj. 自然的　　cause〔kɔz〕n. 原因
drunk〔drʌŋk〕adj. 喝醉的　　**drunk driving**　酒醉駕車
combine〔kəmˈbaɪn〕v. 結合　　condition〔kənˈdɪʃən〕n. 狀況
exist〔ɪgˈzɪst〕v. 存在　　point〔pɔɪnt〕n. 時刻
national〔ˈnæʃənl〕adj. 全國的　　rifle〔ˈraɪfl〕n. 來福槍；步槍
association〔ə͵soʃɪˈeʃən〕n. 聯盟；學會；協會
at some point　在某個時刻　　**go back to**　重新開始；恢復
put out　發表；公布　　valuable〔ˈvæljʊəbl〕adj. 寶貴的；重要的
threat〔θrɛt〕n. 威脅　　face〔fes〕v. 面臨
growing〔ˈgroɪŋ〕adj. 日益增加的　　**no longer**　不再
belong〔bəˈlɔŋ〕v. 屬於；應該在～

33. (**A**) What is the speaker talking about? 說話者在談論什麼？

A. Guns. 槍枝。　　B. Traffic. 交通。
C. Hunting. 打獵。　　D. Living conditions. 生活狀況。

34. (**B**) What is true about the National Rifle Association?
有關「全國來福槍協會」何者為眞？

A. It opposes the ownership of handguns.
他們反對擁有手槍。

B. It used to put out information about gun safety.
他們以前會公布有關槍枝安全的資訊。

C. It is unable to think about the reality of life.
他們無法思考生活的現實面。

D. It faces an enormous threat. 他們面臨極大的威脅。

* oppose〔əˈpoz〕v. 反對　　ownership〔ˈonɚ͵ʃɪp〕n. 所有權
be unable to V. 無法～　　enormous〔ɪˈnɔrməs〕adj. 極大的

Questions 35 and 36 are based on the following report.

The 1992 Consensus is the outcome of a meeting in 1992 between the representatives of the People's Republic of China, the P.R.C. in mainland China, and the Republic of China, the R.O.C. in Taiwan. The Consensus, generally speaking, is that, on the subject of the "One China Principle," both sides agreed to recognize there is only one China—meaning both mainland China and Taiwan belong to the same China—but both sides agree to verbally express the meaning of that one China according to their own individual definition.

　　九二共識是 1992 年，在中國大陸的中華人民共和國，和在台灣的中華民國，雙方代表在會議中所達成的結果。一般說來，此項共識指的是，基於「一個中國的原則」主題，雙方同意承認只有一個中國──意指中國大陸和台灣屬於同一個中國──但雙方同意根據個別不同的定義，來口頭表達一個中國的意義。

**

consensus〔kən'sɛnsəs〕n. 共識　　outcome〔'aut,kʌm〕n. 結果
representative〔,rɛprɪ'zɛntətɪv〕n. 代表
republic〔rɪ'pʌblɪk〕n. 共和國
the People's Republic of China 中華人民共和國
mainland〔'menlənd〕n. 大陸
the Republic of China 中華民國
generally〔'dʒɛnərəlɪ〕adv. 一般地
generally speaking 一般說來　　subject〔'sʌbdʒɪkt〕n. 主題
principle〔'prɪsəpl̩〕n. 原則　　recognize〔'rɛkəg,naɪz〕v. 承認
verbally〔'vɝblɪ〕adv. 口頭上　　express〔ɪk'sprɛs〕v. 表達
individual〔,ɪndə'vɪdʒuəl〕adj. 個別的
definition〔,dɛfə'nɪʃən〕n. 定義

35. (**B**)　What is the 1992 Consensus? 什麼是九二共識？

    A. Speaking generally. 一般說法。

    B. The outcome of a meeting in 1992.

       1992 年的一場會議的結果。

    C. The One China Principle. 一個中國的原則。

    D. An expression of one definition. 一種定義的說法。

    * expression〔ɪkˈsprɛʃən〕*n.* 表達；說法

36. (**B**)　What is true about the 1992 Consensus?

    有關九二共識何者為真？

    A. The P.R.C. said it never happened.

       中華人民共和國說這從未發生。

    B. Both sides agreed to recognize only one China.

       雙方同意承認只有一個中國。

    C. The R.O.C. didn't recognize it. 中華民國不承認它。

    D. Both sides agreed to express the same meaning.

       雙方同意表達相同的意義。

Questions 37 and 38 are based on the following report.

    The Philippines has a tropical climate with two distinct seasons: wet and dry. Typhoons and tropical storms are a common occurrence during the wet season, particularly in the northern part of the Philippines, and occur from late May till early November. The dry season lasts from late November until late April. December to February is a pleasant time to visit the Philippines. Temperatures during this time range from 24-30°C at their peak. From March to May is the hottest period, when temperatures heat up, but it rarely goes above 37°C.

菲律賓屬於熱帶氣候，有兩個不同的季節：雨季和乾季。在雨季期間，颱風和熱帶暴風經常發生，尤其是在菲律賓北部地區，時間從五月底到十一月初。乾季則由十一月底持續到四月底。十二月到二月是造訪菲律賓最愉快的時間。這個時期的最高溫是在攝氏 24 到 30 度。從三月到五月是最熱的時候，溫度會逐漸升高，但很少超過攝氏 37 度。

**

tropical〔ˈtrɑpɪkḷ〕adj. 熱帶的　　climate〔ˈklaɪmɪt〕n. 氣候
distinct〔dɪˈstɪŋkt〕adj. 不同的；分明的
wet〔wɛt〕adj. 常下雨的　　occurrence〔əˈkɝəns〕n. 發生；事件
particularly〔pɚˈtɪkjələˌlɪ〕adv. 尤其；特別是
northern〔ˈnɔrðən〕adj. 北方的　　late〔let〕adj. 末期的
early〔ˈɝlɪ〕adj. 早期的　　last〔læst〕v. 持續
pleasant〔ˈplɛzṇt〕adj. 令人愉快的
temperature〔ˈtɛmp(ə)rətʃɚ〕n. 溫度
range〔rendʒ〕v.（範圍）包括　　peak〔pik〕n. 最高峰
period〔ˈpɪrɪəd〕n. 時期　　*heat up* 變熱
rarely〔ˈrɛrlɪ〕adv. 很少　　go〔go〕v. 變成

37. (**C**) What is true about the Philippines? 關於菲律賓何者爲眞？

　　A. Typhoons and tropical storms are rare.
　　　颱風和熱帶暴風很少。

　　B. It has a cold climate. 氣候很寒冷。

　　C. It has two seasons: wet and dry.
　　　有兩個季節：雨季和乾季。

　　D. There is snow in the south. 南部會下雪。

　　* rare〔rɛr〕adj. 罕見的；稀有的　　south〔sauθ〕n. 南部

38. (**D**) When is it least likely to rain in the Philippines?
　　菲律賓何時最不可能下雨？

　　A. June. 六月。　　　　　　　B. July. 七月。

C. September. 九月。　　D. December. 十二月。

* least〔list〕adv. 最不　　likely〔'laɪklɪ〕adj. 可能的

Questions 39 and 40 are based on the following report.

Parcopresis can be described as an inability to defecate when other people are likely to be around, meaning in the same public toilet, house or building. This inability limits the sufferers to being able to defecate only in a limited number of what they consider "safe" places—thus restricting their lifestyle. The degree of restriction varies depending on the severity of the individual condition but in extreme cases, people give up their jobs, miss vacations they would love to take, and generally let it dictate and limit most aspects of their lives. It affects both men and women of all ages and backgrounds. It is not clear how many people suffer from the condition.

「排便害羞症」可被描述成當有人可能在附近時，意思是在同一個公共廁所、房子或建築物裡時，就無法排便。這種情況使患者受到限制，只能在他們認為「安全」的有限的地方排便——因此限制了他們的生活。受限制的程度視個別情況的嚴重性，而有所不同，但在有些極度嚴重的案例中，人們會放棄工作、錯失他們很想去的假期，通常會讓這個情況支配並限制他們生活的許多方面。這種情況可能影響不同年齡層和背景的男女。有多少人因這個情況而受苦，我們並不清楚。

** ————————————

parcopresis〔ˌpɑrko'prɛsɪs〕n. 排便害羞症
describe〔dɪ'skraɪb〕v. 描述；形容
inability〔ˌɪnə'bɪlətɪ〕n. 無能力　　defecate〔'dɛfəˌket〕v. 排便

be likely to V. 可能~　　around〔əˋraʊnd〕 *adv.* 在附近
toilet〔ˋtɔɪlɪt〕 *n.* 廁所　　sufferer〔ˋsʌfərɚ〕 *n.* 受害者；受苦者
limited〔ˋlɪmɪtɪd〕 *adj.* 有限的　　restrict〔rɪˋstrɪkt〕 *v.* 限制
lifestyle〔ˋlaɪfˏstaɪl〕 *n.* 生活方式　　degree〔dɪˋgri〕 *n.* 程度
restriction〔rɪˋstrɪkʃən〕 *n.* 限制　　vary〔ˋvɛrɪ〕 *v.* 變化；不同
severity〔səˋvɛrətɪ〕 *n.* 嚴重
extreme〔ɪkˋstrim〕 *adj.* 極端的；極度的　　case〔kes〕 *n.* 案例
give up 放棄　　miss〔mɪs〕 *v.* 錯過
dictate〔ˋdɪktet〕 *v.* 指揮　　aspect〔ˋæspɛkt〕 *n.* 方面
affect〔əˋfɛkt〕 *v.* 影響　　background〔ˋbækˏgraʊnd〕 *n.* 背景
suffer from 罹患…

39. (**D**) Who is most likely to suffer from parcopresis?
    誰最有可能罹患排便害羞症？
    A. Young men. 年輕男性。
    B. Middle-aged women. 中年女性。
    C. Adolescent boys and girls. 青春期的男孩和女孩。
    D. Men and women of all ages. 各種年齡層的男女。

    * middle-aged *adj.* 中年的
      adolescent〔ˏædḷˋɛsṇt〕 *adj.* 青春期的

40. (**D**) What is true about parcopresis? 有關排便害羞症何者為真？
    A. There is no cure for the disease. 這種疾病無藥可醫。
    B. It forces people to find part-time jobs.
       它會迫使人們尋找兼職的工作。
    C. The degree of restriction is consistent.
       受限制的程度是持續的。
    D. It is not clear how many people suffer from the
       condition. 有多少人罹患這種病我們並不清楚。

    * cure〔kjʊr〕 *n.* 治療法　　force〔fors〕 *v.* 強迫；迫使
      part-time *adj.* 兼差的
      consistent〔kənˋsɪstənt〕 *adj.* 一致的；持續的

高中英聽測驗模擬試題 ③ 詳解

一、看圖辨義：第一部分

For question number 1, please look at picture 1.

1. (**C**) A girl is waiting for the train.　She is standing on the
platform as the train arrives.
一個女孩正在等火車。火車到達時，她正站在月台上。
 * platform〔'plæt,fɔrm〕 *n.* 月台

For question number 2, please look at picture 2.

2. (**D**) Terry is up late tonight.　He's studying for tomorrow's
big test.　泰瑞今晚熬夜。他正在準備明天重要的考試。
 * up〔ʌp〕 *adj.* 沒睡覺　　big〔bɪg〕 *adj.* 重要的

For question number 3, please look at picture 3.

3. (**A**) Ms. Jones has a short temper. She cannot believe that
John got a 0 on his math test.

瓊斯女士的脾氣很暴躁。他無法相信約翰數學考 0 分。

　　* temper〔'tɛmpə〕*n.* 脾氣　　***short temper*** 脾氣暴躁

For question number 4, please look at picture 4.

4. (**C**) There is an incredible sale at the mall. People are
literally fighting over the merchandise.

在購物中心裡有一場大特賣。人們眞的爲了商品而大打出手。

　　* incredible〔ɪn'krɛdəbḷ〕*adj.* 不可思議的
　　mall〔mɔl〕*n.* 購物中心
　　literally〔'lɪtərəlɪ〕*adv.* 逐字地；簡直；實質上地
　　fight over 爲…打架；爲…吵架
　　merchandize〔'mɝtʃənˌdaɪz〕*n.* 商品

一、看圖辨義：第二部分

For question number 5, please look at picture 5.

5.（**A、B**）Which TWO of the following are true about the people in the picture?
關於圖片中的人，下列哪兩項敘述為眞？

    A. The girls are students.
       那些女孩是學生。

    B. The man is a teacher.
       這個男人是老師。

    C. The woman is a nurse. 這個女人是護士。

    D. The boy is throwing a ball. 這個男孩正在丟球。

For question number 6, please look at picture 6.

6.（**A、D**）Which TWO of the following are true about the picture? 關於這張圖片，下列哪兩項敘述為眞？

    A. There are five dogs in the picture. 圖片中有五隻狗。

    B. There are three boys in the picture. 圖片中有三個男孩。

    C. There are four cats in the picture. 圖片中有四隻貓。

    D. There are two girls in the picture. 圖片中有兩個女孩。

For question number 7, please look at picture 7.

7.（**B、C**）Which TWO of the following are true about the tree? 關於圖片中的樹，下列哪兩項敘述為眞？

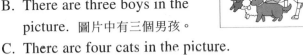

A. It is growing straight and tall.
它長的又直又高。

B. It has a crooked trunk.
它有彎曲的樹幹。

C. It is approximately the same height as the man.
他大約和那個男人一樣高。

D. It has lost all its leaves. 它的樹葉掉光了。

* crooked〔ˋkrʊkɪd〕adj. 彎曲的　　trunk〔trʌŋk〕n. 樹幹
approximately〔əˋprɑksəmɪtlɪ〕adv. 大約
height〔haɪt〕n. 高度

For question number 8, please look at picture 8.

8.（**A、B**）Which TWO of the following are true about the
family? 關於這個家庭，下列哪兩項敘述為真？

A. They are watching television.
他們正在看電視。

B. They are sitting together on a
sofa. 他們正一起坐在沙發上。

C. They are eating popcorn. 他們正吃著爆米花。

D. They are playing video games.
他們正在打電玩。

* popcorn〔ˋpɑpˌkɔrn〕n. 爆米花　　***video game*** 電玩

For question number 9, please look at picture 9.

9.（**C、D**）Which TWO of the following are true about the
girls? 關於這些女孩，下列哪兩項敘述為真？

A. All of them are listening to music.
她們都在聽音樂。

B. All of them are wearing headphones. 她們都戴著耳機。

C. The girl in the middle is reading. 中間的女孩正在閱讀。

D. The girl on the right is listening to music. 右邊的女孩正在聽音樂。

* headphones〔'hɛd,fonz〕*n. pl.* 耳機
  middle〔'mɪdl〕*n.* 中間

For question number 10, please look at picture 10.

10. (**A、C**) Which TWO of the following are true about the picture? 關於這張圖片，下列哪兩項敘述為真？

A. Both students are reading. 兩個學生都在讀書。

B. Both students are in love. 兩個學生都戀愛了。

C. The boy is sweating. 那個男孩正在流汗。

D. The girls is laughing. 那些女孩正在笑。

* ***be in love*** 戀愛　　sweat〔swɛt〕*v.* 流汗

二、對答

11. (**A**) Is your brother old enough to take care of himself? 你的弟弟年紀夠大可以照顧自己了嗎？

A. No, he is too young to be left alone. 不，他還太小了，不能獨自一個人。

B. He is in university. 他在讀大學。

C. My sister doesn't take care of herself. 我妹妹無法照顧她自己。

D. Maybe you can help him. 也許你可以幫助他。

* **take care of** 照顧

leave sb. alone 留下某人單獨一人；不理會某人

12. (**D**) How was the party? 派對如何？

A. It was last night. 在昨天晚上。

B. It was at a restaurant. 在餐廳裡。

C. It was $20. 二十元。

D. It was fun. 很有趣。

* fun〔 fʌn 〕*adj.* 有趣的

13. (**A**) Is there a shuttle bus to the airport? 有到機場的區間車嗎？

A. There is one every half hour. 每隔半小時有一班。

B. We are going to the airport. 我們正要去機場。

C. Wait here for the bus. 在這裡等公車。

D. Buy your ticket on the Internet. 你要在網路上買票。

* shuttle〔ˈʃʌtl̩〕*adj.* 定期往返的；區間的

shuttle bus 區間車 Internet〔ˈɪntɚˌnɛt〕*n.* 網際網路

14. (**A**) Have you ever seen a tornado? 你曾經看過龍捲風嗎？

A. Only on television. 只有在電視上看過。

B. It looks like a tornado. 那看起來像是龍捲風。

C. The wind is very strong. 風非常強。

D. The tornado caused some damage.

這場龍捲風造成一些損害。

* tornado〔tɔrˈnedo〕*n.* 龍捲風 cause〔 kɔz 〕*v.* 造成

damage〔ˈdæmɪdʒ〕*n.* 損害

15. (**B**) Is that your umbrella? 那是你的雨傘嗎？

A. No, it is mine. 不，那是我的。

B. No, it is his. 不，那是他的。

C. Yes, it is raining. 是的，現在正在下雨。

D. Yes, it works fine. 是的，它運作正常。

* work〔wɝk〕v. 運作

16. (**A**) Is your cousin a musician? 你的表哥是一位音樂家嗎？

A. No, he's a painter. 不，他是一位畫家。

B. Yes, he likes music. 是的，他喜歡音樂。

C. That isn't my cousin. 那不是我的表哥。

D. Musicians are dull. 音樂家都很遲鈍。

* cousin〔'kʌzn̩〕n. 表（堂）兄弟姊妹
musician〔mju'zɪʃən〕n. 音樂家　　painter〔'pentə〕n. 畫家
dull〔dʌl〕adj. 遲鈍的；乏味的

17. (**C**) Have you ever been to New York City?

你曾經去過紐約市嗎？

A. New York is a big city. 紐約是個大都市。

B. There are many famous sights to see.

那裡有很多著名景點可看。

C. No, I have never been there.

沒有，我從來沒去過那裡。

D. He is from New York City. 他來自紐約市。

* *have ever been to* 曾經去過　　famous〔'feməs〕adj. 有名的
sight〔saɪt〕n. 風景；名勝

18. (**C**) Did you review your previous lessons?

你有複習之前的課程嗎？

A. That was covered in the previous lesson.

那涵蓋在前一課裡。

B. It has a few lukewarm reviews. 有一些冷淡的評論。

C. I went over them several times. 我複習過好幾次了。

D. He was my previous teacher. 他是我之前的老師。

* review〔rɪˈvju〕v. 複習　n. 評論
previous〔ˈprivɪəs〕adj. 之前的　　lesson〔ˈlɛsn̩〕n. 課；課程
cover〔ˈkʌvə〕v. 涵蓋；包含
lukewarm〔ˈlukˈwɔrm〕adj. 冷淡的　　**go over** 複習

19. (**A**) Who is your friend? 你的朋友是誰？

A. This is Jim. 這是吉姆。

B. That's not Jim. 那不是吉姆。

C. I find it difficult to make friends. 我覺得交朋友很難。

D. Are you Jim? 你是吉姆嗎？

* **make friends** 交朋友

20. (**B**) Would you like to leave a message? 你要留言嗎？

A. I didn't get your message. 我沒有收到你的留言。

B. Yes, if you don't mind. 好的，如果你不介意的話。

C. I left a message. 我留言了。

D. I am not too fond of you. 我不是非常喜歡你。

* message〔ˈmɛsɪdʒ〕n. 訊息；留言
leave a message 留言　　**be fond of** 喜歡

三、簡短對話

For question 21, you will listen to a short conversation.

M：How's the pork chop? 豬排吃起來如何？

W：It's a little undercooked but otherwise fantastic! Very tasty! 有一點不夠熟，但其他都很棒！非常好吃！

* pork〔pork〕n. 豬肉　　chop〔tʃɑp〕n. 肉片

undercooked〔ˋʌndɚˏkʊkt〕*adj.* 煮得不夠熟的

otherwise〔ˋʌðɚˏwaɪz〕*adv.* 在其他方面

fantastic〔fænˋtæstɪk〕*adj.* 很棒的   tasty〔ˋtestɪ〕*adj.* 好吃的

21. (**D**) Q：What does the woman say about her pork chop?

這位女士說她的豬排如何？

A. It is overcooked. 煮過久太老了。

B. It is too salty. 太鹹。

C. It is burned to a crisp. 烤到酥脆。

D. It is delicious. 很好吃。

＊ overcooked〔ˋovɚˏkʊkt〕*adj.* 煮過久的

salty〔ˋsɔltɪ〕*adj.* 鹹的   burn〔bɝn〕*v.* 燒烤

crisp〔krɪsp〕*n.* 酥脆的東西

For question 22, you will listen to a short conversation.

M：How are we getting to the concert? 我們要怎麼去演唱會？

W：We can take the MRT. It's about a ten-minute walk

from here. 我們可以搭捷運。從這裡走路去大約十分鐘。

M：Wouldn't it be easier to take a taxi?

搭計程車不是比較簡單嗎？

W：Yes, but I want to save my money for souvenirs.

是的，但我想把錢省下來買紀念品。

＊ concert〔ˋkɑnsɝt〕*n.* 音樂會；演唱會

MRT 捷運（＝ *Mass Rapid Transit*）

souvenir〔ˏsuvəˋnɪr〕*n.* 紀念品

22. (**D**) Q：Why doesn't the woman want to take a taxi?

為什麼這位女士不想搭計程車？

A. It will take longer.　要花比較久的時間。
B. It is hard to find a taxi in that part of town.
在那個地區很難叫到計程車。
C. The man won't pay his share.
這位男士不付他的費用。
D. She wants to save her money.　她想要把錢省下來。

* share〔ʃɛr〕n. 部分；分攤的費用

For question 23, you will listen to a short conversation.

W : Do you have a detailed map of the city?
你有沒有市區的詳細地圖？

M : No, I don't, but I know the convention center is next to
Taipei 101. We can't miss it.　不，我沒有，但是我知道，
會議中心就在台北 101 旁邊。我們不可能錯過的。

　* detailed〔'diteld〕adj. 詳細的
　convention〔kən'vɛnʃən〕n 會議　　miss〔mɪs〕v. 錯過

23. (**B**) Q : Where do they want to go?　他們要去哪裡？

A. To find a map.　找一張地圖。
B. The convention center.　會議中心。
C. Taipei 101.　台北 101。
D. On a tour of the city.　遊覽市區。

* tour〔tʊr〕n. 旅行；遊覽

For question 24, you will listen to a short conversation.

W : Let's watch the soap opera on TVBS.
我們來看 TVBS 頻道的連續劇吧。

M : Knock yourself out. I'm going to bed.

把妳自己累死吧。我要睡覺了。

 * soap〔sop〕*n.* 肥皂　　opera〔'ɑpərə〕*n.* 歌劇
 soap opera 肥皂劇；連續劇　　***knock out*** 使筋疲力盡

24. (**C**) Q : What does the man mean? 這位男士是什麼意思？

A. He wants to watch the soap opera. 他想要看連續劇。

B. He thinks the woman should punch herself in the face. 他認爲這位女士應該在她自己臉上打一拳。

C. He is tired. 他很累了。

D. He has seen the episode before. 他以前看過這一集了。

 * punch〔pʌntʃ〕*v.* 拳打
 episode〔'ɛpəˌsod〕*n.* 插曲；一集

For questions 25 and 26, you will listen to a short conversation.

W : Do you know where I could find some decent Mexican food in this town?

你知道在這個城鎮哪裡可以找到不錯的墨西哥食物嗎？

M : Ha! Fat chance. 哈！機會渺茫。

W : Really? 眞的嗎？

M : There are thousands of restaurants in Taipei but the one thing you won't find is good Mexican food. There are a few places that claim to be Mexican but I'm afraid you'll be very disappointed. 台北有數千家餐廳，但你唯一找不到的就是好的墨西哥菜。有些餐廳宣稱是墨式，但恐怕妳會很失望。

W : Why is that? 爲什麼呢？

M：That's a very good question.　I don't know the answer to that.　All I know is that I've tried every Mexican joint in Taipei and have yet to find a good one.

那是個很好的問題，但答案我不知道。我只知道，我試過台北的每一家墨西哥餐廳，但還沒找到一家好的。

* decent〔'disn̩t〕*adj.* 高尚的；不錯的
Mexican〔'mɛksɪkən〕*adj.* 墨西哥的
fat chance 機會渺茫　　claim〔klem〕*v.* 宣稱
disappointed〔͵dɪsə'pɔɪntɪd〕*adj.* 失望的
joint〔dʒɔɪnt〕*n.* 地方；餐館；酒吧
have yet to V. 尚未…；還沒有…

25. (**C**) Q：What are the speakers discussing?　說話者在討論什麼？
    A. People.　人。　　　　　B. Animals.　動物。
    C. Food.　食物。　　　　　D. Places.　地方。

26. (**B**) Q：What is true about the woman?
    關於這位女士何者為真？
    A. She has a weight problem.　她有體重問題。
    B. She enjoys Mexican food.　她喜歡墨西哥菜。
    C. She wants to meet a Mexican man.
    她想要認識墨西哥的男生。
    D. She is moving to Mexico.　她要搬去墨西哥。

    * weight〔wet〕*n.* 重量；體重
    Mexico〔'mɛksɪ͵ko〕*n.* 墨西哥

For questions 27 and 28, you will listen to a short conversation.

M：Do you speak any languages other than English?

除了英語之外，妳還會說其他語言嗎？

W : Yes, one.　I am fluent in Italian.

是的，一種。我的義大利語說得很流利。

M : How did you learn to speak Italian?

妳怎麼會學會說義大利語的呢？

W : It was my first language, actually.　My parents and grandparents are from the old country, so they always spoke Italian at home.　Even though I was born here, I really couldn't speak English until I went to kindergarten. The same is true for my brother and sister.

事實上那是我的母語。我的父母和祖父母都來自這個古老的國家，所以他們在家都說義大利語。即使我是在這裡出生的，但我一直到了上幼稚園才會說英語。我的弟弟和妹妹也都一樣。

M : Does your family still speak Italian at home?

妳的家人現在在家仍然說義大利語嗎？

W : Most of the time, but now they speak English whenever I come home.

大部分的時間是的，但現在只要我回家，他們都說英語。

M : Why?　為什麼呢？

W : Well, it's a form of respect.　We are American citizens and my family believes in that old saying, "When in Rome, do as the Romans do."　嗯，是一種尊重。我們都是美國公民，而我的家人相信「入境隨俗」這句古老的諺語。

　　other than 除了～之外　　fluent〔'fluənt〕 *adj.* 流利的
　　Italian〔ɪ'tæljən〕 *n.* 義大利語

first language 第一語言；母語

actually〔'æktʃʊəlɪ〕*adv.* 事實上　　*even though* 即使

not…until~ 直到~才…

kindergarten〔'kɪndə͵gɑrtn̩〕*n.* 幼稚園

respect〔rɪ'spɛkt〕*n.* 尊重　　citizen〔'sɪtəzn̩〕*n.* 公民；國民

saying〔'se·ɪŋ〕*n.* 諺語　　Rome〔rom〕*n.* 羅馬

Roman〔'romən〕*n.* 羅馬人

When in Rome, do as the Romans do. 【諺】入境隨俗。

27. (**B**) Q : How many languages does the woman speak?
　　　　　這位女士會說幾種語言？

　　　A. One. 一種。　　　　B. Two. 兩種。

　　　C. Three. 三種。　　　D. Four. 四種。

28. (**D**) Q : What language does the woman speak at home?
　　　　　這位女士在家說什麼語言？

　　　A. Italian. 義大利語。　　B. Roman. 羅馬人。

　　　C. American. 美語。　　　D. English. 英語。

For questions 29 and 30, you will listen to a short conversation.

M : Pardon me, ma'am, but I think you're in my seat.

　　對不起，小姐，我想妳坐在我的位子上了。

W : Really? 真的嗎？

M : Yes, you're sitting in Row 15, Seat B. See?

　　是的，妳坐的是第 15 排座位 B。看見了嗎？

W : Oh, you're right. Sorry. 噢，你說的對。抱歉。

M : What seat are you supposed to be in?

　　妳應該坐哪個位子呢？

W：Row 16, Seat B.　第 16 排座位 B。

　　* pardon〔ˈpɑrdn〕v. 原諒　　　ma'am〔mæm〕n. 太太；小姐
　　row〔ro〕n. 排　　**be supposed to V.** 應該

29.（**D**）Q：Where are these people? 這些人在哪裡？

　　A. In a supermarket. 在超級市場裡。
　　B. On a roller coaster. 在雲霄飛車上。
　　C. At a horse race. 在賽馬。
　　D. On an airplane. 在飛機上。

　　* **roller coaster** 雲霄飛車　　　race〔res〕n. 比賽
　　horse race 賽馬

30.（**A**）Q：Where is the man's seat? 這位男士的座位在哪裡？

　　A. Row 15, Seat B. 第 15 排座位 B。
　　B. Row B, Seat 15. 第 B 排座位 15。
　　C. Row 16, Seat B. 第 16 排座位 B。
　　D. Row B, Seat 16. 第 B 排座位 16。

四、短文聽解

Questions 31 and 32 are based on the following report.

　　Chandler Fashion Center is the most popular shopping mall in the East Valley. It pumps a lot of money into the local economy and provides jobs for local residents. But now it is facing a challenge. As the economy continues to decline, many consumers are suffering. Their buying habits have changed. Less expendable income translates to fewer trips to the mall. In the past two years, merchant occupancy rates have dropped 30 percent. Sales have dropped to less than $300 per square foot, which is well below the national average of $392 a square foot.

錢得勒時尚中心是東谷市最受歡迎的購物中心,對於當地經濟注入許多金錢,並爲當地居民提供工作。但是它現在正面臨一項挑戰。隨著經濟持續衰退,許多消費者都深受其害,他們的購物習慣改變了。可花費的收入減少,結果就是光臨購物中心的次數減少。在過去兩年來,商場的商家進駐率下降了百分之 30。銷售量下跌至每平方英尺不到 300 美元,遠低於全國平均每平方英尺 392 美元。

**

fashion〔'fæʃən〕n. 流行;時尚　　valley〔'vælı〕n. 山谷
pump〔pʌmp〕v. 打入;注入　　local〔'lokl̩〕adj. 當地的
economy〔ɪ'kɑnəmɪ〕n. 經濟　　provide〔prə'vaɪd〕v. 提供
resident〔'rɛzədənt〕n. 居民　　face〔fes〕v. 面臨
challenge〔'tʃælɪndʒ〕n. 挑戰
decline〔dɪ'klaɪn〕v. 下降;衰退
consumer〔kən'sumɚ〕n. 消費者　　suffer〔'sʌfɚ〕v. 受苦;受害
expendable〔ɪk'spɛndəbl̩〕adj. 可消費的
translate〔træns'let , 'trænslet〕v. 翻譯;結果成爲
merchant〔'mɝtʃənt〕n. 商人　　occupancy〔'ɑkjəpənsɪ〕n. 佔據
rate〔ret〕n. 比率　　drop〔drɑp〕v. 下降
sales〔selz〕n. pl. 銷售量　　square〔skwɛr〕adj. 平方的
foot〔fʊt〕n. 英尺　　below〔bə'lo〕prep. 在~之下
national〔'næʃənl̩〕adj. 全國的　　average〔'æv(ə)rɪdʒ〕n. 平均

31. (**B**) What is Chandler Fashion Center?
錢得勒時尚中心是什麼地方?
A. A modeling agency. 一家模特兒經紀公司。
B. A shopping mall. 一家購物中心。
C. An amusement park. 一座遊樂場。

D. An apartment building. 一棟公寓大樓。

* modeling〔'mɑdḷɪŋ〕*n.* 模特兒
agency〔'edʒənsɪ〕*n.* 經紀公司
amusement〔ə'mjuzmənt〕*n.* 消遣；娛樂
amusement park 遊樂園；遊樂場

32. (**A**) What is happening at Chandler Fashion Mall?
錢得勒時尚中心發生什麼事情？

A. Sales are down. 銷售量下跌。
B. Occupancy rates are up. 商家進駐率上升。
C. Fashion is suffering. 時尚正蒙受傷害。
D. Employers are hiring. 雇主正在招募人才。

* employer〔ɪm'plɔɪɚ〕*n.* 雇主；老闆　　hire〔haɪr〕*v.* 雇用

Questions 33 and 34 are based on the following report.

Cal Callahan was a reporter for a local newspaper that uncovered widespread corruption in the local government. After rejecting a bribe that would have ensured his silence, Cal discovers the funds deposited into his bank account and he is promptly arrested. Now, five years later, he is released from prison. Unemployed, he spends his days in a local bar. Lucy Snow, wife of the richest man in town, asks Cal to help her swindle $5 million with a bogus kidnapping scheme, in which Cal would receive a ten percent cut. Tempted by the prospect of easy money, Cal goes along with the plan. But when Lucy winds up dead, all indications point to Cal as the murderer.

卡爾・卡拉漢是一名地區報社的記者，他揭發了當地政府普遍的貪污現象。在拒絕想封住他的嘴而提出的賄賂之後，卡爾發現有一筆錢存入他的銀行帳戶，他立即被逮捕。五年後的現在，他出獄了。沒有工作的他成天在當地的酒吧裡鬼混。露西・史諾是鎮上最富有的人的太太，要求卡爾幫助她，利用假的綁架案詐騙五百萬元，而從中卡爾可以得到百分之十的贓款。卡爾想到不費勞力可以賺這麼多錢，受到誘惑決定接受這個計劃。但當露西最後死掉時，所有跡象都指向卡爾就是兇手。

** ────────────────────

reporter〔rɪˋportɚ〕n. 記者　　local〔ˋlɑkḷ〕n. 當地的
uncover〔ʌnˋkʌvɚ〕v. 揭發
widespread〔ˋwaɪdˋsprɛd〕adj. 普遍的
corruption〔kəˋrʌpʃən〕n. 貪污；腐敗
reject〔rɪˋdʒɛkt〕v. 拒絕　　bribe〔braɪb〕n. 賄賂
ensure〔ɪnˋʃʊr〕v. 確保　　silence〔ˋsaɪləns〕n. 安靜；沈默
funds〔fʌndz〕n. pl. 資金；錢　　deposit〔dɪˋpɑzɪt〕v. 存入
account〔əˋkaʊnt〕n. 帳戶　　promptly〔ˋprɑmptlɪ〕adv. 立即
arrest〔əˋrɛst〕v. 逮捕　　release〔rɪˋlis〕v. 釋放
prison〔ˋprɪzṇ〕n. 監獄　　unemployed〔ͺʌnɪmˋplɔɪd〕adj. 失業的
bar〔bɑr〕n. 酒吧　　swindle〔ˋswɪndḷ〕v. 詐騙
bogus〔ˋbogəs〕adj. 假的　　kidnapping〔ˋkɪdͺnæpɪŋ〕n. 綁架
scheme〔skim〕n. 計劃　　cut〔kʌt〕n. 分贓
tempt〔tɛmpt〕v. 誘惑；引誘　　prospect〔ˋprɑspɛkt〕n. 希望
easy money 不費勞力賺來的錢　　*go along with* 贊成；合作
wind up 最後　　indication〔ͺɪndəˋkeʃən〕n. 跡象
point to 指向　　murderer〔ˋmɝdərɚ〕n. 謀殺者；兇手

33. (**D**) What is the speaker describing? 說話者在描述什麼？
　　A. Widespread corruption. 普遍的貪污現象。
　　B. Recent business transactions. 最近的商業交易。
　　C. Prison life. 監獄生活。

D.　The plot of a movie.　一部電影的情節。

　* describe〔dɪˈskraɪb〕v. 描述　　recent〔ˈrisn̩t〕adj. 最近的
　　transaction〔trænzˈækʃən , træns-〕n. 交易
　　plot〔plɑt〕n. 情節

34. (**C**) What did Lucy Snow ask Cal Callahan to do?
　　露西・史諾要求卡爾・卡拉漢做什麼？
　　A.　Get released from prison.　從監獄中被釋放。
　　B.　Deposit money into his bank account.
　　　　把錢存入他的銀行帳戶。
　　C.　Steal $5 million.　偷五百萬元。
　　D.　Give up a ten percent cut.　放棄百分之十的贓款。

Questions 35 and 36 are based on the following report.

　　Moon trees are trees grown from hundreds of seeds taken into orbit around the moon by Stuart Roosa during the Apollo 14 mission in 1971. Roosa was the Command Module Pilot on the Apollo 14 mission and was also a former Forest Ranger. He was contacted by Ed Cliff, who was the Chief of the Forest Service at the time, and who proposed the idea of taking the seeds along. Seeds for the experiment were chosen from five different types of trees: Loblolly Pine, Sycamore, Sweetgum, Redwood, and Douglas Fir.

　　月球樹是在 1971 年的阿波羅 14 號任務中，由史都華・陸沙帶上月球軌道的數百顆種子所長出來的樹。陸沙是阿波羅 14 號任務中指揮艙的駕駛員，也是前森林警備隊隊員。當時的林務局局

長艾德・克里夫聯絡他，提議將種子帶上太空。這項實驗中的種子是由五種不同種類的樹選出來的：達德松、美國梧桐、楓香樹、紅杉，和道格拉斯冷杉。

** ─────────────

grow〔gro〕v. 生長；種植　　seed〔sid〕n. 種子

orbit〔'ɔrbɪt〕n. 軌道　　mission〔'mɪʃən〕n. 任務

command〔kə'mænd〕n. 指揮

module〔'mɑdʒul〕n. 太空艙

pilot〔'paɪlət〕n.（飛機、太空艙的）駕駛員

former〔'fɔrmɚ〕adj. 以前的　　forest〔'fɔrɪst〕n. 森林

ranger〔'rendʒɚ〕n. 森林警備隊隊員

contact〔'kɑntækt〕v. 聯絡　　chief〔tʃif〕n. 主管；長官

service〔'sɝvɪs〕n. 政府機關【部、局、處、署等】

propose〔prə'poz〕v. 提議　　along〔ə'lɔŋ〕adv. 連同；一起

experiment〔ɪk'spɛrəmənt〕n. 實驗　　type〔taɪp〕n. 種類

pine〔paɪn〕n. 松樹　　loblolly pine〔'lɑblɑlɪ‚paɪn〕n. 達德松

sycamore〔'sɪkə‚mor〕n. 美國梧桐

sweetgum〔'swit‚gʌm〕n. 楓香樹

redwood〔'rɛd‚wʊd〕n. 紅杉

Douglas Fir〔'dʌgləs‚fɝ〕n. 道格拉斯冷杉；花旗松

35.（**C**）What are moon trees?　什麼是月球樹？

　　A. Trees that grow on the moon.　生長在月球上的樹。

　　B. Trees harvested from the moon and brought back to earth.　從月球上收割，被帶回地球上的樹。

　　C. Trees grown from seeds that were taken on a space mission.　由太空任務中被帶出去的種子長出來的樹。

　　D. Trees sent to the moon by the Forest Service.　由林務局送到月球上的樹。

　　* harvest〔'hɑrvɪst〕v. 收割；收穫

36. (**C**) Which of the following may be a moon tree?
下列何者可能是月球樹之一？
A. Stuart Roosa. 史都華‧陸沙。
B. Ed Cliff. 艾德‧克里夫。
C. Douglas Fir. 道格拉斯冷杉。
D. Annie Oakley. 安妮‧歐克利。

Questions 37 and 38 are based on the following report.

Studies indicate that 10% of British children are described as having ADD—Attention Deficit Disorder. Current estimates suggest that ADD is present throughout the world in about 1-5% of the population. About five times more boys than girls are diagnosed with ADD. This may be partly because of the particular ways they express their difficulties. Boys and girls both have attention problems, but boys are more likely to be overactive and difficult to manage.

研究顯示，有百分之 10 的英國孩童被描述成患有 ADD——注意力不足症。目前的估計顯示，全世界的人口中，大約百分之一至五的人有 ADD。被診斷出有 ADD 的男孩比女孩大約多出五倍，這可能部分是因為男孩表達他們的困難的方式較特殊。男孩和女孩都有注意力的問題，但是男孩比較有可能過動，難以掌控。

** ——————————

study〔'stʌdɪ〕n. 研究　　indicate〔'ɪndə,ket〕v. 顯示
British〔'brɪtɪʃ〕adj. 英國的
describe〔dɪ'skraɪb〕v. 描述；形容

attention〔ə'tɛnʃən〕n. 注意力　　deficit〔'dɛfəsɪt〕n. 不足
disorder〔dɪs'ɔrdə〕n. 疾病　　current〔'kɜənt〕adj. 目前的
estimate〔'ɛstəmɪt〕n. 估計
suggest〔sə(g)'dʒɛst〕v. 顯示
present〔'prɛznt〕adj. 存在的
throughout〔θru'aʊt〕prep. 遍及
population〔,pɑpjə'leʃən〕n. 人口　　time〔taɪm〕n. 倍數
diagnose〔,daɪəg'noz〕v. 診斷　　partly〔'pɑrtlɪ〕adv. 部分地
particular〔pə'tɪkjələ〕adj. 特別的
express〔ɪk'sprɛs〕v. 表達　　**be likely to V.** 可能~
overactive〔,ovə'æktɪv〕adj. 過動的
manage〔'mænɪdʒ〕v. 駕馭；控制；管理

37. (**D**) What is ADD? 何謂 ADD？

A. Andrew Dolan Design. 安德魯‧多倫設計。

B. Adult Diaper Disease. 成人尿布症。

C. Automated Data Developer. 自動化資料顯像劑。

D. Attention Deficit Disorder. 注意力不足症。

* design〔dɪ'zaɪn〕n. 設計
　diaper〔'daɪəpə〕n. 尿布
　automated〔'ɔtə,metɪd〕adj. 自動化的
　data〔'detə , 'dætə〕n. pl. 資料
　developer〔dɪ'vɛləpə〕n. 發展者；顯像劑

38. (**C**) What is true about ADD? 關於 ADD 何者為真？

A. Only British children suffer from the condition.
　　只有英國孩童會罹患這種疾病。

B. People love it in Third World countries.
　　第三世界國家的人超愛它。

C. Boys are more likely to be diagnosed with the
　　disorder. 男孩比較有可能被診斷出有此疾病。

D. It is a way of expressing your difficulties.
這是一種表達困難的方式。

* condition〔kən'dɪʃən〕n. 情況；疾病
Third World 第三世界【尤指亞洲、非洲的不結盟中立國家；開發中國家】

Questions 39 and 40 are based on the following report.

Children from all cultures and social groups are diagnosed with ADD. However, children from certain backgrounds may be particularly likely to be diagnosed with ADD, because of different expectations about how they should behave. If you are a parent, it is therefore important to stay involved in the diagnostic process, and ensure that your child's cultural background is understood and taken into account as part of the assessment.

　　來自各種文化和社會族群的孩童，都會被診斷出患有 ADD。然而，來自某些背景的孩子特別有可能被診斷出患有 ADD，因爲對於他們該有什麼樣的行爲舉止，有不同的期望。因此如果你已爲人父母，參與診斷過程是很重要的，要確保你的孩子的文化背景已被了解，並列入考慮，以作爲評估的一部份。

**　──────────────

　　culture〔'kʌltʃɚ〕n. 文化　　social〔'soʃəl〕adj. 社會的
　　certain〔'sɝtn̩〕adj. 某些
　　background〔'bæk,graʊnd〕n. 背景
　　particularly〔pɚ'tɪkjələⅽlɪ〕adv. 尤其；特別地
　　expectation〔,ɛkspɛk'teʃən〕n. 期望；期待
　　behave〔bɪ'hev〕v. 行爲；舉止　　stay〔ste〕v. 保持
　　involved〔ɪn'vɑlvd〕adj. 牽涉在內的；參與的

diagnostic (͵daɪəgˈnɑstɪk) *adj.* 診斷的
process (ˈprɑsɛs) *n.* 過程
take** sth.* ***into account 把某事列入考慮
assessment (əˈsɛsmənt) *n.* 評估

39. (**C**) What may influence the likelihood of being diagnosed
    with ADD? 什麼因素會影響被診斷出患有 ADD 的可能性？
    A. Diet. 飲食。
    B. Genetics. 遺傳。
    C. Cultural background. 文化背景。
    D. Academic failure. 學術上的失敗。

    * influence (ˈɪnfluəns) *v.* 影響
    likelihood (ˈlaɪklɪ͵hʊd) *n.* 可能性
    diet (ˈdaɪət) *n.* 飲食
    genetics (dʒəˈnɛtɪks) *n.* 遺傳學
    academic (͵ækəˈdɛmɪk) *adj.* 學術的
    failure (ˈfeljɚ) *n.* 失敗

40. (**D**) What is important for parents? 對父母而言什麼很重要？
    A. High-paying jobs. 高薪的工作。
    B. Intensive therapy. 密集的治療。
    C. Spending quality time with their children.
       與孩子共度親子時間。
    D. Being involved in their child's assessment.
       參與孩子的評估。

    * high-paying *adj.* 高薪的   job (dʒɑb) *n.* 工作
    intensive (ɪnˈtɛnsɪv) *adj.* 密集的
    therapy (ˈθɛrəpɪ) *n.* 治療
    quality (ˈkwɑlətɪ) *adj.* 品質好的
    quality time 共處時間；親子時間

高中英聽測驗模擬試題④詳解

一、看圖辨義：第一部分

For question number 1, please look at picture 1.

1. (**D**) Gary is a basketball player. Look, he just made a jump
   shot! 蓋瑞是個籃球員。你看！他剛剛跳投得分。

   　jump shot 跳起投籃；跳投

For question number 2, please look at picture 2.

2. (**D**) Jack and Jill are at the beach. Jack will go surfing.
   傑克和吉兒都在沙灘。傑克將會去衝浪。

   　go surfing 去衝浪

For question number 3, please look at picture 3.

3.（**B**） This is the 235 bus. The old woman sitting in the front
　　 seat will get off at the next stop.

　　　　 這是 235 號公車。坐在前方座位的老太太將會在下一站下車。

　　　　 * ***get off*** 下車　　 stop〔stɑp〕*n.* 停車站

For question number 4, please look at picture 4.

4.（**B**） Big Phil is at the pool. He is stretching before taking a
　　 swim. 大菲爾在游泳池邊。他正在做游泳前的伸展運動。

　　　　 * pool〔pul〕*n.* 游泳池　　 stretch〔strɛtʃ〕*v.* 伸展

　　　　 take a swim 游泳

一、看圖辨義：第二部分

For question number 5, please look at picture 5.

5. (**A**、**B**) Which TWO of the following are true about the dog?

關於這隻狗，下列哪兩項敘述爲眞？

    A. It is chasing after the boy.

      牠正在追那個男孩。

    B. It is wearing a collar.

      牠正戴著一個項圈。

    C. It is chewing on a bone.　牠正在嚼一根骨頭。

    D. It is sleeping on the floor.　牠正在地板上睡覺。

    * chase (tʃes) v. 追　　collar ('kɑlɚ) n. 項圈

      chew (tʃu) v. 嚼

For question number 6, please look at picture 6.

6. (**B**、**D**) Which TWO of the following are true about the people in the picture?

關於圖片中的人，下列哪兩項敘述爲眞？

    A. The man is a plumber.

      那個男人是個水管工人。

    B. The man is a dentist.

      那個男人是位牙醫。

    C. The boy is standing up.　那個男孩正要站起來。

    D. The boy is sitting in a chair.

      那個男孩正坐在椅子上。

    * plumber ('plʌmɚ) n. 水管工人

      dentist ('dɛntɪst) n. 牙醫

For question number 7, please look at picture 7.

7. (**A**、**D**) Which TWO of the following are true about the girl?
關於這位女孩，下列哪兩項敘述爲眞？

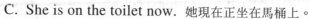

    A. She needs to use the restroom.
      她必須使用廁所。

    B. She is first in line.
      她排在第一位。

    C. She is on the toilet now. 她現在正坐在馬桶上。

    D. She is last in line. 她排在最後一位。

    * toilet〔'tɔɪlɪt〕*n.* 馬桶；洗手間　　*in line* 排隊

For question number 8, please look at picture 8.

8. (**A**、**D**) Which TWO of the following are true about the man
on the right? 關於右方的男士，下列哪兩項敘述爲眞？

    A. He wants a cup of coffee.
      他想要一杯咖啡。

    B. He wants a sandwich.
      他想要一個三明治。

    C. He is wearing a hat. 他正戴著一頂帽子。

    D. He is wearing a tie. 他正打著一條領帶。

    * sandwich〔'sandwɪtʃ〕*n.* 三明治　　tie〔taɪ〕*n.* 領帶

For question number 9, please look at picture 9.

9. (**A**、**B**) Which TWO of the following
are true about the man behind
the counter? 關於櫃台後方的男
士，下列哪兩項敘述爲眞？

A. He's a chef. 他是主廚。

B. He's wearing a robe. 他正穿著一件長袍。

C. He's having dinner. 他正在吃晚餐。

D. He's paying for dinner. 他正在付晚餐的錢。

* counter〔'kaʊntɚ〕n. 櫃台　　chef〔ʃɛf〕n. 主廚
robe〔rob〕n. 長袍　　*pay for* 為…付錢

For question number 10, please look at picture 10.

10. (**A、D**) Which TWO of the following are true about the
woman? 關於這位女士，下列哪兩項敘述為真？

A. She is window shopping.
她正在瀏覽商店櫥窗。

B. She is lying down.
她正在躺下。

C. She is on sale. 她正被拍賣。

D. She is carrying a purse. 她正提著一個手提包。

* *be window shopping* 瀏覽商店櫥窗　　lie〔laɪ〕v. 躺
on sale 拍賣中　　purse〔pɝs〕n. 錢包；手提包

二、對答

11. (**B**) Would you care for something to drink?
你想要喝點什麼嗎？

A. Yes, I am starving. 是的，我快餓死了。

B. No, thanks. 不，謝謝。

C. The water is cold. 這水是冷的。

D. Once a week. 一週一次。

* *care for* 想要　　starve〔stɑrv〕v. 飢餓

12. (**C**) How long does it take you to get home?
你回家需要多久的時間？

    A. I have been at home all day. 我一整天都在家。

    B. Take as many as you want. 你想拿多少就拿多少。

    C. About half an hour by bus. 坐公車大約半小時。

    D. I feel safe at home. 我在家覺得很安全。

13. (**B**) Do you have an e-mail account? 你有電子郵件帳戶嗎？

    A. Not on account of the weather. 不是因為天氣。

    B. Yes, I use Hotmail. 有的，我使用 Hotmail。

    C. Send me an e-mail. 寄一封電子郵件給我。

    D. Maybe you can show me how.
也許你可以告訴我怎麼做。

    * account (ə'kaʊnt) *n.* 帳戶；說明　***on account of*** 因為

14. (**A**) Where did you put my jacket? 你把我的夾克放在哪裡？

    A. It's on the back of the chair. 在椅背上。

    B. It's cold. You should wear a jacket.
天氣很冷。你應該穿件夾克。

    C. I bought it at the night market. 我在夜市買的。

    D. That's a nice jacket. 那是一件不錯的夾克。

    * jacket ('dʒækɪt) *n.* 夾克　***night market*** 夜市

15. (**C**) When will you visit your grandma in Tainan?
你何時要去探望你台南的奶奶？

    A. My grandma lives in Tainan. 我的奶奶住在台南。

    B. We'll take the high-speed rail. 我們會搭高鐵。

    C. Next weekend. 下個週末。

    D. My brother is coming, too. 我的哥哥也會來。

    * rail (rel) *n.* 鐵軌；鐵路　***high-speed rail*** 高速鐵路；高鐵

16. (**C**) Do you prefer home-cooked meals or fast food?

　　　　你比較喜歡吃家裡做的飯菜還是速食？

　　　　A. My mother is a great cook. 我媽媽很會做菜。

　　　　B. I have fast food once or twice a week.

　　　　　　我一個星期會吃一次或兩次的速食。

　　　　C. I prefer to eat at home. 我比較喜歡在家吃。

　　　　D. I think you eat too fast. Slow down and chew your

　　　　　　food. 我認爲你吃東西太快了。吃慢一點，咀嚼你的食物。

　　　　* prefer (prɪ'fɜ) v. 比較喜歡　　meal (mil) n. 一餐
　　　　fast food 速食　　cook (kʊk) n. 廚師
　　　　slow down 放慢速度

17. (**A**) Did you pay full price for that shirt?

　　　　你買那件襯衫沒打折（付全部的價格）嗎？

　　　　A. No, I got it at a discount. 不，我打折買的。

　　　　B. I bought it yesterday. 我昨天買的。

　　　　C. It's not your size. 那不是你的尺寸。

　　　　D. Yes, you can borrow it. 是的，你可以借。

　　　　* discount ('dɪskaʊnt) n. 折扣

18. (**C**) Would you pass the potatoes, please?

　　　　請你把馬鈴薯遞過來好嗎？

　　　　A. On time, as usual. 準時，如往常一般。

　　　　B. They are on the table. 馬鈴薯在桌上。

　　　　C. Sure, here you go. 當然好，拿去吧。

　　　　D. I don't like potatoes. 我不喜歡馬鈴薯。

　　　　* pass (pæs) v. 傳遞　　*on time* 準時
　　　　as usual 如往常一般
　　　　here you go 你要的東西在這裡；拿去吧

19. (**A**) What's the matter? You look upset.

怎麼了？你看來不太高興。

    A. I'm having a bad day. 我今天諸事不順。

    B. That's the most upsetting part.

       那是最令人心煩的部分。

    C. As a matter of fact, he did. 事實上，他是。

    D. Here she comes. 她來了。

    * *the matter* 有問題的   upset〔ʌpˈsɛt〕adj. 不開心的

    upsetting〔ʌpˈsɛtɪŋ〕adj. 令人心煩的

    as a matter of fact 事實上

20. (**A**) How many trains go to Keelung? 到基隆有幾班火車？

    A. There are ten trains per day. 每天有十班火車。

    B. I'll take the train to Keelung. 我會搭這班火車到基隆。

    C. I prefer to take the bus. 我比較喜歡搭公車。

    D. It takes about an hour. 大概要花一小時的時間。

    * per〔pɚ〕prep. 每…

三、簡短對話

For question 21, you will listen to a short conversation.

W：Our team is so lucky to have a leader like Carlos.

    我們這一隊有像卡羅斯這樣的隊長真是幸運。

M：He's the straw that stirs the drink. 他是全隊的靈魂人物。

    * leader〔ˈlidɚ〕n. 領導人；隊長   straw〔strɔ〕n. 吸管

    stir〔stɝ〕v. 攪拌   *the straw that stirs the drink* 字面的意思

    是「攪拌飲料的吸管」，引申為「（團體中的）靈魂人物」。

21. (**C**) Q：What is true about Carlos? 關於卡羅斯何者為真？

    A. Carlos is thirsty. 卡羅斯口很渴。

B. Carlos is a bartender. 卡羅斯是一位酒保。

C. Carlos is the team leader. 卡羅斯是隊長。

D. Carlos is selfish. 卡羅斯很自私。

* thirsty ('θɜstɪ) adj. 口渴的　　bartender ('bɑr,tɛndɚ) n. 酒保

selfish ('sɛlfɪʃ) adj. 自私的

For question 22, you will listen to a short conversation.

M : What is Robert doing here? 羅伯特在這裡做什麼？

W : Why don't you ask him? 你何不問他？

M : Should I? 我應該嗎？

W : Why not? Let him speak for himself.

為什麼不？讓他自己說。

* for oneself 為自己；自己

22. (**A**) Q : What does the woman mean? 這位女士是什麼意思？

A. Robert can speak for himself. 羅伯特可以自己說。

B. She's never met Robert. 她從來沒遇過羅伯特。

C. Perhaps the man is afraid of Robert.

也許這位男士害怕羅伯特。

D. The man asks too many questions.

這位男士問太多問題。

For question 23, you will listen to a short conversation.

M : The size 10 is kind of snug. Do you have it in a 10 and

a half? 十號有點合。你們有十號半的嗎？

W : These shoes don't come in half sizes.

這款鞋子沒有半號的。

　　　* snug〔snʌg〕*adj.* 合身的；剛好的
　　　come in　（商品）有（…尺寸、顏色等）

23.（**B**）Q：Where are these people?　這些人在哪裡？
　　　　A. At a track race.　在徑賽比賽中。
　　　　B. In a shoe store.　在鞋店裡。
　　　　C. On a crowded street.　在擁擠的街上。
　　　　D. In a library.　在圖書館裡。
　　　* track〔træk〕*n.* 徑賽　　race〔res〕*n.* 競賽；比賽
　　　crowded〔ˈkraʊdɪd〕*adj.* 擁擠的

For question 24, you will listen to a short conversation.

　M：Have you met Jessica?　妳和潔西卡見過面了嗎？
　W：We were roommates in college.　我們是大學室友。

　　　* roommate〔ˈrumˌmet〕*n.* 室友

24.（**C**）Q：What does the woman mean?　這位女士是什麼意思？
　　　　A. She is looking for a new roommate.
　　　　　她正在尋找一位新室友。
　　　　B. She didn't go to college.　她沒有上大學。
　　　　C. She has known Jessica for a long time.
　　　　　她認識潔西卡很久了。
　　　　D. She has never met Jessica.　她從來沒見過潔西卡。

For questions 25 and 26, you will listen to a short conversation.

　M：What are you watching?　妳在看什麼？
　W：The Red Sox versus the Yankees.　It's 5 to 4, the bottom
　　　of the ninth.　The Yankees are down by one run.　Two
　　　outs, bases loaded.　紅襪對洋基。現在是五比四，第九局
　　　下半。洋基隊落後一分。兩人出局，滿壘。

M : Wow! I thought you hated baseball.

哇！我以爲妳討厭棒球。

W : I do, kind of. Usually the games are so slow and boring. But a tight game between two archrivals is really exciting to watch! 我是有一點。通常棒球比賽速度都很慢、很無聊。但是，看兩大對手勢均力敵的比賽就眞的很刺激！

M : Who are you rooting for? 妳支持誰呢？

W : I hope the Red Sox hold on to win.

我希望紅襪隊能堅持到獲勝。

* versus〔'vɝsəs〕prep. 對抗
bottom〔'batəm〕n.（棒球）下半局
down〔daʊn〕adj. 被打敗的　　run〔rʌn〕n.（棒球）得分
out〔aʊt〕n. 出局　　base〔bes〕n.（棒球）壘
loaded〔'lodɪd〕adj. 滿壘的　　hate〔het〕v. 討厭
kind of 有一點　　tight〔taɪt〕adj. 緊的；勢均力敵的
archrival〔'artʃ,raɪvḷ〕n. 首要對手；大敵
root〔rut〕v. 支持；加油 <*for*>　　*hold on* 堅持下去

25. (**B**) Q : What does the woman think about baseball?

這位女士對棒球的看法爲何？

A. It is a dangerous sport. 棒球是一種危險的運動。

B. It is usually slow and boring.

棒球通常速度很慢、很無聊。

C. It is her favorite pastime. 棒球是她最喜歡的消遣。

D. It is wild and crazy. 棒球很野蠻、很瘋狂。

* pastime〔'pæs,taɪm〕n. 消遣
wild〔waɪld〕adj. 野蠻的；粗暴的

26. (**D**) Q : What is true about the woman?
　　　　　關於這位女士何者為眞？
　　　A. She wants the Yankees to win the game.
　　　　她希望洋基隊贏得比賽。
　　　B. She doesn't know anything about baseball.
　　　　她對棒球一無所知。
　　　C. She watches a lot of baseball. 她常常看棒球。
　　　D. She wants the Red Sox to win the game.
　　　　她希望紅襪隊贏得比賽。

For questions 27 and 28, you will listen to a short conversation.

　M : Did you hear about Carl Carlson, the movie star who got arrested for drug smuggling? They caught him at the airport with two kilos of cocaine in his luggage, trying to board a plane to Hawaii. 你有聽說卡爾・卡爾森，那個因為走私毒品而被捕的電影明星嗎？他們在機場逮到他，行李裡面藏了二公斤古柯鹼，試圖搭上飛機前往夏威夷。

　W : How stupid do you have to be to think you can get away with that? 要蠢到什麼地步，才會認為做那種事可以逍遙法外？

　M : I guess Carlson isn't the brightest lantern at the festival, but he did hire some big-shot, high-profile defense attorney. 我想卡爾森不是最聰明的，但他確實雇用了某個大牌、有名的辯護律師。

　W : That's a pretty serious crime. He's looking at jail time. 那是很嚴重的罪。他應該會坐牢吧。

M : Well, you never know.　Lawyers can work miracles.

嗯，很難說。律師可能會創造奇蹟。

W : Innocent until proven guilty.

被證明有罪之前，都被視為無罪。

M : Though it's a little different when they get caught red-handed.　不過如果是當場被捕的現行犯，就有點不同了。

W : Yes, and I hope Carlson doesn't get off with a slap on the wrist.　A lot of celebrities act like they're above the law.　是啊，而且我希望卡爾森不會只得到輕罰就脫身了。有很多名人都以為自己是超越法律、不受法律約束的。

* arrest〔əˋrɛst〕v. 逮捕　　drug〔drʌg〕n. 毒品
smuggle〔ˋsmʌg!〕v. 走私　　kilo〔ˋkɪlo〕n. 公斤
cocaine〔koˋken〕n. 古柯鹼　　luggage〔ˋlʌgɪdʒ〕n. 行李
board〔bord〕v. 上（車、船、飛機等）
get away with　（做壞事卻）不受處罰；逍遙法外
bright〔braɪt〕adj. 明亮的　　lantern〔ˋlæntən〕n. 燈籠
festival〔ˋfɛstəv!〕n. 節慶
the brightest lantern at the festival　字面意思是「節慶中最明亮的一盞燈」，引申為「群體中最聰明的人」。
hire〔haɪr〕v. 雇用　　some〔sʌm〕adj. 某個
big-shot adj. 重要的；大牌的
profile〔ˋprofaɪl〕n. 側面；輪廓
high-profile adj. 高姿態的；高調的；有名的
defense〔dɪˋfɛns〕n. 防衛；辯護　　attorney〔əˋtɜnɪ〕n. 律師
pretty〔ˋprɪtɪ〕adv. 相當地　　jail〔dʒel〕n. 監獄；監禁
be looking at jail time　可能會坐牢（ = *may be sentenced to jail* ）
you never know　很難說；難以預料
miracle〔ˋmɪrək!〕n. 奇蹟　　***work miracles***　創造奇蹟
innocent〔ˋɪnəsn̩t〕adj. 無罪的　　prove〔pruv〕v. 證明
guilty〔ˋgɪltɪ〕adj. 有罪的　　red-handed adj. 現行犯的

get off 脫身；倖免　　slap〔slæp〕*n. v.* 打耳光；掌擊
wrist〔rɪst〕*n.* 手腕　　*a slap on the wrist* 手腕上拍一下；輕罰
celebrity〔sə'lɛbrətɪ〕*n.* 名人
act〔ækt〕*v.* 行為；舉止；表現得
above the law 超越法律；法律管不到

27. (**B**) Q : What does the woman imply?　這位女士暗示什麼？

A. Celebrities should be beaten.　名人應該被打。

B. Everyone has to obey the law.　人人都應該守法。

C. The movie star doesn't use drugs.
這位電影明星沒有吸毒。

D. The movie star should get special treatment.
這位電影明星應該得到特殊待遇。

* imply〔ɪm'plaɪ〕*v.* 暗示　　beat〔bit〕*v.* 打
obey〔ə'be〕*v.* 遵守　　*use drug* 吸毒
treatment〔'tritmənt〕*n.* 對待

28. (**C**) Q : What was Carl Carlson arrested for?
卡爾・卡爾森因為什麼事情被逮捕？

A. Hiring a high-profile attorney.　雇用一位有名的律師。

B. Lighting lanterns at the festival.　在節慶時點燈籠。

C. Smuggling drugs.　走私毒品。

D. Slapping someone's wrist.　輕拍某人的手腕。

* light〔laɪt〕*v.* 點火；點亮

For questions 29 and 30, you will listen to a short conversation.

W : I'm surprised this place is so crowded on a Monday
night.　我很驚訝，這個地方星期一晚上竟然人這麼多。

M : This is nothing. You should see it on the weekends.
這沒什麼。妳應該週末來看看。

W：I can imagine. We probably wouldn't be able to get a table. 我可以想像。我們可能沒辦法有桌子坐了。

M：Well, I know the manager, so he'd find something for us. 嗯，我認識經理，所以他會幫我們想辦法的。

W：Wow! So you come here often. 哇！所以你常來這裡囉。

M：Oh, sure. I'm a regular customer. 噢，當然。我是常客。

　*imagine〔ɪ'mædʒɪn〕v. 想像　　manager〔'mænɪdʒɚ〕n. 經理
　regular〔'rɛgjələ〕adj. 經常的；固定的
　customer〔'kʌstəmɚ〕n. 顧客

29. (**C**) Q：Where are the speakers? 說話者在哪裡？
　　A. They are on a bus. 他們在公車上。
　　B. They are in a classroom. 他們在教室裡。
　　C. They are in a restaurant. 他們在餐廳裡。
　　D. They are in a doctor's office. 他們在醫生的診所裡。
　　*office〔'ɔfɪs〕v. 診所

30. (**A**) Q：What is true about the man? 關於這位男士何者爲眞？
　　A. He dines there often. 他經常在那裡用餐。
　　B. He makes trouble for the manager.
　　　他爲經理製造麻煩。
　　C. He avoids the place on weekends.
　　　他週末會避開那個地方。
　　D. He is surprised it is so crowded.
　　　他很驚訝那裡人那麼多。
　　*dine〔daɪn〕v. 用餐　　***make trouble*** 製造麻煩
　　avoid〔ə'vɔɪd〕v. 避免；避開

四、短文聽解

Questions 31 and 32 are based on the following report.

We must help parents protect their children from the worst health threat that they face—an epidemic of teen smoking, spread by multimillion-dollar marketing campaigns. We need to challenge Congress to pass legislation that will improve public health and change the way tobacco companies do business forever. Let's do what it takes to control teen smoking. Let's raise the tax on cigarettes up to $5.00 a pack over the next 2 years, and penalize the tobacco industry if it keeps marketing to our children.

我們必須幫助父母們保護他們的孩子，免於他們所面臨最嚴重的健康威脅——青少年吸煙的流行，這是因為數百萬美元的行銷活動而傳播開來的。我們必須要求國會通過法令，來改善公共衛生，並永久改變香菸公司做生意的方式。讓我們做所需要做的事，來控制青少年吸煙的問題。讓我們在未來的兩年內，將香菸稅提高到一包五元，而如果香菸業者繼續對我們的孩子銷售的話，就處罰他們。

** ────────────────

threat〔θrɛt〕n. 威脅　　face〔fes〕v. 面臨
epidemic〔͵ɛpə'dɛmɪk〕n. 流行
teen〔tin〕adj. 十幾歲的；青少年的（= teenage）
spread〔sprɛd〕v. 傳播；散播
multimillion〔͵mʌltə'mɪljən〕adj. 數百萬的
marketing〔'markɪtɪŋ〕n. 行銷　　campaign〔kæm'pen〕n. 活動
challenge〔'tʃælɪndʒ〕v. 挑戰；要求
Congress〔'kaŋgrəs〕n.（美國）國會　　pass〔pæs〕v. 通過
legislation〔͵lɛdʒɪs'leʃən〕n. 立法；法律
public health 公共衛生　　tobacco〔tə'bæko〕n. 香菸；煙草

what it takes 所需要的一切   raise〔rez〕*v.* 提高
tax〔tæks〕*n.* 稅   ***up to*** 高達
pack〔pæk〕*n.* (煙) 一包；一盒   penalize〔'pinḷ,aɪz〕*v.* 處罰
industry〔'ɪndəstrɪ〕*n.* 產業   market〔'markɪt〕*v.* 銷售；販賣

31. (**B**) Who is the speaker? 說話者是誰？
A. An engineer. 一位工程師。
B. A politician. 一位政治人物。
C. A tobacco user. 一位吸煙者。
D. A marketing executive. 一位行銷主管。

* politician〔,palə'tɪʃən〕*n.* 政治人物
executive〔ɪg'zɛkjətɪv〕*n.* 主管

32. (**A**) What does the speaker suggest? 說話者建議什麼？
A. Raising the taxes on cigarettes. 提高香菸稅。
B. Penalizing teen smokers. 處罰少年吸煙者。
C. Pretending the problem doesn't exist.
假裝這個問題不存在。
D. Changing the way Congress markets to children.
改變國會銷售給小孩的方式。

* suggest〔sə(g)'dʒɛst〕*v.* 建議   pretend〔prɪ'tɛnd〕*v.* 假裝
exist〔ɪg'zɪst〕*v.* 存在

Questions 33 and 34 are based on the following report.

The cost of a human life is a common tool employed in the analysis of regulations for everything from drug bottle warning labels to the standards on the strength of car roofs. Every policy decision that can save lives or prevent injuries can be equated to a monetary value that represents the life saved or injury avoided—hence, the price of life. What adds an element of confusion to these formulas is that this value changes. Every presidential administration, every government agency and every corporation determines its own number to equate to a human life. According to *The New York Times*, the numbers fall into the $5 million to $10 million range.

　　人命的代價是一個常見的工具，應用在各種規定的分析中，從藥瓶上的警告標籤，到汽車車頂的強度標準等。每一項能夠拯救人命或避免傷害的政策決定，都等同於一個金錢上的價值，代表著被拯救的人命或被避免的傷害——因此，這就是生命的價格。在這些公式中有些許的困惑是，這個價值是會變的。每個總統府團隊、每個政府機關，和每家公司，都有他們自己等同於一條人命的數字。根據紐約時報的說法，這些數字落在五百萬到一千萬元的範圍內。

**

cost〔kɔst〕*n.* 價格；代價　　　tool〔tul〕*n.* 工具
employ〔ɪm'plɔɪ〕*v.* 應用　　analysis〔ə'næləsɪs〕*n.* 分析
regulation〔ˌrɛgjə'leʃən〕*n.* 規定　　drug〔drʌg〕*n.* 藥
bottle〔'batḷ〕*n.* 瓶子　　label〔'lebḷ〕*n.* 標籤
standard〔'stændəd〕*n.* 標準　　strength〔strɛŋθ〕*n.* 強度
roof〔ruf〕*n.* 屋頂；車頂　　policy〔'paləsɪ〕*n.* 政策
injury〔'ɪndʒərɪ〕*n.* 傷害
equate〔ɪ'kwet〕*v.* 把…視為同等；使相等；相等
monetary〔'mʌnəˌtɛrɪ〕*adj.* 金錢的
represent〔ˌrɛprɪ'zɛnt〕*v.* 代表　　avoid〔ə'vɔɪd〕*v.* 避免
hence〔hɛns〕*adv.* 因此；所以　　add〔æd〕*v.* 添加
element〔'ɛləmənt〕*n.* 些微　　***an element of*** 些微；有些
confusion〔kən'fjuʒən〕*n.* 困惑　　formula〔'fɔrmjələ〕*n.* 公式
presidential〔ˌprɛzə'dɛnʃəl〕*adj.* 總統的
administration〔ədˌmɪnə'streʃən〕*n.* 管理；政府
agency〔'edʒənsɪ〕*n.* (政府) 機關

corporation〔,kɔrpə'reʃən〕*n.* 公司
determine〔dɪ'tɜmɪn〕*v.* 決定
fall into 落入；屬於　　range〔rendʒ〕*n.* 範圍

33. (**A**) What is the price of life? 什麼是生命的價格？

   A. A monetary value that represents a life saved or injury avoided.
     代表被拯救的生命或被避免的傷害的金錢價值。

   B. The value of warning labels. 警告標籤的價值。

   C. About $10 million on a good day.
     天氣好時大約一千萬元。

   D. The amount a family pays to give birth to a child.
     一個家庭生一個小孩所付的金額。

   * *give birth to* 生（小孩）

34. (**A**) According to the article, what is confusing about the cost of a life? 根據本文，關於生命的代價，何者是令人困惑的？

   A. Its value changes. 它的價值會變動。

   B. The cost doesn't rise when a life is saved.
     當一條人命被拯救時，費用不會增加。

   C. Presidential administrations often ignore the formula.
     總統府團隊經常忽視這個公式。

   D. The New York Times is a daily paper.
     紐約時報是一份日報。

   * rise〔raɪz〕*v.* 上升；增加　　ignore〔ɪg'nor〕*v.* 忽視
    daily〔'delɪ〕*adj.* 每日的

Questions 35 and 36 are based on the following report.

   While some have suggested a standardized value for the cost of a life, others believe that the price of life really does vary. It might be worth more or less depending on how the person died and how much suffering was involved; so some might feel that a life that ends after a long battle with cancer should be given a different value from one that ended quickly in a car crash. The lack of a standard number allows for a degree of flexibility in the process. However, those decisions should not just be made based on hard numbers; we hope that politicians and policy makers—those who ultimately determine the price—strive only to make all of us safer.

　　雖然有些人建議，生命的代價要有標準化的價值，但也有些人相信，生命的價格確實是會變動的。它的價值較多或較少，都取決於一個人如何死亡，以及其中包含多少痛苦來決定；所以，有些人可能會覺得，在長期與癌症搏鬥後結束的生命，和在車禍中快速結束的生命，應該給予不同的價值。沒有一個標準的數字，正是考慮到在這個過程中有一點彈性。然而，那些決定也不該只根據具體硬梆梆的數字來做；我們希望政治人物和決策者——那些最終決定價格的人——只是努力讓我們大家更安全一點。

**

while〔hwaɪl〕conj. 雖然　　**some…others~** 有些…有些~
standardized〔'stændəd,aɪzd〕adj. 標準化的
vary〔'vɛrɪ〕v. 變化；不同　　worth〔wɝθ〕adj. 有…價值的
depend on 視~而定；取決於　　suffering〔'sʌf(ə)rɪŋ〕n. 痛苦
involve〔ɪn'vɑlv〕v. 包含；牽涉在內
battle〔'bætḷ〕n. 戰鬥　　crash〔kræʃ〕n. 墜毀；相撞
standard〔'stændəd〕adj. 標準的　　**allow for** 考慮到；斟酌
degree〔dɪ'gri〕n. 程度　　flexibility〔,flɛksə'bɪlətɪ〕n. 彈性
process〔'prɑsɛs〕n. 過程　　**based on** 根據
hard〔hɑrd〕adj. 具體的；硬梆梆的　　**policy maker** 決策者
ultimately〔'ʌltəmɪtlɪ〕adv. 最後　　strive〔straɪv〕v. 努力

35. (**A**) What might cause the price of life to vary?

何者可能會造成生命價格的變動？

A. How the person died and how much suffering was involved. 一個人如何死亡，以及其中包含多少痛苦。

B. How many survivors are left behind. 留下多少生還者。

C. The degree of flexibility among policy makers. 在決策者之間的彈性程度。

D. The type of cancer that ends up being fatal. 最後會致命的癌症種類。

* survivor〔sɚ'vaɪvɚ〕n. 生還者　*leave behind* 遺留
end up 最後　fatal〔'fetḷ〕adj. 致命的

36. (**B**) What is true about the cost of a life?

關於生命的價格何者為真？

A. It is an exact science. 這是一門精確的科學。

B. It is generally determined by politicians and policy makers. 這通常由政治人物和決策者來決定。

C. It is better to die quickly to keep the prices high. 為了要保持高價，最好很快就死亡。

D. It is worth more if you die on a Sunday. 如果在星期日死亡會價值高一點。

* exact〔ɪg'zækt〕adj. 精確的
generally〔'dʒɛnərəlɪ〕adv. 通常

Questions 37 and 38 are based on the following report.

Americans have more freedom than citizens of almost any other nation in the world, including the freedom to criticize their government and their elected officials. But we do not have the right to resort to violence—or the threat of violence—when we don't get our way. Our system of

government is designed to let reason prevail over fear.
Without the law there is no freedom. Criticism is part of
the lifeblood of democracy. No one is right all the time.
But we should remember that there is a big difference
between criticizing a policy or a politician and demonizing
the government that guarantees our freedoms and the public
servants who enforce our laws.

美國人比世界上幾乎任何國家的國民，擁有更多的自由，包括
批評他們的政府，和所選出的官員的自由。但是當我們無法照自己
的意思做事時，我們沒有訴諸於暴力——或威脅使用暴力——的權
力。我們的政府體系的設計，就是要讓理性戰勝恐懼。沒有法治就
沒有自由。批評是民主政治的原動力之一。沒有人永遠是對的。但
是我們應該要記得，批評政策或政治人物，以及將保障我們自由的
政府和為我們執法的公僕妖魔化，是有極大的不同的。

**

freedom ('fridəm) n. 自由　citizen ('sɪtəzṇ) n. 國民
criticize ('krɪtə,saɪz) v. 批評　elected (ɪ'lɛktɪd) adj. 被選出的
official (ə'fɪʃəl) n. 官員　right (raɪt) n. 權利
resort (rɪ'zɔrt) v. 訴諸 < to >　violence ('vaɪələns) n. 暴力
get one's way 想怎樣就怎樣；隨心所欲
system ('sɪstəm) n. 系統；制度　design (dɪ'zaɪn) v. 設計
reason ('rizṇ) n. 理性　prevail (prɪ'vel) v. 勝過 < over >
criticism ('krɪtə,sɪzəm) n. 批評
lifeblood ('laɪf,blʌd) n. 維持生命所需的血；生命；原動力
democracy (dɪ'mɑkrəsɪ) n. 民主政治
demonize ('dimən,aɪz) v. 妖魔化
guarantee (,gærən'ti) v. 保證　servant ('sɝvənt) n. 僕人
public servant 公僕；公務人員　enforce (ɪn'fors) v. 執行

37. (**C**) Which of the following is not something Americans
　　have? 下列何者不是美國人所擁有的？

A. The freedom to criticize their government.
批評他們政府的自由。
B. A system of government.　一套政府體系。
C. The right to resort to violence. 訴諸暴力的權利。
D. Democracy. 民主政治。

38. (**C**) What is true about freedom? 關於自由何者爲眞？
A. It doesn't prevail over fear. 自由不能戰勝恐懼。
B. It carries the threat of violence. 自由具有暴力的威脅。
C. It cannot exist without law. 自由沒有法治就無法存在。
D. It demonizes the government. 自由將政府妖魔化。
* carry〔ˈkærɪ〕v. 具有

Questions 39 and 40 are based on the following report.

Humor is infectious. The sound of roaring laughter is far more contagious than any cough, sniffle, or sneeze. When laughter is shared, it binds people together and increases happiness and intimacy. In addition to the domino effect of joy and amusement, laughter also triggers healthy physical changes in the body. Humor and laughter strengthen your immune system, boost your energy, diminish pain, and protect you from the damaging effects of stress. Best of all, this priceless medicine is fun, free, and easy to use.

幽默是會傳染的。轟隆的笑聲比任何的咳嗽、吸鼻子，或打噴嚏的聲音，更加具有感染力。當笑聲被分享時，可以把大家結合在一起，增加快樂和親密感。除了快樂和娛悅的骨牌效應之外，笑也會引發身體裡的健康的生理變化。幽默和笑可以增強免疫系統、提升精力、減少痛苦，並且保護你免於壓力帶來的有害影響。最好的是，這種珍貴的藥物是有趣、免費，而且是容易使用的。

**

humor〔'hjumɚ〕*n.* 幽默　　infectious〔ɪn'fɛkʃəs〕*adj.* 會傳染的
roaring〔'rorɪŋ〕*adj.* 轟隆作響的；喧鬧的
contagious〔kən'tedʒəs〕*adj.* 會傳染的　　cough〔kɔf〕*n.* 咳嗽
sniffle〔'snɪfḷ〕*n.* 抽鼻子；鼻塞 (= *snuffle*)
sneeze〔sniz〕*n.* 打噴嚏　　bind〔baɪnd〕*v.* 捆綁；束縛
intimacy〔'ɪntəməsɪ〕*n.* 親密　　***in addition to*** 除了～之外
domino〔'dɑmə‚no〕*n.* 骨牌　　effect〔ɪ'fɛkt〕*n.* 效果；效應
trigger〔'trɪgɚ〕*v.* 引發　　amusement〔ə'mjuzmənt〕*n.* 娛樂
physical〔'fɪzɪkḷ〕*adj.* 身體的；生理的
strengthen〔'strɛŋθən〕*v.* 加強　　immune〔ɪ'mjun〕*adj.* 免疫的
boost〔bust〕*v.* 提升　　energy〔'ɛnɚdʒɪ〕*n.* 精力；能量
diminish〔də'mɪnɪʃ〕*v.* 減少
damaging〔'dæmɪdʒɪŋ〕*adj.* 有害的　　stress〔strɛs〕*n.* 壓力
best of all 最好的是　　priceless〔'praɪslɪs〕*adj.* 無價的；珍貴的
fun〔fʌn〕*adj.* 有趣的　　free〔fri〕*adj.* 免費的

39. (**C**) What happens when laughter is shared?
當笑聲被分享時會發生什麼事？
　　A. It pulls people apart. 會使人們分離。
　　B. It knocks children to the ground. 會把小孩打倒在地。
　　C. It brings people together. 會使人們結合在一起。
　　D. It crushes the spirit. 會摧毀精神。
　　* ***pull apart*** 拉開；使分離　　knock〔nɑk〕*v.* 打擊
　　ground〔graʊnd〕*n.* 地面　　crush〔krʌʃ〕*v.* 壓碎；摧毀
　　spirit〔'spɪrɪt〕*n.* 精神

40. (**A**) What is true about humor? 關於幽默何者為眞？
　　A. It is contagious. 它是會傳染的。
　　B. It is expensive. 它是很昂貴的。
　　C. It is unhealthy. 它是不健康的。
　　D. It is painful. 它是很痛苦的。
　　* painful〔'penfəl〕*adj.* 使人痛苦的

高中英聽測驗模擬試題 ⑤ 詳解

一、看圖辨義：第一部分

For question number 1, please look at picture 1.

1. (**C**)　A woman is cleaning the window.　A boy is mopping the floor.　有個女士正在清潔窗戶。有個男孩正在拖地。

　　　* mop〔map〕v.（用拖把）拖（地）

For question number 2, please look at picture 2.

2. (**D**)　These kids are in a cafeteria.　Henry and Fred are looking for a place to sit and eat.　這些孩子在一間自助餐廳裡。亨利和弗瑞德正在找地方坐下來吃飯。

　　　* cafeteria〔͵kæfə'tɪrɪə〕n. 自助餐廳　　*look for* 尋找

For question number 3, please look at picture 3.

3. (**B**) Marie is an excellent baker. She's making a birthday
cake for a friend.

　　瑪莉是個優秀的麵包師父。她正在替朋友做生日蛋糕。

　　　* excellent〔ˈɛkslənt〕 *adj.* 優秀的
　　　　baker〔ˈbekɚ〕 *n.* 麵包師父

For question number 4, please look at picture 4.

4. (**C**) Little John is an active boy. He is especially fond of
swinging from trees.

　　小約翰是個活潑的男孩。他特別喜歡搖盪在樹上。

　　　* active〔ˈæktɪv〕 *adj.* 活潑的
　　　　especially〔əˈspɛʃəlɪ〕 *adv.* 特別地
　　　　be fond of 喜歡　　swing〔swɪŋ〕 *v.* 搖擺;搖盪

一、看圖辨義：第二部分

For question number 5, please look at picture 5.

5. (**B**、**C**) Which TWO of the following are true about the
man? 關於這位男士，下列哪兩項敘述為眞？

    A. He is staying in room 703.

       他正住在 703 房。

    B. He is delivering room service to room 703.

       他正在為 703 房送上客房服務。

    C. He is knocking on the door.

       他正在敲門。

    D. He is ringing the bell.

       他正在按門鈴。

    * stay〔 ste 〕*v.* 暫住   deliver〔 dɪ'lɪvə 〕*v.* 遞送
    room service 客房服務   knock〔 nɑk 〕*v.* 敲
    ring the bell 按門鈴

For question number 6, please look at picture 6.

6. (**A**、**B**) Which TWO of the following are true about the
woman? 關於這位女士，下列哪兩項敘述為眞？

    A. She is about to have a meal.

       她正準備用餐。

    B. She is alone. 她是獨自一個人。

    C. She is about to get dressed.

       她正要穿衣服。

    D. She is asleep. 她正在睡覺。

    * ***be about to V***. 正要～   have〔 hæv 〕*v.* 吃
    meal〔 mil 〕*n.* 一餐   alone〔 ə'lon 〕*v.* 獨自地
    get dressed 穿衣服

For question number 7, please look at picture 7.

7. (**A、B**) Which TWO of the following are true about the
man? 關於這位男士，下列哪兩項敘述為眞？

   A. He has touched the woman's
butt. 他碰了那個女人的臀部。

   B. He has one hand behind his
back. 他一隻手放在背後。

   C. He has spilled his drink.
他灑出了他的飲料。

   D. He has offended the other customers.
他冒犯了其他的顧客。

  * butt〔bʌt〕*n.* 臀部　　spill〔spɪl〕*v.* 灑出；潑出
    offend〔əˋfɛnd〕*v.* 冒犯；觸怒
    customer〔ˋkʌstəmɚ〕*n.* 顧客

For question number 8, please look at picture 8.

8. (**B、C**) Which TWO of the following are true about the
people in the picture?
關於圖片中的人，下列哪兩項敘述為眞？

   A. The boy is excited.
那個男孩很興奮。

   B. The man is angry.
那個男人很憤怒。

   C. The boy is upset. 那個男孩很不高興。

   D. The man is pleased. 那個男人很開心。

  * upset〔ʌpˋsɛt〕*adj.* 不高興的
    pleased〔plizd〕*adj.* 高興的

For question number 9, please look at picture 9.

9. (**A、B**) Which TWO of the following are true about the girl?

關於這個女孩，下列哪兩項敘述為眞？

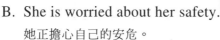

　　A. She is walking alone at night.

　　　她在晚上獨自一人走路。

　　B. She is worried about her safety.

　　　她正擔心自己的安危。

　　C. She is having a casual stroll in the park.

　　　她正在公園悠閒地散步。

　　D. She is accompanied by her boyfriend.

　　　她的男朋友陪伴著她。

　be worried about　擔心　　safety〔ˋseftɪ〕*n.* 安全
　casual〔ˋkæʒuəḷ〕*adj.* 悠閒的
　stroll〔strɔl〕*n.* 漫步；散步
　accompany〔əˋkʌmpənɪ〕*v.* 陪伴

For question number 10, please look at picture 10.

10. (**A、B**) Which TWO of the following are true about the boy?

關於這個男孩，下列哪兩項敘述為眞？

　　A. He is late for class.

　　　他上學遲到了。

　　B. He is a student.

　　　他是個學生。

　　C. He is angry with his teacher.　他在生老師的氣。

　　D. He is yelling at his teacher.

　　　他正對著老師吼叫。

　be angry with sb. 對某人生氣
　yell〔jɛl〕*v.* 吼叫

二、對答

11. (**D**) Do you want chicken or pork? 你要吃雞肉還是豬肉？

       A. I had the fish. 我吃了魚了。

       B. Medium rare. 四分熟。

       C. I don't speak Chinese. 我不說中文。

       D. I'll have the chicken. 我要吃雞肉。

       * pork〔pork〕*n.* 豬肉
         medium〔'midɪəm〕*adj.* （牛排）五分熟的
         rare〔rɛr〕*adj.* （牛排）三分熟的

12. (**C**) Why is the door unlocked? 門鎖爲什麼打開了？

       A. Close the door. 把門關上。

       B. I just bought the lock. 我剛剛買了鎖。

       C. I must have forgot to lock it. 我一定是忘記鎖門了。

       D. Open a window then. 那麼打開一扇窗戶吧。

       * unlock〔ʌn'lɑk〕*v.* 開鎖　　lock〔lɑk〕*n.* 鎖　*v.* 鎖上

13. (**C**) Is that John's bike? 那是約翰的腳踏車嗎？

       A. I don't know how to ride a bike.

         我不知道如何騎腳踏車。

       B. I found it in the street. 我在街上發現它的。

       C. Yes, it is John's bike. 是的，那是約翰的腳踏車。

       D. We can ride there together. 我們可以一起騎去那裡。

14. (**A**) Is there an ATM nearby? 這附近有提款機嗎？

       A. There's one on the next block. 下一條街有一台。

       B. I have plenty of cash. 我有很多現金。

       C. No, they aren't. 不，它們不是。

D. Ask someone if there is an ATM nearby.

找個人問這附近有沒有提款機。

* **ATM** 自動櫃員機；提款機 (= *Automated Teller Machine*)
nearby (ˈnɪrˈbaɪ) *adv.* 在附近　　block (blɑk) *n.* 街區
plenty of 很多的　　cash (kæʃ) *n.* 現金

15. (**C**) What time is it? 現在幾點了？

A. We are out of time. 我們沒有時間了。
B. It's Tuesday. 星期二。
C. It's six-fifteen. 六點十五分。
D. It's my time. 這是我的時間。

* **be out of** 沒有；缺乏

16. (**A**) How's the pizza? 披薩好吃嗎？

A. It's delicious. Would you like a slice?
很好吃。你想要來一片嗎？
B. Cheese and sausage. 起司和臘腸。
C. He is at home. 他現在在家。
D. I ordered a pizza. 我點了一個披薩。

* pizza (ˈpitsə) *n.* 披薩　　**would like** 想要
slice (slaɪs) *n.* 一片　　sausage (ˈsɔsɪdʒ) *n.* 香腸；臘腸
order (ˈɔrdɚ) *v.* 點 (菜)

17. (**D**) Are you a good student? 你是個好學生嗎？

A. I'm in the fifth grade. 我五年級。
B. I like my teachers. 我喜歡我的老師。
C. My classmates are disruptive.
我的同學很會搗蛋。
D. Yes, I study hard and get good grades.
是的，我用功讀書，成績也很好。

* grade 〔 gred 〕 *n.* 年級；成績
disruptive 〔 dɪsˈrʌptɪv 〕 *adj.* 引起混亂的

18. (**A**) Would you like a ride home? 你想要我載你回家嗎？

    A. No, thanks. I would prefer to walk.

       不，謝謝。我比較喜歡走路。

    B. They took me for a ride. 他們載我去兜風。

    C. She likes him. 她喜歡他。

    D. No, he doesn't. 不，他不是。

    * ride 〔 raɪd 〕 *n.* 搭乘　　prefer 〔 prɪˈfɝ 〕 *v.* 比較喜歡
    take sb. for a ride 載某人去兜風

19. (**B**) Is it raining? 現在正在下雨嗎？

    A. It's the rainy season. 現在是雨季。

    B. No, it's not. 不，沒有。

    C. We could use the rain. 下點雨也不錯。

    D. My clothes are wet from the rain.

          我的衣服因為下雨都濕了。

    * rainy 〔ˈrenɪ〕 *adj.* 下雨的　　season 〔ˈsizn̩〕 *n.* 季節
    could use 可以有點～；有點～也不錯
    wet 〔 wɛt 〕 *adj.* 濕的

20. (**C**) She's a nice lady, isn't she?

    她是一位很不錯的淑女，不是嗎？

    A. Yes, they are. 是的，他們是的。

    B. No, he isn't. 不，他不是。

    C. Yes, she is. 是的，她是。

    D. No, I didn't. 不，我沒有。

三、簡短對話

For question 21, you will listen to a short conversation.

M : Good evening, ma'am. Would you care to hear about tonight's specials?

　　晚安，女士。您想要聽聽今日特餐的內容嗎？

W : Not tonight. I'll have the blackened tuna and a glass of Pinot noir.

　　今晚不要。我想要香煎鮪魚排，和一杯黑比諾葡萄酒。

　　* care〔kɛr〕v. 想要　　***hear about*** 聽聽有關～的事
　　special〔'spɛʃəl〕n. 特餐
　　blacken〔'blækən〕v.（使）變黑【源自法國的一個烹飪方法，
　　　是在肉類或是魚類上抹一層厚厚的香料粉，再大火去煎或烤到香料
　　　變黑的菜餚】　　tuna〔'tunə〕n. 鮪魚
　　Pinot noir　n. 黑比諾【釀造紅葡萄酒的葡萄品種之一】

21.（**B**） Q : Where are these people?　這些人在哪裡？

　　A. They are in an auditorium.　他們在大禮堂。
　　B. They are in a restaurant.　他們在餐廳。
　　C. They are in the ocean.　他們在海洋裡。
　　D. They are in a winery.　他們在葡萄酒釀造廠。

　　* auditorium〔͵ɔdə'torɪəm〕n. 大禮堂
　　winery〔'waɪnərɪ〕n. 葡萄酒釀造廠

For question 22, you will listen to a short conversation.

M : How's your soup?　妳的湯如何？

W : It's really salty. I think I'm going to send it back.

　　真的很鹹。我想我要退回去。

M : Let me taste it first. 先讓我嚐嚐看。

W : Here, try it. Tell me if it is as salty as I think it is.

來，試試看。告訴我是否和我想的一樣鹹。

　　* salty〔'sɔltɪ〕 adj. 鹹的　　taste〔test〕v. 品嚐　n. 味道

22.（**B**） Q : What's wrong with the woman's soup?

這位女士的湯有什麼問題？

A. It doesn't have enough salt. 鹽放得不夠多。

B. It may be too salty. 可能太鹹了。

C. It is definitely too salty. 確實太鹹了。

D. It has no taste. 沒味道。

　　* salt〔sɔlt〕 n. 鹽　　definitely〔'dɛfənɪtlɪ〕 adv. 確實地

For question 23, you will listen to a short conversation.

W : How was the meeting? 會開得怎樣？

M : Like having a tooth pulled without painkillers.

很像拔牙沒有打止痛藥。

　　* pull〔pʊl〕v. 拔出　　painkiller〔'pen,kɪlɚ〕 n. 止痛藥

23.（**B**） Q : What does the man say about the meeting?

這位男士說會議進行得如何？

A. The meeting was productive. 會議很有收穫。

B. The meeting was unpleasant. 會議很不愉快。

C. The meeting was cancelled. 會議被取消了。

D. The meeting was painless. 會議很輕鬆。

　　* productive〔prə'dʌktɪv〕 adj. 有生產力的；有收穫的
　　unpleasant〔ʌn'plɛznt〕 adj. 不愉快的
　　painless〔'penlɪs〕 adj. 無痛苦的；容易的

For question 24, you will listen to a short conversation.

W：How was the movie? 電影好看嗎？

M：A lot like my first marriage; it went on way too long and had a terrible ending.

很像我的第一段婚姻；拖得太長了，結局很糟。

　　＊ marriage〔ˈmærɪdʒ〕 n. 婚姻　　　***go on*** 進行
　　way〔we〕 adv. 非常地　　 ending〔ˈɛndɪŋ〕 n. 結局

24. (**C**) Q：What does the man think about the movie?

這位男士覺得這部電影如何？

　　A. It was romantic. 很浪漫。

　　B. It made him want to get married again.

很使他想要再婚。

　　C. It wasn't very good. 不是很好。

　　D. It didn't remind him of anything.

沒有使他想起任何事情。

　　＊ romantic〔roˈmæntɪk〕 adj. 浪漫的
　　remind〔rɪˈmaɪnd〕 v. 提醒；使想起

For questions 25 and 26, you will listen to a short conversation.

W：You're sure working late tonight. What's going on?

你今天真的工作到很晚。發生了什麼事？

M：Oh, I've got a lot of paperwork to do. I figured I might as well get it over with. I don't want anything to spoil the weekend. 噢，我有很多文書工作要做。我想最好把它處理完。我不想有任何事破壞了週末。

W：Are you going somewhere this weekend?

你這個週末要去哪裡嗎？

M：Yes, I'm going on a fishing trip with my brother-in-law.

是的，我要和我的姐夫去釣魚。

W：I didn't know you were interested in fishing.

我不知道你對釣魚有興趣。

M：I'm not.　But it's a chance to get out of the city and

breathe some fresh air.

我沒有。但這是個可以遠離都市，呼吸一些新鮮空氣的機會。

* **go on** 發生　　paperwork〔'pepɚ,wɝk〕n. 文書工作
figure〔'fɪɡɚ〕v. 料想
might as well + V. 最好~ (= had better + V.)
get sth. over with 處理掉某事　　spoil〔spɔɪl〕v. 破壞
brother-in-law n. 姐夫；妹夫　　breathe〔brið〕v. 呼吸
fresh〔frɛʃ〕adj. 新鮮的

25. (**B**) Q：Where are these people?　這些人在哪裡？

　　　A. They're on a fishing trip.　他們正在釣魚。

　　　B. They're in an office.　他們在辦公室裡。

　　　C. They're out of the city.　他們離開了都市。

　　　D. They're at a business convention.

　　　　　他們正在開商業會議。

　　　* convention〔kən'vɛnʃən〕n. 會議

26. (**C**) Q：What is the man doing?　這位男士正在做什麼？

　　　A. Fishing.　釣魚。

　　　B. Talking to his brother.　和他的兄弟說話。

C. Paperwork. 文書工作。

D. Leaving the city. 離開都市。

For questions 27 and 28, you will listen to a short conversation.

W : How much beer did you order for the party?

舞會要用的啤酒你訂了多少？

M : Three cases each of Heineken and Budweiser.

海尼根和百威啤酒各三箱。

W : Six cases? That's not nearly enough. A lot of these
guys are serious drinkers.

才六箱嗎？那幾乎是不夠的。這些人當中有許多都是很會喝的。

M : Then how much do you think I should order?

那妳認為我應該訂多少？

W : Double it. Twelve cases total. 兩倍吧。總共十二箱。

M : We're going to need double the ice, too.

那我們也需要兩倍的冰塊。

W : Whatever it takes. Money is not an object.

該買的就買。錢不是問題。

M : OK, so I'll order a couple of extra cases, just in case.
We don't want to run out of anything. 好的，所以為了
以防萬一，我再多訂幾箱。我們不想有什麼不夠的。

---

* beer〔 bɪr 〕*n.* 啤酒　　order〔'ɔrdɚ〕*v.* 訂購
case〔 kes 〕*n.* 箱　　nearly〔'nɪrlɪ〕*adv.* 幾乎
serious drinker 酗酒者；很會喝酒的人（= *hard drinker*）
double〔'dʌbḷ〕*v.* 使加倍

total〔'totḷ〕adj. 總計的【這裡等於 in total (總共)】

double the ~ 兩倍的~　　**whatever it takes** 不惜一切

is not an object 不成問題 (= *is no object*)

a couple of 幾個　　extra〔'ɛkstrə〕adj. 額外的

just in case 以防萬一　　**run out of** 用完

27. (**B**) Q : What did the man do? 這位男士做了什麼事？

    A. He ordered three cases of beer. 他訂了三箱啤酒。

    B. He ordered six cases of beer. 他訂了六箱啤酒。

    C. He forgot to order the ice. 他忘了訂冰塊。

    D. He ran out of money. 他的錢用完了。

28. (**C**) Q : What is the man going to do?

        這位男士將要做什麼事？

    A. Cancel the order. 取消訂單。

    B. Run out of ice. 把冰塊用完。

    C. Order at least eight more cases of beer.

        至少再多訂八箱啤酒。

    D. Order twenty-four cases of beer. 訂二十四箱啤酒。

For questions 29 and 30, you will listen to a short conversation.

M : Did you finish sending out all the wedding invitations?

    妳把所有喜宴的邀請函都寄出去了嗎？

W : I sent them out last week. Why?

    我上週就寄了。你為什麼問？

M : We need to send one more. My cousin Jeffery in Spain
wants to come.

    我們必須在多寄一張。我在西班牙的表哥傑佛瑞要來。

W : Jeffery? Who's Jeffery? This is the first I'm hearing about a cousin named Jeffery.

傑佛瑞？誰是傑佛瑞？這是我第一次聽到有個叫傑佛瑞的表哥。

M : I haven't seen him for 20 years. He's on my father's side of the family.

我和他二十年沒見了。他是我爸爸那邊的親戚。

W : Well, that's going to affect more than just the invitations. Now I'll have to adjust the seating arrangements to accommodate your cousin. 嗯，不只是邀請函會受到影響。

我現在還必須調整座位的安排，以容納你的表哥。

* wedding〔'wɛdɪŋ〕n. 婚禮
  invitation〔͵ɪnvə'teʃən͵〕n. 請帖；邀請函
  cousin〔'kʌzn〕n. 表（堂）兄弟姊妹
  side〔saɪd〕n. 血統；家系　　affect〔ə'fɛkt〕v. 影響
  more than just 不只是　　adjust〔ə'dʒʌst〕v. 調整
  seating〔'sitɪŋ〕n. 座位　　arrangement〔ə'rendʒmənt〕n. 安排
  accommodate〔ə'kɑmə͵det〕v. 容納

29. (**D**) Q: Who are these people? 這些人是誰？

　　A. Brother and sister. 兄妹。

　　B. A married couple about to get divorced.
　　　即將要離婚的夫妻。

　　C. Father and daughter. 父女。

　　D. A couple about to get married.
　　　即將要結婚的一對男女。

* married〔'mærɪd〕adj. 已婚的　　**be about to** + V. 即將～
  divorce〔də'vors〕v., n. 離婚　　**get married** 結婚

30. (**B**) Q: Who is Jeffery? 誰是傑佛瑞？

　　　　A. The woman's brother. 這位女士的哥哥。
　　　　B. The man's cousin. 這位男士的表哥。
　　　　C. The woman's father. 這位女士的爸爸。
　　　　D. The man's uncle. 這位男士的叔叔。

四、短文聽解

Questions 31 and 32 are based on the following report.

　　I used to think we were in good financial shape. We save a good percentage of our income. We don't have any debt beyond our mortgage. We probably spend a bit too much on food and pet care, but we don't run up credit card bills to do it. The counselor was warm and welcoming as we entered the office. But as soon as we were seated, it was all business. The counselor said that we did not have enough life or disability insurance. We both have insurance that would cover about three or four years of earnings if one of us died. This seemed sufficient to get past a few years of sorting things out. The counselor disagreed. Going from two incomes to one would mean a radical rethinking of our life.

　　我以前認為我們的財務狀況良好。我們的收入有一定的比率都存起來。除了抵押貸款以外，我們沒有負債。也許我們在食物和照顧寵物上花費有一點太多，但我們並沒有累積信用卡帳單。當我們走進辦公室時，那位顧問很親切的歡迎我們。但等我們一坐下，就

全是生意話了。顧問說我們沒有足夠的壽險或殘障保險。我們倆都
有保險,如果我們其中一人死亡,還可以彌補大約三四年的收入。
這樣要過個幾年解決一些問題似乎還是足夠的。但顧問不同意。從
兩人的收入變成一人的收入,意味著要徹底重新考慮我們的生活方
式。

** ————————————

financial〔fəˋnænʃəl, faɪ-〕*adj.* 財務的
shape〔ʃep〕*n.* 狀況　　***in good shape*** 狀況良好
percentage〔pɚˋsɛntɪdʒ〕*n.* 百分比
a good percentage of 大部分的
income〔ˋɪn͵kʌm〕*n.* 收入　　debt〔dɛt〕*n.* 債務
beyond〔bɪˋjɑnd〕*prep.* 除了⋯以外
mortgage〔ˋmɔrgɪdʒ〕*n.* 抵押貸款　　pet〔pɛt〕*n.* 寵物
care〔kɛr〕*n.* 照顧　　***run up*** 增加;累積
bill〔bɪl〕*n.* 帳單　　counselor〔ˋkaunslɚ〕*n.* 顧問
warm〔wɔrm〕*adj.* 熱心的;親切的　　***be seated*** 就座
disability〔͵dɪsəˋbɪlətɪ〕*n.* 無能力;殘障
insurance〔ɪnˋʃurəns〕*n.* 保險
life insurance 人壽保險;壽險　　cover〔ˋkʌvɚ〕*v.* 涵蓋;彌補
earnings〔ˋɝnɪŋz〕*n. pl.* 賺得的錢;收入;薪水
sufficient〔səˋfɪʃənt〕*adj.* 足夠的　　past〔pæst〕*prep.* 經過
sort out 整理;解決　　disagree〔͵dɪsəˋgri〕*v.* 不同意
go〔go〕*v.* 變成;變為　　radical〔ˋrædɪkl̩〕*adj.* 徹底的
rethink〔riˋθɪŋk〕*v.* 重新考慮

31.（**A**）What is true about the speaker? 有關說話者何者正確?
　　A. He is married. 他已婚。
　　B. He is unemployed. 他失業。
　　C. He is an insurance salesman. 他是一位保險業務員。
　　D. He is a financial counselor. 他是一位財務顧問。

* unemployed〔͵ʌnɪmˈplɔɪd〕*adj.* 失業的
　　　　　salesman〔ˈselzmən〕*n.* 業務員；推銷員

32. (**D**) What did the counselor say? 這位顧問說了什麼？

　　　A. They should sell their house. 他們應該賣掉房子。
　　　B. They should quit their jobs. 他們應該辭掉工作。
　　　C. They should get rid of their pets.
　　　　　他們應該丟掉寵物。
　　　D. They should buy more life insurance.
　　　　　他們應該購買更多壽險。

　　　* quit〔kwɪt〕*v.* 辭（職）；擺脫　　***get rid of*** 除去

Questions 33 and 34 are based on the following report.

　　A good night's sleep isn't just about waking up refreshed in the morning. If you get the seven to nine hours experts advise, you can expect added benefits. People who get less than seven hours per night are three times likelier to catch colds. The reason? Sleep boosts immunity; too little impairs it. People who logged seven to nine hours a night had an average body mass almost 2 points lower than those who slept less. Not enough sleep may throw off hormones that regulate appetite, raise blood pressure and affect glucose metabolism.

　　一夜好眠不只是早上起床時神清氣爽而已。如果你如專家所建議的睡七到九小時，你可以期待有額外的好處。每晚睡眠少於七小時的人，感冒的可能性變成三倍。原因為何？睡覺可以提高免疫

力；太少則有損免疫力。每晚睡七到九小時的人，比起睡得比較少的人，平均身體質量減少兩個百分點。睡眠不足可能會使控制食慾的荷爾蒙減少、血壓升高，並影響葡萄糖的代謝。

** ————————————————

refreshed〔rɪ'frɛʃt〕 *adj.* 神清氣爽的
expert〔'ɛkspɝt〕 *n.* 專家　　advise〔əd'vaɪz〕 *v.* 建議
expect〔ɪk'spɛkt〕 *v.* 期待；期望
added〔'ædɪd〕 *adj.* 更多的
benefit〔'bɛnəfɪt〕 *n.* 利益；好處
likely〔'laɪklɪ〕 *adj.* 可能的　　boost〔bust〕 *v.* 提高；增加
immunity〔ɪ'mjunətɪ〕 *n.* 免疫力　　impair〔ɪm'pɛr〕 *v.* 損害
log〔lɑg, lɔg〕 *v.* 記錄　　average〔'ævərɪdʒ〕 *adj.* 平均的
mass〔mæs〕 *n.* 質量　　*body mass* 身體質量
point〔pɔɪnt〕 *n.* 度；點　　*throw off* 甩掉；擺脫掉
hormone〔'hɔrmon〕 *n.* 荷爾蒙　　regulate〔'rɛgjə,let〕 *v.* 控制
appetite〔'æpə,taɪt〕 *n.* 食慾；胃口　　raise〔rez〕 *v.* 提高
pressure〔'prɛʃɚ〕 *n.* 壓力　　*blood pressure* 血壓
affect〔ə'fɛkt〕 *v.* 影響　　glucose〔'glukos〕 *n.* 葡萄糖
metabolism〔mə'tæbḷ,ɪzəm〕 *n.* 新陳代謝

33. (**C**) What is true about a good night's sleep?
　　　有關一夜好眠何者正確？

　　A. It throws off hormones that regulate appetite.
　　　　它會使控制食慾的荷爾蒙減少。

　　B. It lowers the body mass. 它會使身體質量降低。

　　C. It comes with added benefits. 它會帶來額外的好處。

　　D. It wakes up refreshed. 它起床時會神清氣爽。

34. (**C**) What may happen if someone doesn't get enough sleep?
　　　一個人如果睡眠不足可能會發生什麼事？

A. They will lose weight. 他們體重會下降。
B. They will wake up feeling refreshed.
   他們起床時會感到神清氣爽。
C. They will be more likely to catch a cold.
   他們更有可能會感冒。
D. They will have impaired vision.
   他們可能會視力受損。

* vision ('vɪʒən) n. 視力

Questions 35 and 36 are based on the following report.

The economy may now be in recession, but when it recovers, confidence will increase, jobs will return and the Great Recession will become an unpleasant memory. Even so, some industries will never recover because they're destined to go the way of milkmen and carriage makers. There are 10 industries in America that had a steep decline in revenue in the last decade and are forecasted to lose more money in the next one. Extinction is a hard word, but unfortunately that's what all these industries are facing, due to external competition, technological change and lack of innovation.

經濟現在也許是處於不景氣之中,但當景氣復甦時,信心就會增加,工作機會就會回復,而大蕭條就將變成一段不愉快的回憶。即使如此,有些產業永遠無法恢復,因為它們注定要走上和送牛奶的人以及馬車製造商相同的路。在美國有十種產業,過去十年來歲收銳減,根據預測在未來的十年裡還會賠更多錢。滅亡是一個殘酷

的字眼，但不幸的是，那正是這些產業現在所面臨的，因為外來的
競爭、科技的改變，還有缺乏創新。

** —————————————————

economy〔ɪˋkɑnəmɪ〕 *n.* 經濟
recession〔rɪˋsɛʃən〕 *n.* 不景氣；蕭條
recover〔rɪˋkʌvɚ〕 *v.* 恢復
confidence〔ˋkɑnfədəns〕 *n.* 信心
unpleasant〔ʌnˋplɛznt〕 *adj.* 不愉快的
memory〔ˋmɛmərɪ〕 *n.* 記憶；回憶
industry〔ˋɪndəstrɪ〕 *n.* 產業
destined〔ˋdɛstɪnd〕 *adj.* 注定的
go the way of 和～走上相同之路
milkman〔ˋmɪlk͵mæn〕 *n.* 送牛奶的人
carriage〔ˋkærɪdʒ〕 *n.* 四輪馬車
steep〔stip〕 *adj.* 陡峭的；急遽的
decline〔dɪˋklaɪn〕 *n.* 衰退；下跌
revenue〔ˋrɛvə͵nju〕 *n.* 歲收；收入
decade〔ˋdɛked〕 *n.* 十年
forecast〔ˋfor͵kæst〕 *v.* 預測
extinction〔ɪkˋstɪŋkʃən〕 *n.* 絕種；滅亡
unfortunately〔ʌnˋfortʃənɪtlɪ〕 *adv.* 不幸地
due to 因為；由於　　external〔ɪkˋstɝnl〕 *adj.* 外部的
competition〔͵kɑmpəˋtɪʃən〕 *n.* 競爭
technological〔͵tɛknəˋlɑdʒɪkl〕 *adj.* 科技的
lack〔læk〕 *n.* 缺乏　　innovation〔͵ɪnəˋveʃən〕 *n.* 創新；革新

35. (**C**) What does the speaker say about the economy?
　　　　說話者說到有關經濟的什麼事？

　　　A. It is driven by milkmen and carriage makers.
　　　　　它受到送牛奶的人和馬車製造商的驅使。

　　　B. It is a pleasant memory. 它是一個愉快的回憶。

C. It is in recession. 它正處於不景氣之中。

D. It is forecasted to lose money in the next decade.
它被預測在未來的十年中都會賠錢。

* drive〔draɪv〕v. 驅使；驅策

36. (**D**) Which of the following is NOT a reason certain
industries are facing extinction?
下列何者不是某些產業面臨滅亡的原因之一？

A. External competition. 外來的競爭。

B. Technological change. 科技的改變。

C. Lack of innovation. 缺乏創新。

D. Unpleasant memories. 不愉快的回憶。

* certain〔'sɝtn〕adj. 某些

Questions 37 and 38 are based on the following report.

Summer is here, and the time is right for some
4-wheeled fun in the sun. Known as Route 1 in California
and as Highway 101 farther north, the Pacific Coast
Highway is possibly the most picturesque stretch of road
ever constructed. It follows the coastline from the sandy
beaches of Southern California to the rugged Olympic
Peninsula in northern Washington, passing through quaint
coastal towns, lush national parks and idyllic wildlife
refuges. It is therapeutic as well as scenic; the meandering
track has an uncanny way of making your troubles fade
away.

夏天來了，這個時候正適合在陽光下來點四輪的樂趣。太平洋沿岸公路，在加州被稱爲 1 號公路，再往北一點被稱爲 101 號公路，可能是有史以來所建築的最風景如畫的一段路了。它順著海岸線，從南加州的沙灘，一直到北華盛頓州崎嶇的奧林匹克半島，經過古色古香的沿岸小鎮、翠綠茂盛的國家公園，以及田園般的野生動物保留區。這段路具有療效，而且風景優美；這條蜿蜒的路徑有種神奇的方法，可以消除你的煩惱。

**

right〔raɪt〕*adj.* 適當的　　wheel〔hwil〕*n.* 輪子

in the sun 在陽光下　　***be known as*** 被稱爲

route〔rut, raʊt〕*n.* 路線；公路

highway〔'haɪˌwe〕*n.* 公路　　farther〔'fɑrðɚ〕*adv.* 更遠地

Pacific〔pə'sɪfɪk〕*adj.* 太平洋的

coast〔kost〕*n.* 海岸；沿岸

picturesque〔ˌpɪktʃə'rɛsk〕*adj.* 如圖畫般的

stretch〔strɛtʃ〕*n.* 延伸；一段　　***a stretch of road*** 一段路

construct〔kən'strʌkt〕*v.* 建造　　follow〔'fɑlo〕*v.* 順著（路）

coastline〔'kostˌlaɪn〕*n.* 海岸線　　sandy〔'sændɪ〕*adj.* 沙地的

southern〔'sʌðən〕*adj.* 南方的　　rugged〔'rʌgɪd〕*adj.* 崎嶇的

Olympic〔o'lɪmpɪk〕*adj.* 奧林匹克的

peninsula〔pə'nɪnsələ〕*n.* 半島

northern〔'nɔrðən〕*adj.* 北方的

quaint〔kwent〕*adj.* 古色古香的

coastal〔'kostḷ〕*adj.* 沿海的；沿岸的

lush〔lʌʃ〕*adj.* 翠綠茂盛的　　idyllic〔aɪ'dɪlɪk〕*adj.* 田園般的

wildlife〔'waɪldˌlaɪf〕*n.* 野生動物

refuge〔'rɛfjudʒ〕*n.* 避難所

wildlife refuge 野生動物保留區（= *wildlife sanctuary* = *reserve*）

therapeutic〔ˌθɛrə'pjutɪk〕*adj.* 有療效的

as well as 以及　　scenic〔'sinɪk〕*adj.* 風景優美的

meandering〔mɪ'ændərɪŋ〕*adj.* 蜿蜒的（= *winding*）

track〔træk〕 n. 路徑   uncanny〔ʌn'kænɪ〕 adj. 神奇的
troubles〔'trʌblz〕 n. pl. 煩惱   ***fade away*** 逐漸消失

37. (**C**) What is the Pacific Coast Highway also known as?
太平洋沿岸公路又被稱爲什麼？

    A. A quaint coastal town. 一座古色古香的沿岸小鎮。

    B. The sandy beaches of Southern California.
南加州的沙灘。

    C. Highway 101. 101 號公路。

    D. Lush national parks. 翠綠茂盛的國家公園。

38. (**C**) When is this report being made? 這篇報導是何時做的？

    A. Winter. 冬天。

    B. Spring. 春天。

    C. Summer. 夏天。

    D. Fall. 秋天。

Questions 39 and 40 are based on the following report.

Studies have found that dominant individuals—bosses,
for instance—use humor more than their subordinates.
If you've often thought that everyone in the office laughs
when the boss laughs, you're very perceptive. In such
cases, controlling the laughter of a group becomes a way
of exercising power by controlling the emotional climate
of the group. So laughter, like much human behavior,
must have evolved to change the behavior of others. For
example, in an embarrassing or threatening situation,

laughter may serve as a conciliatory gesture or as a way
to deflect anger. If the threatening person joins the laughter,
the risk of confrontation may lessen.

研究已經發現，處於支配地位的人──例如老板──比他們的
部屬更經常使用幽默。如果你常常認爲，辦公室裡的人會跟著老板
笑，那你的感覺很敏銳。在這些情況中，控制群體的笑聲，變成一
種藉由控制全場情緒來運用權力的一種方法。所以笑就像許多人類
的行爲一樣，一定已經逐漸演變成能改變他人的行爲。例如，在一
個很尷尬或有威脅性的情況之中，笑可能可以當作一種安撫的表
示，或是轉移憤怒的方法。如果帶有威脅性的那個人和大家一起
笑，衝突的風險可能就會降低。

** ───────────────────

dominant〔'dɑmənənt〕adj. 支配的；佔優勢的
individual〔ˌɪndə'vɪdʒuəl〕n. 個人　　*for instance*　例如
humor〔'hjumɚ〕n. 幽默　　subordinate〔sə'bɔrdn̩ɪt〕n. 部屬
perceptive〔pɚ'sɛptɪv〕adj. 有知覺的；敏銳的
case〔kes〕n. 情況　　exercise〔'ɛksɚˌsaɪz〕v. 運用
emotional〔ɪ'moʃən̩〕adj. 情緒的；感情的
climate〔'klaɪmɪt〕n. 氣候；情勢；氛圍
behavior〔bɪ'hevjɚ〕n. 行爲
evolve〔ɪ'vɑlv〕v. 進化；演變
embarrassing〔ɪm'bærəsɪŋ〕adj. 令人尷尬的
threatening〔'θrɛtn̩ɪŋ〕adj. 威脅的；脅迫的
situation〔ˌsɪtʃu'eʃən〕n. 情況　　*serve as*　充當；擔任
conciliatory〔kən'sɪlɪəˌtorɪ〕adj. 安撫的；調解的
gesture〔'dʒɛstʃɚ〕n. 姿勢；表示
deflect〔dɪ'flɛkt〕v. 使偏離
confrontation〔ˌkɑnfrən'teʃən〕n. 衝突；對立
lessen〔'lɛsn̩〕v. 減輕；減少；降低

39. (**C**) What does the speaker say about dominant individuals?

關於處理支配地位的人，說話者提到什麼？

   A. They're very perceptive.

     他們感覺很敏銳。

   B. They're confrontational.

     他們很容易起衝突。

   C. They use humor more often than others.

     他們比其他人更常使用幽默。

   D. They laugh when the boss laughs.

     當老闆笑的時候他們會跟著笑。

   * confrontational〔͵kɑnfrən'teʃṇḷ〕 *adj.* 衝突的；對立的

40. (**A**) How does laughter become a way of exercising power?

笑如何成爲一種運用權力的方法？

   A. By controlling the emotional climate of the group.

     藉由控制全場的情緒。

   B. By threatening a person to join the group.

     藉由威脅一個人加入團體。

   C. By evolving to deflect anger.

     藉由逐漸演變，得以轉移憤怒。

   D. By serving as a conciliatory gesture.

     藉由當作安撫的表示。

高中英聽測驗模擬試題 ⑥ 詳解

一、看圖辨義：第一部分

For question number 1, please look at picture 1.

1. (**D**) A man is driving his new car. He likes it very much.
     一位男士在開他的新車。他非常喜歡它。

For question number 2, please look at picture 2.

2. (**A**) A woman is upset with her son. She's trying to prepare dinner.　一位女士正在跟她的兒子生氣。她正試著準備晚餐。

　 * upset〔ʌpˋsɛt〕*adj.* 不高興的

For question number 3, please look at picture 3.

3. (**A**) The boy has been having trouble with his vision lately. He's getting an eye examination.

這男孩最近視力有一些問題。他正在做視力檢查。

* trouble (ˋtrʌbḷ) n. 疾病；（身體上的）痛苦；不適
vision (ˋvɪʒən) n. 視力　　lately (ˋletlɪ) adv. 最近
examination (ɪgˌzæməˋneʃən) n. 檢查

For question number 4, please look at picture 4.

4. (**C**) A lifeguard is watching the swimmers in the water. Other people are playing on the beach.

一個救生員正在看水裡的游泳者。其他的人正在海灘上玩。

* lifeguard (ˋlaɪfˌgɑrd) n. 救生員

一、看圖辨義：第二部分

For question number 5, please look at picture 5.

5. (**B、D**) Which TWO of the following are true about the people in the picture?

關於圖片中的人，下列哪兩項敘述為眞？

    A. They are in a math class.

      他們正在上數學課。

    B. They are in a drawing class.

      他們正在上繪畫課。

    C. The boy in the middle is very talented.

      中間的男孩很有天分。

    D. The boy in the middle is out of ideas.

      中間的男孩沒有點子。

    * talented〔'tæləntɪd〕*adj.* 有才能的；有天分的

    be out of 沒有；缺乏

For question number 6, please look at picture 6.

6. (**C、D**) Which TWO of the following are true about the boy?

關於這位男孩，下列哪兩項敘述為眞？

    A. He is at the post office.

      他在郵局。

    B. He is mailing a letter.

      他正在寄信。

    C. He is at the library.　他在圖書館。

    D. He is taking a book from the shelf.

      他正從書架上拿了一本書。

    * ***post office*** 郵局　　mail〔mel〕*v.* 郵寄

    shelf〔ʃɛlf〕*n.* 架子

For question number 7, please look at picture 7.

7. (**B、D**) Which TWO of the following are true about the
picture? 關於這張圖片，下列哪兩項敘述爲眞？

    A. The woman is sewing a dress.
這女士正在縫一件洋裝。

    B. The woman is watching
television. 這女士正在看電視。

    C. It's three o'clock in the afternoon.
時間是下午三點。

    D. It's three o'clock in the morning.
時間是上午三點。

    * sew〔so〕v. 縫製　　dress〔drɛs〕n. 洋裝

For question number 8, please look at picture 8.

8. (**A、C**) Which TWO of the following are true about the
picture? 關於這張圖片，下列哪兩項敘述爲眞？

    A. They are shopping. 他們在購物。

    B. They are driving. 他們在開車。

    C. The store is having a big sale.
這家店正在舉行大拍賣。

    D. The roads are crowded. 這些道路很擁擠。

    * sale〔sel〕n. 拍賣；廉價出售
    crowded〔ˈkraʊdɪd〕adj. 擁擠的

For question number 9, please look at picture 9.

9. (**B、C**) Which TWO of the following are true about the
woman behind the desk?
關於在桌子後面的女士，下列哪兩項敘述爲眞？

A. She's a cashier. 她是收銀員。
B. She's a librarian. 她是圖書館員。
C. She's wearing glasses. 她戴著眼鏡。
D. She's talking on the phone.
   她正在講電話。

* cashier〔kæ'ʃɪr〕n. 收銀員
  librarian〔laɪ'brɛrɪən〕n. 圖書館員

For question number 10, please look at picture 10.

10. (**A、D**) Which TWO of the following are true about the people in the picture?
   關於圖片中的人，下列哪兩項敘述爲眞？
   A. They are celebrating Chinese New Year.
      他們正在慶祝農曆新年。
   B. They are celebrating Christmas. 他們在慶祝聖誕節。
   C. They are indoors. 他們在室內。
   D. They are outdoors. 他們在戶外。

   * celebrate〔'sɛlə,bret〕v. 慶祝
     indoors〔'ɪn'dorz〕adv. 在室內
     outdoors〔'aʊt'dorz〕adv. 在戶外

二、對答

11. (**C**) Have you seen Dennis lately? 你最近有見到丹尼斯嗎？
   A. I'm glad you enjoyed it. 我很高興你喜歡它。
   B. Seeing is believing. 眼見爲憑。
   C. No, I haven't seen him in a while.
      沒有，我有一陣子沒見到他了。
   D. Yes, that's Dennis. 是的，那是丹尼斯。

Seeing is believing. 【諺】眼見爲憑。
in a while 一段時間

12. (**A**) Does your mother always make dinner?
　　　你的媽媽總是會做晚餐嗎？
　　　　A. No, sometimes we eat out.　不，我們有時候會出去吃。
　　　　B. You're invited to dinner.　你被邀請來吃晚餐。
　　　　C. We're having beef noodles.　我們正在吃牛肉麵。
　　　　D. My father is a great cook.　我的父親很會做菜。
　　　　* ***eat out*** 出去吃　　***beef noodles*** 牛肉麵
　　　　cook〔kʊk〕*n.* 廚師

13. (**C**) Can you make it to my party this weekend?
　　　你這個週末能來我的派對嗎？
　　　　A. I brought snacks to the party.　我帶了點心去派對。
　　　　B. No, he's right over there.　不，他就在那邊。
　　　　C. Yes, I'll be there.　是的，我會去。
　　　　D. You should come to the party.　你應該要來參加派對。
　　　　* ***make it to*** 準時抵達；能參加；能出席
　　　　snake〔snek〕*n.* 點心　　right〔raɪt〕*adv.* 恰好；正好

14. (**C**) Were you late for school again?　你上學又遲到了嗎？
　　　　A. He's always late.　他總是遲到。
　　　　B. She is never late.　她從不遲到。
　　　　C. Yes, I was.　是的，我又遲到了。
　　　　D. No, I was at school.　不，我那時在學校。

15. (**A**) I'll take a shower before we go out.
　　　在我們出門前我會先淋浴。
　　　　A. Don't take too long.　別花太多時間。

B. That's how they do it. 他們就是這樣做的。

C. So was I. 我也是。【要改成 So will I.】

D. I fell asleep on the couch. 我在長沙發上睡著了。

* **take a shower** 沖澡；淋浴　　**fall asleep** 睡著
  couch〔kautʃ〕n. 長沙發

16. (**B**) You look tired.　Did you get enough sleep?
　　　你看起來很疲倦。你有睡飽嗎？

A. I'm tired of asking him. 我厭倦問他問題了。

B. No, I tossed and turned all night.
　　不，我整晚翻來覆去睡不著。

C. Of course.　Feel free. 當然，請隨意。

D. She tires easily. 她很容易就感到疲倦了。

* tired〔taɪrd〕adj. 疲倦的　　**be tired of** 厭倦
  toss and turn 翻來覆去；睡不著　　**feel free** 別拘束；請隨意
  tire〔taɪr〕v. 疲倦

17. (**A**) Please help your father with the dishes.
　　　請幫你的爸爸洗碗。

A. Yes, Mother. 好的，媽媽。

B. The dishes are dirty. 這些碗盤很髒。

C. Dinner was fantastic. 晚餐真是太棒了。

D. My father is washing the dishes. 我的爸爸正在洗碗。

* **help sb. with sth.** 幫助某人做某事　　dish〔dɪʃ〕n. 碗盤
  fantastic〔fæn'tæstɪk〕adj. 很棒的

18. (**A**) I'll go to the beach with my family this weekend.
　　　這個週末我將會和我的家人去海邊。

A. Have fun! 玩得愉快！

B. I got sand in my shoes. 我的鞋子進了沙。

C. I don't know how to swim. 我不會游泳。
D. No, I'll stay home this weekend.
　　不，我這個週末會待在家。

* **have fun** 玩得愉快

19. (**C**) I love your new hairstyle. 我喜歡你的新髮型。
　　A. I'm getting a haircut this afternoon.
　　　　我今天下午會去剪頭髮。
　　B. I just washed my hair. 我才剛洗過頭髮。
　　C. Thanks. It's very kind of you to notice.
　　　　謝謝。你能注意到真是太好了。
　　D. OK, I'll wait here. 好的，我會在這裡等。

* hairstyle (ˈhɛrˌstaɪl) n. 髮型　　haircut (ˈhɛrˌkʌt) n. 理髮

20. (**B**) What did you have for breakfast? 你早餐吃了什麼？
　　A. I'm going to breakfast. 我正要去吃早餐。
　　B. Scrambled eggs and toast. 炒蛋和吐司。
　　C. I don't drink coffee. 我不喝咖啡。
　　D. I don't have it anymore. 我不再擁有它了。

* breakfast (ˈbrɛkfəst) n. 早餐　v. 吃早餐
　　have (hæv) v. 吃；擁有　　**scrambled eggs** 炒蛋
　　toast (tost) n. 吐司　　**not…anymore** 不再…

三、簡短對話

For question 21, you will listen to a short conversation.

　　M：Have you met the new secretary? 你見過新來的秘書嗎？
　　W：I've been out of town for the last two weeks.
　　　　我過去這兩週都不在城裡。

* secretary (ˈsɛkrəˌtɛrɪ) n. 秘書　　**out of town** 出城

21. (**C**) Q : What does the woman mean?　那個女士的意思是什麼？

　　A. She fired the new secretary two weeks ago.

　　　她兩週前開除了那個新來的秘書。

　　B. She has been too busy to meet anybody.

　　　她一直都很忙，無法與人碰面。

　　C. She has not met the new secretary yet.

　　　她還沒見過那個新秘書。

　　D. She will introduce herself to the new secretary

　　　tomorrow.　她明天將會向新秘書介紹自己。

　　　* fire〔faɪr〕v. 開除　　introduce〔͵ɪntrə'djus〕v. 介紹

For question 22, you will listen to a short conversation.

M : I heard you had an accident the other day.

　　我聽說前幾天你發生車禍。

W : Yes, it was a minor collision but my car suffered some

　　body damage.　It's not bad enough to file an insurance

　　claim, so I have to pay out of pocket.

　　是的，那是個小擦撞，但我的車身受了一些損傷。情況沒有糟到

　　能申請保險理賠，所以我得自掏腰包付錢。

M : So how much do you think it's going to cost to fix your

　　car?　那你認為修好你的車得花多少錢？

W : Well, my brother is a mechanic and he said the parts

　　alone are going to cost $500.　That doesn't include labor.

　　嗯，我的哥哥是一名技工，他說光是零件就得花上五百元美元，

　　而這還不包括工錢。

　　* accident〔'æksədənt〕n. 意外；車禍　　***the other day*** 前幾天

　　minor〔'maɪnɚ〕adj. 輕微的　　collision〔kə'lɪʒən〕n. 碰撞

suffer (ˈsʌfɚ) v. 遭受　　body (ˈbɑdɪ) n. 車身
damage (ˈdæmɪdʒ) n. 損害　　file (ˈfaɪl) v. 申請；提出
insurance (ɪnˈʃʊrəns) n. 保險　　claim (klem) n. (保險) 索賠
out of pocket 自掏腰包賠錢　　fix (fɪks) v. 修理
mechanic (məˈkænɪk) n. 技工；機械工人
part (pɑrt) n. (汽車、機械等的) 零件
include (ɪnˈklud) v. 包括　　labor (ˈlebɚ) n. 勞動；勞力

22. (**B**) Q：How much will it cost to fix the car?
　　　　　修好車得花多少錢？
　　A. No more than $500.　不會多於五百美元。
　　B. At least $500.　至少五百美元。
　　C. Exactly $500.　五百美元整。
　　D. Nothing.　The woman's brother is a mechanic.
　　　　免費。那個女士的哥哥是位技工。

　　* ***no more than***　不超過；僅僅　　***at least***　至少
　　　exactly (ɪgˈzæktlɪ) *adv.* 正好
　　　nothing (ˈnɑθɪŋ) *pron.* 沒有東西；零

For question 23, you will listen to a short conversation.

W：Isn't Lester supposed to be here?
　　萊斯特不是應該來這裡嗎？

M：He is, but his flight was delayed by the typhoon.　Let's
　　give him until after lunch and then start the meeting
　　without him.　是啊，但是他的班機因為颱風而誤點了。我們
　　就等他到午餐結束，接著就自己開會吧。

　　* ***be supposed to V.*** 應該～　　flight (flaɪt) n. 班機
　　　delay (dɪˈle) v. 使延誤
　　　give (gɪv) v. 給 (某人) (時間)；等待 (= *wait for*)

23. (**C**) Q：What will happen after lunch?　午餐後會發生什麼事？

A. Lester will arrive. 萊斯特將會抵達。

B. Lester's flight will be delayed.
萊斯特的班機將會誤點。

C. The meeting will begin. 這場會議將會開始。

D. The meeting will be over. 這場會議將會結束。

For question 24, you will listen to a short conversation.

W : Would you like another drink? 你想要再喝一杯飲料嗎？

M : The last thing I need is another drink.
我最不想要的就是再喝一杯飲料。

* last〔læst〕*adj.* 最不可能的

24. (**C**) Q : What does the man mean? 這個男人的意思是什麼？

A. He's thirsty. 他渴了。　　B. He's hungry. 他餓了。

C. He's had enough to drink. 他已經有足夠的飲料了。

D. He always needs another drink.
他總是需要再一杯飲料。

For questions 25 and 26, you will listen to a short conversation.

W : How was your vacation in Greece? 你的希臘之旅如何？

M : It was wonderful! 太棒了！

W : What did you do? 你做了甚麼？

M : Well, of course we visited a lot of the famous tourist
sights in Athens, like the Parthenon. Then we went on
a tour of a few nearby islands. That had to be the
highlight of the trip. 嗯，我們當然拜訪了很多在雅典有名的
旅遊景點，例如巴特農神殿。接著我們到幾個附近的島旅遊。
那是我們這趟旅行最精彩的地方。

W : Sounds like fun. Do you have any plans to go back?

聽起來很有趣。你有計畫要再回去嗎？

M : Do I?! My dream is to live there.

我嗎？！我的夢想是住在那裡。

> * Greece〔gris〕*n.* 希臘　　tourist〔'tʊrɪst〕*adj.* 旅遊的；觀光的
> sights〔saɪts〕*n. pl.* 名勝；觀光地
> Parthenon〔'pɑrθə,nɑn〕*n.* 巴特農神殿【位於希臘雅典】
> ***go on a tour*** 去旅行　　island〔'aɪlənd〕*n.* 島
> highlight〔'haɪ,laɪt〕*n.* 最精彩的部分
> ***Sounds like***…. 聽起來…。(= *It sounds like*…)
> fun〔fʌn〕*n.* 樂趣；有趣

25. (**A**) Q : What are the speakers discussing?

　　　　　　　說話者正在討論什麼？

　　　　　　A. The man's recent vacation. 那個男士最近的旅行。

　　　　　　B. The woman's experience in Greece.
　　　　　　　那個女士的希臘經驗。

　　　　　　C. The man's retirement plans. 那個男士的退休計畫。

　　　　　　D. The woman's dreams. 那個女士的夢。

> * recent〔'risṇt〕*adj.* 最近的　　retirement〔rɪ'taɪrmənt〕*n.* 退休

26. (**D**) Q : What is true about the man?

　　　　　　　有關那個男士，何者正確？

　　　　　　A. He is easily amused. 要逗他開心很容易。

　　　　　　B. He doesn't enjoy tourist activities.
　　　　　　　他不喜歡旅遊活動。

　　　　　　C. He prefers to travel alone. 他比較喜歡獨自旅遊。

　　　　　　D. He wishes to return to Greece. 他希望能回到希臘。

> * amuse〔ə'mjuz〕*v.* 娛樂；逗樂　　activity〔æk'tɪvətɪ〕*v.* 活動
> prefer〔prɪ'fɝ〕*v.* 比較喜歡　　alone〔ə'lon〕*adv.* 獨自地

For questions 27 and 28, you will listen to a short conversation.

W：Do you know anything about computers? 你懂電腦嗎？

M：A little bit. Why? 一點點。爲何這麼問？

W：Oh, my laptop isn't working properly.

喔，我的筆記型電腦出了點問題。

M：What seems to be the problem? 看來是什麼問題呢？

W：Well, it freezes up whenever I try to open a program.

嗯，當我要開啓程式的時候，它就當機了。

M：Sounds like you might have caught a virus.

聽起來像是你的電腦可能已經中毒了。

W：Is that bad? Is there anything you might be able to do?

那是很糟的狀況嗎？你能幫我任何的忙嗎？

M：I suppose I could take a look at it, but I'm not an expert

or anything.

我想我可以幫你看看，但是我並不是專家之類的喔。

* laptop〔'læp͵tɑp〕*n.* 筆記型電腦　　work〔wɜk〕*v.* 運作
properly〔'prɑpɚlɪ〕*adv.* 適當地　　seem〔sim〕*v.* 似乎；看來
freeze up 停止；當機　　program〔'progræm〕*n.* 節目；程式
virus〔'vaɪrəs〕*n.* 病毒　　*catch a virus* 染上病毒；中毒
suppose〔sə'poz〕*v.* 猜想　　*take a look at* 看一看
expert〔'ɛkspɜt〕*n.* 專家　　*or anything* 或別的什麼

27.（ **D** ）Q：What is the woman's problem?

那女士的問題是什麼？

A. She is sick. 她生病了。

B. She is unemployed. 她失業了。

C. Her favorite program was cancelled.

她最喜愛的節目被取消了。

D. Her computer isn't working. 她的電腦無法運作。

* unemployed〔ˏʌnɪmˈplɔɪd〕*adj.* 失業的
program〔ˈprogræm〕*n.* 節目　　cancel〔ˈkænsḷ〕*v.* 取消

28. (**D**) Q : What does the man say? 那個男士說了什麼？

A. He is an expert in computers. 他是位電腦專家。

B. The woman may be coming down with the flu.

那個女士可能罹患流行性感冒。

C. The woman should seek professional help.

那個女士應該尋求專業的協助。

D. He will try to help the woman solve her problem.

他會試著幫助那個女士解決問題。

* ***come down with*** 罹患　　flu〔flu〕*n.* 流行性感冒
seek〔sik〕*v.* 尋求　　professional〔prəˈfɛʃənḷ〕*adj.* 專業的
solve〔sɑlv〕*v.* 解決

For questions 29 and 30, you will listen to a short conversation.

M : Were you able to get in touch with Kim?

你能夠與金聯繫上嗎？

W : No. I've tried calling several times but she never picks

up. 不行。我試著打了好幾次電話給她，但她都沒接。

M : That's strange. I've called her at least a dozen times

over the last two days.

那太奇怪了。我在這兩天內，至少打給她十幾次了

W : Do you think something happened?

你想會不會發生了什麼事情？

M : I can't be sure. But it is unusual for her not to answer the phone. 我不確定。但是，對她來說，不接電話很不尋常。

W : If she doesn't answer today, I think someone should go over to her house and make sure everything is OK. 如果她今天再不接電話，我認為該有人過去她家，確定一切沒問題。

* *get in touch with* 和～聯繫　　*pick up* 接電話
dozen〔ˈdʌzn̩〕*n.* 一打的；十二（個、次）的
time〔taɪm〕*n.* 次數　　unusual〔ʌnˈjuʒʊəl〕*adj.* 不尋常的
answer the phone 接電話　　*make sure* 確定

29. (**C**) Q: Who are the speakers? 說話者是誰？
    A. Brother and sister. 兄妹。
    B. Kim's roommates. 金的室友。
    C. Friends of Kim. 金的朋友。
    D. Strangers. 陌生人。

    * roommate〔ˈrumˌmet〕*n.* 室友
    stranger〔ˈstrendʒɚ〕*n.* 陌生人

30. (**A**) Q: What is true about the woman?
    關於那個女士，何者正確？
    A. She has tried to contact Kim. 她試著要聯絡金。
    B. She went to Kim's house the previous day.
    她前一天去了金的家。
    C. She had a fight with Kim. 她和金吵了一架。
    D. She rarely answers her phone. 她很少接電話。

    * contact〔ˈkɑntækt〕*v.* 聯繫；接觸
    previous〔ˈpriviəs〕*adj.* 之前的　　fight〔faɪt〕*n.* 打架；吵架
    rarely〔ˈrɛrlɪ〕*adv.* 很少

四、短文聽解

Questions 31 and 32 are based on the following report.

Picture the gorgeous beach you spent a week on this summer. Now picture that same beach next summer, destroyed. Beach destinations around the world are in danger of disappearing forever due to forces such as erosion, pollution, rising sea levels, overdevelopment, and sand mining. If we don't curb global warming, insist on sustainable development, and protect the world's beaches against pollution and mismanagement, the idyllic shorelines we cherish will be preserved only in memory.

想像一下今年夏天你待了一個禮拜的美麗沙灘。現在再想像同樣一片沙灘，在明年的夏天就被摧毀了。因為各種外力因素，包含侵蝕、污染、海平面上升、過度開發，以及採集砂石，世界各地的海灘景點正面臨永遠消失的危險。如果我們不抑制全球暖化、堅持永續的發展，並且保護全世界的海灘免於污染與不當的管理，這些我們所珍惜、美麗寧靜的海岸線，將會只存於我們記憶當中。

**

picture〔ˈpɪktʃɚ〕v. 想像
gorgeous〔ˈgɔrdʒəs〕adj. 華麗的；很美的
destroy〔dɪˈstrɔɪ〕v. 摧毀
destination〔ˌdɛstəˈneʃən〕n. 目標；目的地
in danger of 處於…的危險中　　disappear〔ˌdɪsəˈpɪr〕v. 消失
forever〔fɚˈɛvɚ〕adv. 永遠地　　*due to* 因為；由於
force〔fɔrs〕n. 力量　　erosion〔ɪˈroʒən〕n. 侵蝕
pollution〔pəˈluʃən〕n. 污染　　rising〔ˈraɪzɪŋ〕adj. 上升的
sea level 海平面

overdevelopment〔͵ovɚdɪ'vɛləpmənt〕n. 過度開發
mining〔'maɪnɪŋ〕n. 採礦　　curb〔kɝb〕v. 抑制；阻止
global〔'globḷ〕adj. 全球的　　*global warming* 全球暖化
insist〔ɪn'sɪst〕v. 堅持 < to >
sustainable〔sə'stenəbḷ〕adj. 能持續的；永續的
protect…against~ 保護…免於~
mismanagement〔mɪs'mænɪdʒmənt〕n. 不當管理
idyllic〔aɪ'dɪlɪk〕adj. 牧歌的；美麗寧靜的
shoreline〔'ʃɔr͵laɪn〕n. 海岸線　　cherish〔'tʃɛrɪʃ〕v. 珍惜
preserve〔prɪ'zɝv〕v. 保存　　memory〔'mɛmərɪ〕n. 記憶

31. (**C**) What is in danger of disappearing forever?
　　下列何者正處於永遠消失的危險中？

　　A. Pollution. 污染。　　B. Sea levels. 海平面。

　　C. Beaches. 海灘。　　D. Global warming. 全球暖化。

32. (**B**) What may be a cause of the disappearance?
　　造成沙灘消失的原因可能是什麼？

　　A. Forces such as evil. 像是邪惡之類的力量。

　　B. Mismanagement. 不當管理。

　　C. Declining sea levels. 下降的海平面。

　　D. Conservation. 自然保育。

　　* cause〔kɔz〕n. 原因　　disappearance〔͵dɪsə'pɪrəns〕n. 消失
　　evil〔'ivḷ〕n. 邪惡　　decline〔dɪ'klaɪn〕v. 下降；衰退
　　conservation〔͵kɑnsɚ'veʃən〕n.（動植物、森林等）保護

Questions 33 and 34 are based on the following report.

　　For all its benefits, the Internet can be a hassle when it comes to remembering passwords for e-mail, banking, social networking and shopping. Many people use just a single password across the Web. That's a bad idea, say many online security experts. Having the same password for everything is like having the same key for your house, your car, your gym locker, your office. Users should have different passwords for their e-mail accounts, financial websites, banks and credit cards, and shopping sites such as Amazon.com.

儘管網路有很多好處，但一談到要記得電子郵件、銀行業務、社交網站，和購物網站的密碼時，網路也可能是一件麻煩的事。很多人在網路上只使用一個密碼。這實在是個壞主意，很多網路安全專家說。老是使用同一個密碼，就好像你的屋子、車子、健身房置物櫃，以及辦公室都使用同一把鑰匙一樣。使用者應該針對電子郵件帳戶、財金網站、銀行及信用卡，以及購物網站，像是亞馬遜網路書店，使用不同的密碼。

** ─────────────────

for all 儘管 (= *in spite of*)　　benefit〔'bɛnəfɪt〕*n.* 利益；好處
Internet〔'ɪntə͵nɛt〕*n.* 網際網路　　hassle〔'hæsl̩〕*n.* 麻煩的事
when it comes to 一提到　　password〔'pæs͵wɝd〕*n.* 密碼
banking〔'bæŋkɪŋ〕*n.* 銀行業務　　social〔'soʃəl〕*adj.* 社交的
networking〔'nɛt͵wɝkɪŋ〕*n.* 人際關係網　　*the Web* 網際網路
single〔'sɪŋgl̩〕*adj.* 單一的　　across〔ə'krɔs〕*prep.* 遍及
online〔͵ɑn'laɪn〕*adj.* 線上的；網路的
security〔sɪ'kjʊrətɪ〕*n.* 安全　　gym〔dʒɪm〕*n.* 健身房
locker〔'lɑkə〕*n.* 置物櫃　　account〔ə'kaʊnt〕*n.* 帳戶
financial〔faɪ'nænʃəl〕*adj.* 金融的；財務的
credit card 信用卡　　site〔saɪt〕*n.* 網站　　*such as* 像是

33. (**C**) Why is the Internet somewhat of a hassle?
為什麼網路會有點麻煩？

A. There's too much spam. 有太多的垃圾郵件。
B. The broadband connections are too slow.
   寬頻連線的速度太慢。
C. Passwords are difficult to remember. 密碼很難記住。
D. Major shopping sites are impractical.
   主要的購物網站太不實用。

* somewhat (ˈsʌmˌhwɑt) pron. 有點　*somewhat of* 有點…
  spam (spæm) n. 垃圾郵件
  broadband connection 寬頻連線
  major (ˈmedʒɚ) adj. 主要的；較大的
  impractical (ɪmˈpræktɪkḷ) adj. 不實用的

34. (**A**) What does the speaker suggest? 說話者建議什麼？
    A. Internet users should use different passwords for
       different sites.
       網路的使用者應該針對不同的網站使用不同的密碼。
    B. Internet users should use only one password across
       the Web. 網路的使用者在網路上應該只使用一個密碼。
    C. Internet users should publish their passwords online.
       網路的使用者應該將他們的密碼公布在網路上。
    D. Internet users should use credit cards at Amazon.com.
       網路的使用者應該在亞馬遜網路書店使用信用卡。

    * publish (ˈpʌblɪʃ) v. 發表；公布

Questions 35 and 36 are based on the following report.

The most dangerous thing most people do in a typical
day is get behind the wheel. Car crashes are the leading
cause of death for Americans ages 5 to 34, reports the
Centers for Disease Control. Globally, motor vehicle

accidents claim more than 1.3 million lives a year, and cause
20 to 50 million injuries—prompting the United Nations to
declare 2011 to 2020 the decade of action for road safety with
upwards of 70 countries pledging to initiate new programs to
save lives on their roads.

　　對大部分的人來說，平常日子裡最危險的事情就是開車。根據
疾病管制中心的報告，五歲到三十四歲的美國人，主要死因就是車
禍。全世界每一年死於車禍的人數超過了一千三百萬，車禍導致的
傷殘者更多達兩千到五千萬人——促使了聯合國宣布從 2011 年到
2020 年為道路安全行動十年，有超過七十個國家宣誓，要著手開始
新的計畫，來拯救馬路上的生命。

**　**

typical〔ˈtɪpɪkl̩〕adj. 典型的；平常的
wheel〔hwil〕n. 輪子；方向盤　　**get behind the wheel** 開車
car crash 車禍　　leading〔ˈlidɪŋ〕adj. 主要的
cause of death 死因　　report〔rɪˈport〕v. 報導；報告
disease〔dɪˈziz〕n. 疾病
the Centers for Disease Control 疾病管制局
globally〔ˈglobl̩ɪ〕adv. 全球地
motor〔ˈmotɚ〕adj. 動力的；汽車的
vehicle〔ˈviɪkl̩〕n. 車輛；交通工具　　**motor vehicle** 機動車輛
claim〔klem〕v. 奪去（性命）　　injury〔ˈɪndʒərɪ〕n. 傷害
prompt〔prɑmpt〕v. 促使　　**the United Nations** 聯合國
declare〔dɪˈklɛr〕v. 宣布　　decade〔ˈdɛked〕n. 十年
action〔ˈækʃən〕n. 行動　　**upwards of** 超過（= more than）
pledge〔plɛdʒ〕v. 發誓；宣誓
initiate〔ɪˈnɪʃɪˌet〕v. 創始；開始　　program〔ˈprogræm〕n. 計畫

35.（ **D** ）What is the most dangerous thing most people do in a
　　　　typical day?
　　　　大多數人在日常生活所做的事情中，何者是最危險的？

A. Walk down the street. 走在街上。
B. Drink water from the tap. 喝自來水。
C. Declare bankruptcy. 宣告破產。
D. Drive a car. 開車。

* down〔daʊn〕*prep.* 沿著（= *along*）
  tap〔tæp〕*n.* 水龍頭   bankruptcy〔'bæŋkrʌptsɪ〕*n.* 破產

36. (**D**) How many people are hurt every year in motor vehicle accidents? 每年有多少人因為車禍而受傷？

A. 5. 五人。   B. 34. 三十四人。
C. 1.3 million. 一千三百萬人。
D. 20 to 50 million. 兩千萬到五千萬人。

* hurt〔hɝt〕*adj.* 受傷的

Questions 37 and 38 are based on the following report.

If they were only allowed to have one child, more Americans would prefer it be a boy rather than a girl. The Gallup polling agency asked a random sample of 1,000 American adults whether they'd prefer to have a girl or a boy if they could only choose one. Forty percent said they'd pick a boy, 28 percent said they would want a girl, and the rest didn't mind either way or weren't sure. The preference for boys over girls is driven by men, 49 percent of whom said they'd want a son; 22 percent said they'd prefer a daughter. Women, in contrast, showed no significant preference to gender, with 31 percent preferring a boy and 32 percent preferring a girl.

如果只能允許擁有一個孩子的話，多數的美國人會偏好是男孩而不是女孩。蓋洛普民調機構隨機採樣地詢問了一千位美國成人，如果只能選擇一個，他們偏好男孩還是女孩。百分之四十的人說他們會選擇男孩，百分之二十八的人說他們會要女孩，剩下的人表示不介意或是不確定。對男孩的偏好勝過女孩是男人，他們之中有百分之四十九的人說想要個兒子；而百分之二十二的想要女兒。對比之下，女人並沒有展現出對孩子性別顯著的偏好，有百分之三十一的女人偏好男孩，而百分之三十二的女人偏好女孩。

** ─────────────────────

allow〔ə'laʊ〕v. 允許　　***rather than*** 而不是
polling〔'polɪŋ〕n. 民意調查
agency〔'edʒənsɪ〕n. 機構；代辦處
random〔'rændəm〕adj. 隨機的
sample〔'sæmpḷ〕n. 樣本；樣品
percent〔pə'sɛnt〕n. 百分之…　　***the rest*** 其餘的人或物
mind〔maɪnd〕v. 介意
either way　（兩極中的）任一樣都；兩邊都
preference〔'prɛfərəns〕n. 偏好　　drive〔draɪv〕v. 驅使；促使
in contrast 對比之下　　show〔ʃo〕v. 顯示；表現
significant〔sɪg'nɪfəkənt〕adj. 顯著的
gender〔'dʒɛndə〕n. 性別

37. (**C**) What question did Gallup ask American adults?
　　蓋洛普機構問了美國成年人什麼問題？

　　A. If they could change one thing about their partner,
　　　 what it would be. 如果他們能夠改變他們的夥伴一件事，
　　　 那會是什麼事。

　　B. If they had four hours to live, how they would spend
　　　 the time.
　　　 如果只剩四小時能活，他們會如何度過那段時間。

  C. If they'd prefer a girl or a boy if they could only choose only one.
如果只能選擇一個，他們會偏好男孩還是女孩。

  D. If they'd prefer all girls to all boys if they could have any choice. 如果能夠選擇的話，他們是否會偏好都生女孩甚於都生男孩。

38. (**B**) Who showed no significant preference to gender?
誰並未表現出對性別顯著的偏好？

  A. Men. 男人。   B. Women. 女人。

  C. Boys. 男孩。   D. Girls. 女孩。

Questions 39 and 40 are based on the following report.

  If only we all had a mirror to see ourselves when we're out on a date. Without realizing it, you can come off as overly defensive to your dates. All it takes is one inquiring mind asking about aspects of your life that should be acceptable topics of conversation. Then, what should be a harmless comment instead upsets you for reasons you may not even understand at the time. If you think this might be you, know that the first step in changing such counter-productive dating behavior is self-awareness.

  要是我們外出約會時，有面鏡子能看見自己的樣子就好了。你沒察覺到，你對於你的約會對象，顯得有過度的防備。這只要有個人好奇地問你一些應該是與你的生活各方面有關，而且應該是可接受的問題。然後，原本應該是無害的評論，反而會讓你感到不高興，而你可能甚至在當時也不了解原因為何。如果你認為這可能就是你，那你就要知道，改變這種適得其反的約會行為的第一步，就是自覺。

** ———————————————

if only 要是…就好了　　mirror (ˈmɪrɚ) n. 鏡子
date (det) n. 約會;約會對象　　**on a date** 約會
realize (ˈriəˌlaɪz) v. 了解
come off as 看起來;顯得 (= *appear*)
overly (ˈovɚlɪ) adv. 過度地;非常
defensive (dɪˈfɛnsɪv) adj. 有防衛心的　　take (tek) v. 需要
inquiring (ɪnˈkwaɪrɪŋ) adj. 愛打聽的;追根究底的
mind (maɪnd) n. …的人　　aspect (ˈæspɛkt) n. 方面
acceptable (əkˈsɛptəbḷ) adj. 可接受的
topic (ˈtɑpɪk) n. 主題　　conversation (ˌkɑnvɚˈseʃən) n. 對話
harmless (ˈhɑrmlɪs) adj. 無害的
comment (ˈkɑmənt) n. 評論　　instead (ɪnˈstɛd) adv. 反而
upset (ʌpˈsɛt) v. 使心煩;使不高興
counter-productive (ˌkaʊntɚprəˈdʌktɪv) adj. 適得其反的
behavior (bɪˈhevjɚ) n. 行為　　self-awareness n. 自覺

39. (**B**) What is this report about? 這篇報導是關於什麼?

   A. Self-defense. 自我防衛。

   B. Dating. 約會。　　　C. Psychics. 靈媒。

   D. Acceptable topics of conversation. 適合的聊天主題。

  * defense (dɪˈfɛns) n. 防禦　　psychic (ˈsaɪkɪk) n. 靈媒;巫師

40. (**B**) Who is the speaker talking to? 說話者的對象是什麼人?

   A. Married couples. 已婚的夫妻。

   B. Single adults. 單身的成人。

   C. Retirees. 退休的人。

   D. Preschoolers. 學齡前兒童。

  * married (ˈmærɪd) adj. 結婚的;已婚的
   retiree (rɪˌtaɪˈri) n. 退休的人
   preschooler (ˈpriˈskulɚ) n. 學齡前兒童

高中英聽測驗模擬試題 ⑦ 詳解

一、看圖辨義：第一部分

For question number 1, please look at picture 1.

1. (**C**) A woman is carrying a bag.　She is chasing the garbage
truck.　一位女士正提著一個袋子。她正在追垃圾車。

　　　　* chase〔tʃes〕v. 追逐　　garbage〔'gɑrbɪdʒ〕n. 垃圾
　　　　truck〔trʌk〕n. 卡車　　*garbage truck* 垃圾車

For question number 2, please look at picture 2.

2. (**A**) A street is filled with cars.　A man is directing them.
街上都是車。一位男士正在指揮這些車。

　　　　* *be filled with* 充滿了　　direct〔də'rɛkt〕v. 指揮

For question number 3, please look at picture 3.

3. (**A**) Two children are on a roller coaster. They are screaming
in delight. 有兩個兒童在雲霄飛車上。他們正高興地尖叫著。

　　* roller〔'rolɚ〕*n.* 滾筒　　coaster〔'kostɚ〕*n.* 平底雪橇
　　roller coaster 雲霄飛車　　scream〔skrim〕*v.* 尖叫
　　delight〔dɪ'laɪt〕*n.* 高興　　***in delight*** 高興地

For question number 4, please look at picture 4.

4. (**B**) A tornado has hit a town. There is a lot of damage.
　　　　有個龍捲風侵襲了一座城鎮。造成很多損害。

　　　　* tornado〔tɔr'nedo〕*n.* 龍捲風　　hit〔hɪt〕*v.* 侵襲
　　　　damage〔'dæmɪdʒ〕*n.* 損害

一、看圖辨義：第二部分

For question number 5, please look at picture 5.

5. (**B**、**C**) Which TWO of the following are true about the
people in the picture?
關於圖片中的人，下面哪兩項為眞？

　　A. They are at a football game.
　　　他們正在打美式足球。

　　B. They are at a dance. 他們在一場舞會裡。

　　C. They are wearing formal clothing.
　　　他們穿著正式服裝。

　　D. They are dressed casually. 他們穿得很休閒。

　　* football〔ˋfʊtˏbɔl〕n. 美式足球　　dance〔dæns〕n. 舞會
　　　formal〔ˋfɔrml̩〕adj. 正式的　　clothing〔ˋkloðɪŋ〕n. 衣服
　　　dress〔drɛs〕v. 使穿著
　　　casually〔ˋkæʒjʊəlɪ〕adv. 休閒地

For question number 6, please look at picture 6.

6. (**C**、**D**) Which TWO of the following are true about the
picture? 關於這張圖片，下面哪兩項為眞？

　　　A. The woman is surrounded
　　　　by dogs. 這位女士被狗圍繞。

　　　B. The children are playing a
　　　　game. 這些小孩正在玩遊戲。

　　C. The woman is in distress. 這位女士很苦惱。

　　D. The children are begging for money.
　　　這些小孩正在乞討錢。

　　* surround〔səˋraʊnd〕v. 圍繞
　　　distress〔dɪˋstrɛs〕n. 苦惱　　*in distress* 苦惱
　　　beg〔bɛg〕v. 乞討

For question number 7, please look at picture 7.

7. (**B、D**) Which TWO of the following are true about the people in the picture?
關於圖片中的人，下面哪兩項為眞？

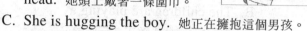

A. All of them are seated on the sofa. 他們全部都坐在沙發上。

B. The girl is standing behind the sofa.
這女孩正站在沙發後面。

C. All of them are playing video games.
他們全部都在打電玩。

D. The old man is playing video games.
這老人正在打電玩。

* *be seated* 坐 (= *sit*)　　*video game* 電玩

For question number 8, please look at picture 8.

8. (**A、B**) Which TWO of the following are true about the woman? 關於這位女士，下面哪兩項為眞？

A. She is a fortune teller.
她是個算命師。

B. She is wearing a scarf on her head. 她頭上戴著一條圍巾。

C. She is hugging the boy. 她正在擁抱這個男孩。

D. She is painting her nails. 她正在塗她的指甲。

* fortune〔'fɔrtʃən〕*n.* 命運
teller〔'tɛlɚ〕*n.* 敘述者　　*fortune teller* 算命師
scarf〔skarf〕*n.* 圍巾　　hug〔hʌg〕*v.* 擁抱
paint〔pent〕*v.* 畫；塗　　nail〔nel〕*n.* 指甲

For question number 9, please look at picture 9.

9. (**A** 、 **C**)　Which TWO of the following are true about the
picture?　關於這張圖片，下面哪兩項為真？

A. They are at the beach.
他們在沙灘上。
B. They are having a fight.
他們在打架。
C. They are having a picnic.　他們在野餐。
D. They are on the moon.　他們在月球上。

　* fight〔faɪt〕*n.* 打架　　picnic〔ˈpɪknɪk〕*n.* 野餐

For question number 10, please look at picture 10.

10. (**A** 、 **D**)　Which TWO of the following
are true about the picture?
關於這張圖片，下面哪兩項為真？

A. The girl is crashing her
motorcycle.　這女孩正在撞毀她的摩托車。
B. The girl is riding a horse.　這女孩正在騎馬。
C. The girl is wearing safety goggles.
這女孩正在戴安全護目鏡。
D. The girl is wearing a helmet.
這女孩正在戴安全帽。

　* crash〔kræʃ〕*v.* 撞毀
motorcycle〔ˈmotəˌsaɪkḷ〕*n.* 摩托車
safety〔ˈseftɪ〕*n.* 安全
goggles〔ˈgɑgḷz〕*n. pl.* 護目鏡
helmet〔ˈhɛlmɪt〕*n.* 安全帽

二、對答

11. (**C**) What is today's date? 今天幾月幾號？

    A. I am going on a date tonight. 我今天晚上要去約會。

    B. It is Friday. 今天是禮拜五。

    C. June sixteenth. 六月十六號。

    D. Don't be late. 別遲到。

    * date〔det〕n. 日期；約會　　***go on a date*** 去約會
    June〔dʒun〕n. 六月

12. (**B**) Where were you born? 你在哪裡出生的？

    A. I am in Taipei. 我現在在台北。

    B. I was born in Tokyo. 我在東京出生。

    C. I went to school in Beijing. 我在北京上學。

    D. I will visit Taiwan next year. 我明年會來造訪台灣。

    * Tokyo〔'tokɪ,o〕n. 東京　　Beijing〔'be'dʒɪŋ〕n. 北京

13. (**D**) What is your favorite color? 你最喜歡的顏色是什麼？

    A. Water. 水。

    B. Heat. 熱。

    C. Screams. 尖叫。

    D. Blue. 藍色。

    * heat〔hit〕n. 熱　　scream〔skrim〕n. 尖叫

14. (**C**) Will you go to the concert this weekend?
    你這個週末會去音樂會嗎？

    A. I don't mind at all. 我一點也不介意。

    B. It's much too loud. 眞的太大聲了。

    C. Yes, I will. 是的，我會去。

D. They didn't tell me. 他們沒告訴我。

* concert〔'kansɜt〕*n.* 音樂會　　mind〔maɪnd〕*v.* 介意

not~at all 一點也不~　　**much too** 太…

15. (**C**) Can I borrow a pen? 我可以借一枝筆嗎？

A. Sign on the dotted line. 在虛線上簽名。

B. I'm left-handed. 我是左撇子。

C. Sure, there's one on my desk.

當然可以，我桌上有一枝。

D. This is a new pencil. 這是一枝新的鉛筆。

* borrow〔'baro〕*v.* 借　　sign〔saɪn〕*v.* 簽名

dotted〔'datɪd〕*adj.* 點狀的　　line〔laɪn〕*n.* 線

dotted line 虛線　　left-handed *adj.* 左撇子的

16. (**D**) Did you draw this picture? 這張圖是你畫的嗎？

A. I don't need it. 我不需要它。

B. My arm hurts. 我的手臂很痛。

C. Who are you? 你是誰？

D. Yes, I did. 是的，是我畫的。

* draw〔drɔ〕*v.* 畫　　arm〔arm〕*n.* 手臂

hurt〔hɜt〕*v.* 疼痛

17. (**C**) Can you speak Japanese? 你會說日語嗎？

A. I was there once. 我曾經去過那裡。

B. Who asked you? 誰問你的？

C. No, I can't. 不，我不會。

D. He is speaking Japanese. 他正在說日語。

* Japanese〔,dʒæpə'niz〕*n.* 日語

once〔wʌns〕*adv.* 一次；曾經

18. (**D**) The phone is ringing. Would you mind answering it?

電話正在響。請你接一下電話好嗎？

   A. The phone is ringing. 電話正在響。

   B. I'll see who is there. 我會去看誰在那裡。

   C. I have been calling you all day.

      我已經打給你打了一整天了。

   D. Sure, I'll do it. 當然，我會接。

   * ring〔rɪŋ〕v. 響（鈴）

   Would you mind + V-ing? 你介不介意…？；請你…好嗎？

   answer〔'ænsɚ〕v. 接（電話）

19. (**A**) You look great today! What's the occasion?

你今天起來很不錯！是什麼特別的日子嗎？

   A. It's my birthday. 今天是我的生日。

   B. Don't look. 別看。

   C. It's hot in here. 這裡好熱。

   D. Green is my favorite color. 綠色是我最喜歡的顏色。

   * occasion〔ə'keʒən〕n. 時刻；場合；特別的大事

   favorite〔'fevərɪt〕adj. 最喜愛的

20. (**C**) George, I'd like you to meet my friend, Kevin.

喬治，我想讓你見見我的朋友凱文。

   A. Hi George, I'm Kevin. 嗨！喬治，我是凱文。

   B. You're my best friend. 你是我最要好的朋友。

   C. Hi Kevin. Nice to meet you.

      嗨！凱文，很高興認識你。

   D. George and Kevin will be there.

      喬治和凱文會在那裡。

   * ***Nice to meet you.*** 很高興認識你。

三、簡短對話

For question 21, you will listen to a short conversation.

M：Congratulations! I heard you are pregnant. Do you know if it's a boy or a girl?

恭喜！我聽說你懷孕了。你知道是男孩還是女孩嗎？

W：Thanks! I'm having a girl. 謝謝！我懷的是個女孩。

* congratulations〔kən͵grætʃə'leʃənz〕*n. pl.* 恭喜
pregnant〔'prɛgnənt〕*adj.* 懷孕的　　have〔hæv〕*v.* 懷（孩子）

21. (**D**) Q：What is true about the woman?
關於這位女士何者為真？
A. She just bought a new car. 她剛買了部新車。
B. She got a promotion at work. 她工作獲得了晉升。
C. She won the lottery. 她中樂透了。
D. She is having a baby. 她懷了一個小孩。

* promotion〔prə'moʃən〕*n.* 晉升；升遷
lottery〔'lɑtərɪ〕*n.* 彩券；樂透彩

For question 22, you will listen to a short conversation.

M：Have you filed your taxes yet? 你已經報稅了嗎？

W：No. When is the filing deadline?
還沒。報稅期限是什麼時候？

M：June 15th. You have exactly a week left.
六月十五日。你正好剩下一個禮拜的時間。

W：Can I file online? 我可以線上報稅嗎？

*file〔faɪl〕v. 申報　　tax〔tæks〕n. 稅
　　deadline〔'dɛd,laɪn〕n. 截止日期
　　exactly〔ɪg'zæktlɪ〕adv. 正好　　left〔lɛft〕adj. 剩下的
　　online〔'ɑn,laɪn〕adv. 在網路上；線上

22.（**C**）Q：When is this conversation taking place?
　　　　這段對話發生在什麼時候？
　　　　A．On June 15th. 在六月十五日。
　　　　B．A week after June 15th. 六月十五後一個禮拜。
　　　　C．On June 8th. 在六月八日。
　　　　D．Two weeks before June 15th. 六月十五前兩個禮拜。

For question 23, you will listen to a short conversation.

　　W：What's wrong with Oscar? He looks like he's about to
　　　　cry. 奧斯卡怎麼了？他看起來像快要哭了。
　　M：Oh, he lost the Parker account. I wouldn't be surprised
　　　　if Dorothy fires him. 噢，他失去了派兒這個客戶。如果
　　　　桃樂西開除他的話我不意外。

　　　　* **What's wrong with ~?** ～怎麼了？
　　　　be about to V. 快要～　　account〔ə'kaʊnt〕n. 客戶
　　　　surprised〔sə'praɪzd〕adj. 驚訝的　　fire〔faɪr〕v. 開除

23.（**C**）Q：Who are these people? 這些人是誰？
　　　　　A．Classmates. 同學。
　　　　　B．Brother and sister. 兄妹。
　　　　　C．Co-workers. 同事。
　　　　　D．Volunteers. 志工。

　　　　　* co-worker〔'ko,wɝkə〕n. 同事（= colleague）
　　　　　　volunteer〔,vɑlən'tɪr〕n. 志工；志願者

For question 24, you will listen to a short conversation.

W : Where is the blueberry pie I left out on the kitchen counter? It's for the bake sale tomorrow. 我遺漏在廚房櫃檯台上的藍莓派在哪裡？那是明天的糕點義賣要用的。

M : I don't know what you're talking about. I haven't set foot in the kitchen all day.

我不知道你在說什麼。我一整天都沒踏進廚房。

* blueberry〔'blu͵bɛrɪ〕n. 藍莓　　pie〔paɪ〕n. 派
  leave out 忽略；遺漏　　counter〔'kaʊntɚ〕n. 櫃台式長桌
  bake sale 糕點義賣　　*set foot in* 進入；踏進

24. (**A**) Q : What does the man mean? 這位男士的意思是什麼？

A. He doesn't know anything about the blueberry pie.
他不知道任何關於藍莓派的事。

B. He won't attend the bake sale because of a foot injury. 因爲腳受傷，所以他不會參加糕點義賣。

C. He left the blueberry pie on the kitchen counter.
他把藍莓派留在廚房櫃台上。

D. He accidentally stepped on the blueberry pie.
他意外地踩在藍莓派上。

* attend〔ə'tɛnd〕v. 參加　　injury〔'ɪndʒərɪ〕n. 傷害
  accidentally〔͵æksə'dɛntl̩ɪ〕adv. 偶然地；意外地
  step〔stɛp〕v. 踩

For questions 25 and 26, you will listen to a short conversation.

W : Are you taking your family to the Fourth of July parade?
你會帶你家人去七月四日的遊行嗎？

M : No, not this year. Unfortunately, I have to work.

不，今年不會。很遺憾地，我必須工作。

W : Really? But it's a national holiday.

真的嗎？可是那天是國定假日。

M : I know, but I've got a very important project that has to
be finished. 我知道，但我有個非常重要的計畫必須要完成。

W : That's too bad. Your family must be disappointed.

真是太糟了。你家人一定很失望。

M : Not really. My wife is taking the kids to Disney World,
so they won't miss me. 其實沒有。我太太會帶孩子們去迪
士尼樂園，所以他們是不會想我的。

* July〔ˋdʒuˋlaɪ〕n. 七月
the Fourth of July 七月四日（美國獨立紀念日；國慶日）
parade〔pəˋred〕n. 遊行
unfortunately〔ʌnˋfɔrtʃənɪtlɪ〕adv. 不幸地；遺憾地
national〔ˋnæʃənḷ〕adj. 國家的   *national holiday* 國定假日
project〔ˋprɑdʒɛkt〕n. 計畫   finish〔ˋfɪnɪʃ〕v. 完成
disappointed〔͵dɪsəˋpɔɪntɪd〕adj. 失望的
not really 不完全是；不盡然   Disney〔ˋdɪznɪ〕n. 迪士尼
miss〔mɪs〕v. 想念

25. (**B**) Q : Why isn't the man going to the parade?

為什麼這男士不去參加遊行？

A. He is taking his family to Disney World.

他要帶他的家人去迪士尼樂園。

B. He has to work. 他必須工作。

C. He doesn't observe national holidays.

他不慶祝國定假日。

D. He doesn't feel well. 他覺得不太舒服。

* observe〔əb'zɜv〕v. 慶祝（節日）　　well〔wɛl〕adj. 健康的

26.（**D**）Q：What is true about the man's family?
　　　　　關於這男士的家人何者為真？

A. They are very disappointed. 他們非常失望。

B. They will miss him during the holiday.
　　他們在放假期間會想他。

C. They always attend the Fourth of July parade.
　　他們一定會參加國慶遊行。

D. They are going to Disney World without him.
　　他們不會和他一起去迪士尼樂園。

For questions 27 and 28, you will listen to a short conversation.

W：Something smells good in here. What's cooking?
　　這裡有東西聞起來好香。在煮什麼啊？

M：I'm making my special Texas chili.
　　我在煮我的特製德州辣醬湯。

W：Wow! Can I have some? 哇！我可以喝一些嗎？

M：Sure, but it won't be ready until tomorrow.
　　當然，但要到明天才會煮好。

W：Really? Why is that? 真的嗎？為什麼？

M：Well, first of all, it takes five hours of preparation. I
　　have to chop the vegetables, measure the seasonings,
　　soak the beans, and brown the meat. Then it takes a
　　good 12 hours over a low flame before all the
　　ingredients start to blend together.

嗯，首先，它需要五個小時來準備。我必須把蔬菜切成細絲，調個調味料，浸泡豆子，再用大火把肉煮成焦黃色。然後，還要用小火煮整整十二小時後，所有食材才會開始混合在一起。

W：Sounds like a lot of work. 聽起來眞費工。

M：It is a labor of love, especially if I follow the traditional family recipe.

這是充滿愛的工作，尤其我是遵照傳統家庭食譜來做的。

* cook〔kʊk〕v.（食物）在煮（燒）著
Texas〔ˈtɛksəs〕n. 德州　　　chili〔ˈtʃɪlɪ〕n. 辣椒；辣醬湯
wow〔waʊ〕interj. 哇　　have〔hæv〕v. 吃；喝
not~until… 直到～才…
preparation〔ˌprɛpəˈreʃən〕n. 準備
chop〔tʃɑp〕v. 切細；切絲　　measure〔ˈmɛʒɚ〕v. 測量；調整
seasoning〔ˈsizṇɪŋ〕n. 佐料；香辣調味料
soak〔sok〕v. 浸泡　　bean〔bin〕n. 豆子
brown〔braʊn〕v. 用大火煮成焦黃色　　meat〔mit〕n. 肉
good〔gʊd〕adj. 充分的；完整的　　flame〔flem〕n. 火焰
a low flame 小火　　ingredient〔ɪnˈgridɪənt〕n. 食材
blend〔blɛnd〕v. 混合　　labor〔ˈlebɚ〕n. 勞動；工作
especially〔əˈspɛʃəlɪ〕adv. 尤其；特別是
follow〔ˈfɑlo〕v. 遵循
traditional〔trəˈdɪʃənḷ〕adj. 傳統的　　recipe〔ˈrɛsəpɪ〕n. 食譜

27.（**C**）Q：Where are these people? 這些人在哪裡？

A. In a post office. 在郵局裡。

B. In a bathroom. 在浴室裡。

C. In a kitchen. 在廚房裡。

D. In a produce market. 在菜市場裡。

* produce〔ˈprɑdjus〕n. 農產品

28. (**C**) Q : What is true about the man? 關於這位男士何者為眞？

    A. He is the only member of his family who can cook.
       他是他家中唯一會煮菜的成員。

    B. He never follows the recipe when he cooks.
       他做菜時從不遵循食譜。

    C. He puts a lot of work into making Texas chili.
       他費了很多的功夫來做德州辣醬湯。

    D. He would prefer not to work for love.
       他寧可不要因爲愛而工作。

    put…into ~ 投入…到~　　prefer (prɪˈfɝ) *v.* 偏好
    would prefer to V. 寧願~

For questions 29 and 30, you will listen to a short conversation.

M : Do you think it's OK to park here? I don't see any no
    parking signs. 你覺得把車子停在這裡可以嗎？我沒看到任何
    禁止停車的標誌。

W : I don't see any other cars parked here and the streets are
    dark. 我沒看到任何其他車子停在這裡，而且街道很暗。

M : Yes, you're right. It's probably not safe.
    是的，你是對的。這裡可能不安全。

W : I have an idea. We could try the parking garage at
    Macy's. 我有個想法。我們可以試試停在梅西百貨的停車場。

M : Yeah, and then walk across the park to the theater.
    對，然後穿過公園走到電影院。

W : As long as you don't mind paying 15 dollars to park the
    car. 只要你不介意付十五美元來停車。

* park〔pɑrk〕v. 停車　　sign〔saɪn〕n. 標誌
probably〔'prɑbəblɪ〕adv. 可能　　garage〔gə'rɑʒ〕n. 車庫
parking garage 室內停車場　　theater〔'θiətə〕n. 電影院
as long as 只要　　mind〔maɪnd〕v. 介意

29. (**C**) Q : What do these people want to do? 這些人想做什麼？

　　A. They want to go to Macy's. 他們想去梅西百貨。
　　B. They want to go to the park. 他們想去公園。
　　C. They want to park the car. 他們想要停車。
　　D. They want to exit the theater. 他們想離開劇院。

　　* exit〔'ɛgzɪt〕v. 離開

30. (**B**) Q : What is true about Macy's? 關於梅西百貨何者為真？

　　A. It is next to the theater. 它在電影院隔壁。
　　B. It costs 15 dollars to park in their garage.
　　　　在他們的停車場停車要花十五美元。
　　C. It isn't safe. 它不安全。
　　D. It is located in a park. 它位在公園裡。

　　* cost〔kɔst〕v. 花費　　*be located in* 位於

四、短文聽解

Questions 31 and 32 are based on the following report.

　　When the mail carriers went on strike last month, they hoped to force the postal service to back down from a proposal to reduce wages. It got me thinking just how much our modern cyber-connected society needs the post office anyway. If I get my mail, that's nice, but if I really have to do something, I go on the Internet.　True, some businesses say they have had problems filling orders and receiving payments that would usually be sent by mail, and some say charities are missing out on donations.　But by going on strike, postal workers have likely sealed their own fate by proving it's possible to function without daily mail delivery.

　　當郵差上個月進行罷工時，他們希望能迫使郵政服務退回一個減薪的提案。這讓我開始思考，究竟我們現代網路連結的社會到底有多需要郵局。如果是我收到郵件，是很好沒錯，但如果我眞的得要做某件事，我會上網。的確，有些行業表示他們已經在塡寫訂單，以及通常是靠郵寄的收款上，遇到了問題，有人指出慈善機構沒有得到捐贈。但藉著進行罷工，郵政人員可能已經決定了他們自己的命運，證明了即便沒有每日遞送郵件，還是有可能正常運作。

** —————————————————

carrier (ˈkærɪɚ) n. 運送人員；郵差　　***mail carrier*** 郵差
strike (straɪk) n. 罷工　　***go on strike*** 進行罷工
force (fors) v. 強迫　　postal (ˈpostl̩) adj. 郵政的
back down from 放棄；退回　　proposal (prəˈpozl̩) n. 提議
reduce (rɪˈdjus) v. 減少　　wage (wedʒ) n. 工薪
get sb. V-ing 讓某人開始～　　just (dʒʌst) adv. 確切地；究竟
modern (ˈmɑdɚn) adj. 現代的　　cyber (ˈsaɪbɚ) n. 網路
connect (kəˈnɛkt) v. 連接　　cyber-connected adj. 網路連結的
anyway (ˈɛnɪˌwe) adv. 到底；究竟　　business (ˈbɪznɪs) n. 行業
have problems (in) + V-ing 做…有困難　　fill (fɪl) v. 塡寫
order (ˈɔrdɚ) n. 訂單　　payment (ˈpemənt) n. 付款
charity (ˈtʃærətɪ) n. 慈善機構　　***miss out on*** 漏掉；未得到
donation (doˈneʃən) n. 捐贈　　likely (ˈlaɪklɪ) adv. 可能地
seal one's own fate 決定某人的命運（常指產生不愉快的結果）
prove (pruv) v. 證明　　function (ˈfʌŋkʃən) v. 運作
daily (ˈdelɪ) adj. 每天的　　delivery (dɪˈlɪvərɪ) n. 遞送

31. (**B**)　Who went on strike?　誰進行罷工？

　　　A. Charity donations.　慈善捐款。
　　　B. Postal workers.　郵政人員。
　　　C. Internet servers.　網路伺服器。
　　　D. Carrier pigeons.　信鴿。

　　　* Internet〔ˈɪntɚˌnɛt〕 *n.* 網際網路
　　　　server〔ˈsɝvɚ〕 *n.* 伺服器　　pigeon〔ˈpɪdʒɪn〕 *n.* 鴿子
　　　　carrier pigeon　信鴿

32. (**B**)　What does the speaker say about daily mail delivery?
　　　說話者認為日常郵件遞送如何？

　　　A. It is too slow.　它太慢。
　　　B. It is possible to function without it.
　　　　沒有它也可以正常運作。
　　　C. It is essential to modern life.　它對現代生活是必要的。
　　　D. It is missing out on donations.　它沒收到捐贈。

　　　* essential〔ɪˈsɛnʃəl〕 *adj.* 必要的；不可或缺的

Questions 33 and 34 are based on the following report.

　　If you're a dedicated shopper, a new discovery could help you justify browsing for hours on end. Studies show that shopping isn't just about materialism; it's actually good for your mental and physical health. It releases mood-lifting endorphins, boosts your immune system, keeps your brain nimble, and even fulfills basic social needs. There already is a well-established link between shopping and a heightened sense of happiness. Maybe browsing at Macy's isn't quite as strenuous as 60 minutes on the treadmill, but shopping will give you the same kind of high by releasing a flood of endorphins—the feel-good chemicals in your brain.

　　如果你是個愛好購物的人，有一個新的發現可以幫你合理化連續逛個好幾小時的行為。研究顯示，購物不只和物質主義有關；它實際上對心理及身體上的健康很有幫助。它能釋放提振心情的腦內啡、增強你的免疫系統、使你的大腦保持靈活，甚至可以滿足基本的社會需求。購物與提升幸福感之間確實有關。或許逛梅西百貨不像在跑步機上跑六十分鐘一樣費力，但購物卻能釋出大量讓人感到心情好的化學物質——腦內啡，而給你同樣的快感。

** ———————————————————

dedicated〔ˋdɛdə͵ketɪd〕*adj.* 投入的；獻身的
shopper〔ˋtʃɑpɚ〕*n.* 購物者　　discovery〔dɪˋskʌvərɪ〕*n.* 發現
justify〔ˋdʒʌstə͵faɪ〕*v.* 合理化；使成為正當
browse〔brauz〕*v.* 瀏覽；隨意逛逛　***on end*** 連續地
study〔ˋstʌdɪ〕*n.* 研究
materialism〔məˋtɪrɪəl͵ɪzəm〕*n.* 物質主義；享樂主義
actually〔ˋæktʃʊəlɪ〕*adv.* 實際上
mental〔ˋmɛntḷ〕*adj.* 心理上的
physical〔ˋfɪzɪkḷ〕*adj.* 身體上的　　release〔rɪˋlis〕*v.* 釋放
mood〔mud〕*n.* 心情；情緒　　lift〔lɪft〕*v.* 提升；鼓舞
mood-lifting *adj.* 提振心情的
endorphin〔ɛnˋdɔrfən〕*n.* 腦內啡【一種可於生物體內合成的類嗎啡
　　生物化合物，與嗎啡受體結合可止痛與產生欣快感，為天然的鎮痛劑】
boost〔bust〕*adj.* 促進；增強　　immune〔ɪˋmjun〕*adj.* 免疫的
immune system 免疫系統　　nimble〔ˋnɪmbḷ〕*adj.* 靈活的
fulfill〔fulˋfɪl〕*v.* 滿足；實現
social〔ˋsoʃəl〕*adj.* 社會的；社交的
social needs 社會需求【追求被他人接受和歸屬感】
establish〔əˋstæblɪʃ〕*v.* 建立

well-established *adj.* 確實的；根深蒂固的
link〔lɪŋk〕*n.* 連結；關係
heightened〔'haɪtn̩d〕*adj.* 提高的；增加的
sense〔sɛns〕*n.* 感覺　strenuous〔'strɛnjʊəs〕*adj.* 費力的
treadmill〔'trɛd,mɪl〕*n.* 跑步機　high〔haɪ〕*n.* 快感
a flood of 大量的；滔滔不絕的　feel-good *adj.* 令人愉悅的
chemical〔'kɛmɪkl̩〕*n.* 化學物質

33. (**B**) What is true about shopping? 關於購物何者為真？

   A. It is as strenuous as 60 minutes on the treadmill.
   它像在跑步機上跑六十分鐘一樣費力。

   B. It is good for your mental and physical health.
   它對心理上及身體上的健康有好處。

   C. It is justified by materialism.
   它可以用物質主義來合理化。

   D. It is a feel-good chemical in your brain.
   它是在你腦中讓你感到心情好的化學物質。

34. (**B**) Which of the following is NOT a benefit of shopping?
   下列何者「不是」購物的好處？

   A. The release of mood-lifting endorphins.
   釋放提振情緒的腦內啡。

   B. The heightened sense of materialism.
   提升的物質享樂感。

   C. The fulfillment of basic social needs.
   基本社交需求的滿足。

   D. The boosting of the immune system.
   免疫系統的強化。

   * benefit〔'bɛnəfɪt〕*n.* 利益；好處

Questions 35 and 36 are based on the following report.

Cars are not supposed to be good investments but many people have recently turned a profit selling their used vehicles. The rule of thumb says that a new or used car loses at least 10 percent of its value the moment it leaves the dealership. But soaring used-car values are destroying that formula. Fuel-efficient vehicles are suddenly in high demand as Americans fret about escalating gas prices and do not want to pay for a new car. Used cars overall are retaining a higher percentage of their original value than ever before. Compact cars that are one to five years old are worth, on average, about 30 percent more on the wholesale market now than just six months ago.

汽車被認爲不是好的投資，但最近許多人因爲賣二手車而獲利。經驗法則指出，當車子一離開經銷商時候，新車或二手車都會折損至少百分之十的價值。但激增的二手車價值正在破壞那個行情公式。當美國人擔心不斷上升的油價，而且不想花錢買一台新車時，省油車的需求便突然升高。整體來看，二手車保留了比以前更高比例的原始價值。一到五年的小型車現在在批發市場，平均比六個月前的價值還高百分之三十。

** ————————————————

suppose〔səˋpoz〕 v. 認爲
investment〔ɪnˋvɛstmənt〕 n. 投資
recently〔ˋrisṇtlɪ〕 adv. 最近　　profit〔ˋprɑfɪt〕 n. 利潤
turn a profit 賺錢；獲利　　used〔just〕 adj. 二手的
thumb〔θʌm〕 n. 姆指　　***rule of thumb*** 經驗法則
at least 至少　　value〔ˋvælju〕 n. 價值

the moment 一…就 (= *as soon as*)
dealership ('dilɚ,ʃɪp) *n.* 經銷商
soaring ('sorɪŋ) *adj.* 高飛的；激增的；暴漲的
destroy (dɪ'strɔɪ) *v.* 破壞　　formula ('fɔrmjələ) *n.* 公式
fuel ('fjuəl) *n.* 燃料　　efficient (ɪ'fɪʃənt) *adj.* 有效率的
fuel-efficient *adj.* 燃料消耗低的；省油的
vehicle ('viɪkḷ) *n.* 車輛　　suddenly ('sʌdṇlɪ) *adv.* 突然地
demand (dɪ'mænd) *n.* 需求
in high demand 需求量大；很搶手　　fret (frɛt) *v.* 煩惱
escalating ('ɛskə,letɪŋ) *adj.* 升高的　　gas (gæs) *n.* 汽油
overall ('ovɚ,ɔl) *adv.* 整體來說　　retain (rɪ'ten) *v.* 保持
percentage (pɚ'sɛntɪdʒ) *n.* 百分比
original (ə'rɪdʒənḷ) *adj.* 原來的　　**than ever before** 比以前
compact (kəm'pækt) *adj.* 小型的
worth (wɝθ) *adj.* 有…價值的　　average ('ævərɪdʒ) *n.* 平均
on average 平均而言　　wholesale ('hol,sel) *adj.* 批發的

35. (**B**) Why are cars not supposed to be good investments?
　　 為什麼汽車被認為不是好的投資？

　　A. Gasoline is not free. 汽油不是免費的。

　　B. They lose at least 10 percent of their value when
　　　 purchased.
　　　 當車子被購買時，它們就損失了至少百分之十的價值。

　　C. No one wants to pay for a new car.
　　　 沒人想付錢買一台新車。

　　D. Five-year-old cars are worth more.
　　　 五年車的價值更高。

　　＊ gasoline ('gæsḷ,in) *n.* 汽油　　free (fri) *adj.* 免費的
　　　 percent (pɚ'sɛnt) *n.* 百分之…
　　　 purchase ('pɝtʃəs) *v.* 購買

36. (**A**) Why are fuel-efficient vehicles in high demand?
　　　爲什麼省油的車子需求量很大？
　　　A. Escalating gas prices. 攀升的油價。
　　　B. Soaring insurance rates. 激增的保險費用。
　　　C. Sluggish wholesale markets. 蕭條的批發市場。
　　　D. Exploding profits. 爆增的利潤。

　　　* insurance〔ɪnˋʃʊrəns〕 *n.* 保險　　　rate〔ret〕 *n.* 價格；費用
　　　sluggish〔ˋslʌgɪʃ〕 *adj.* 蕭條的　　explode〔ɪkˋsplod〕 *v.* 爆發

Questions 37 and 38 are based on the following report.

　　It's not known how many parents have the opportunity to select what sex they'd like their baby to be, but sex-selective abortions have skewed the gender balance. Normally, 105 baby boys are born for every 100 girls. According to China's census, 118 baby boys were born for every 100 girls in 2010. Kits that promise to reveal the sex of a baby at just a few weeks' gestation have raised fears of similar sex-selective abortions in Western countries.

　　我們不知道有多少父母有機會來選擇他們所希望孩子的性別，但「選擇性別的墮胎」已經使性別平衡失衡了。通常每生 100 個女孩，就會生 105 個男孩。依據中國人口調查顯示，在 2010 年，每生一百個女孩，就會生 118 個男孩。保證在懷孕前面幾週就顯示出孩子性別的設備，已經讓西方國家開始害怕，會發生類似「選擇性別的墮胎。」

** ————————————

　　opportunity〔ˌɑpɚˋtjunətɪ〕 *n.* 機會　　select〔səˋlɛkt〕 *v.* 選擇
　　selective〔ˌsəˋlɛktɪv〕 *adj.* 選擇性的

abortion〔ə'bɔrʃən〕n. 墮胎　　skew〔'skju〕v. 使偏斜
gender〔'dʒɛndɚ〕n. 性別　　balance〔'bæləns〕n. 平衡
normally〔'nɔrml̩ɪ〕adv. 通常　　*according to* 根據
census〔'sɛnsəs〕n. 人口普查　　kit〔kɪt〕n. 設備
promise〔'prɑmɪs〕v. 保證　　reveal〔rɪ'vil〕v. 顯示
gestation〔dʒɛs'teʃən〕n. 懷孕　　raise〔rez〕v. 引起
fear〔fɪr〕n. 恐懼；擔心　　similar〔'sɪmələ〕adj. 類似的
Western〔'wɛstɚn〕adj. 西方的；西洋的；歐美的

37. (**B**) What has skewed the gender balance?
　　是什麼使性別平衡失衡？

　　　A. China's census. 中國的人口普查。

　　　B. Sex-selective abortions. 選擇性別的墮胎。

　　　C. 118 baby boys. 118 個男嬰。

　　　D. Western countries. 西方國家。

38. (**A**) What is the normal birthrate ratio of boys to girls?
　　何者是正常的男孩比女孩的出生比率？

　　　A. 105 boys for every 100 girls.
　　　　每 100 個女孩有 105 個男孩。

　　　B. 118 boys for every 105 girls.
　　　　每 105 個女孩有 118 個男孩。

　　　C. 100 boys for every 118 girls.
　　　　每 118 個女孩有 100 個男孩。

　　　D. 118 boys for every 100 girls.
　　　　每 100 個女孩有 118 個男孩。

　　* normal〔'nɔrml̩〕adj. 正常的
　　　birthrate〔'bɝθ,ret〕n. 出生率
　　　ratio〔'reʃo〕n. 比例

Questions 39 and 40 are based on the following report.

About one in five U.S. drivers—36.9 million
Americans—couldn't meet the basic requirements to get a
driver's license if they had to take the written test today,
according to a shocking insurance survey released in May.
Kansas topped the list with the most knowledgeable drivers,
while Washington, D.C. drivers scored the worst on a test of
basic driving skills, based on questions from state DMV
exams. The survey also found that California drivers are the
most likely to fail the written test on their first attempt.

依據一份五月發表的一項驚人的保險調查，大約每五個美國駕
駛人中就有一個——三千六百九十萬個美國人——假使今天要考駕
照的筆試的話，他們無法符合考取駕照的必備條件。擁有「最多駕
駛知識的駕駛人」的堪薩斯州，在這份名單中位居首位，而根據州
機動車輛管理局的測驗，華盛頓特區的駕駛人在基本駕駛技術考試
中，得到最差的分數。這個調查也發現，加州駕駛人是最有可能在
他們第一次嘗試考駕照筆試時考不及格。

** ————————————————————

driver (ˈdraɪvɚ) *n.* 駕駛人　　meet (mit) *v.* 滿足；符合
basic (besɪk) *adj.* 基本的
requirement (rɪˈkwaɪrmənt) *n.* 必備條件；要求的事物
license (ˈlaɪsn̩s) *n.* 執照　　**driver's license** 駕照
written (ˈrɪtn̩) *adj.* 寫下的；書面的　　**written test** 筆試
shocking (ˈʃɑkɪŋ) *adj.* 令人震驚的
insurance (ɪnˈʃʊrəns) *n.* 保險　　survey (ˈsɚˌve) *n.* 調查
release (rɪˈlis) *v.* 釋放；發表
Kansas (ˈkænzəs) *n.* 堪薩斯州【位於美國正中心，是世界最大且重要
的小麥生產區】

top〔tɑp〕v. 居首位；位於…的頂端　　list〔lɪst〕n. 名單
knowledgeable〔'nɑlɪdʒəbl̩〕adj. 有知識的
Washington〔'wɑʃɪŋtən〕n. 華盛頓
Washington, D.C. 華盛頓哥倫比亞特區【為美國首都，常簡稱華府。
　　D.C. 為哥倫比亞特區 District of Columbia 的簡稱】
state〔stet〕adj. 州的　　score〔skor〕v. 得分
skill〔skɪl〕n. 技術；技巧　　**based on** 根據
DMV 機動車輛管理局（= Department of Motor Vehicles）
California〔͵kælə'fɔrnjə〕n. 加州
fail〔fel〕v.（考試）不及格
attempt〔ə'tɛmpt〕n. 企圖；嘗試

39. (**A**) What is the report based on?　這份報告是根據什麼？

A. The results of an insurance survey.
保險調查的結果。

B. One in five U.S. drivers.
每五個美國駕駛人中就有一個。

C. Driving skills.　駕駛技術。

D. Basic requirements.　基本的必備條件。

* result〔rɪ'zʌlt〕n. 結果

40. (**D**) Who is most likely to fail the written test on their first
attempt?　誰最有可能在第一次嘗試考筆試時考不及格？

A. About one in ten U.S. drivers.
大約十個美國駕駛人中就有一個。

B. Kansas drivers.　堪薩斯州的駕駛人。

C. Washington, D.C. drivers.　華盛頓特區的駕駛人。

D. California drivers.　加州的駕駛人。

高中英聽測驗模擬試題 ⑧ 詳解

一、看圖辨義：第一部分

For question number 1, please look at picture 1.

1. (**A**) A woman is sitting at a computer. A man is shouting at her. 一個女人正坐在電腦旁。一個男人正對她吼叫。

　　* shout〔ʃaut〕v. 吼叫

For question number 2, please look at picture 2.

2. (**B**) A man is angry with his daughter. She burned his dinner. 一個男士對他的女兒很生氣。她把他的晚餐弄燒焦了。

　　* burn〔bɜn〕v. 燃燒；燒焦

For question number 3, please look at picture 3.

3. (**D**) A woman made a big mistake. She threw some water on her neighbor.

一個女士犯了一個大錯誤。她潑了一些水在她的鄰居身上。

* throw〔θro〕*v.* 拋；丟；噴
  neighbor〔'nebɚ〕*n.* 鄰居

For question number 4, please look at picture 4.

4. (**B**) A boy and a girl are at the beach. The girl is covering the boy with sand.

一個男孩與一個女孩在沙灘上。這女孩正在用沙掩蓋這男孩。

* cover〔'kʌvɚ〕*v.* 掩蓋   sand〔sænd〕*n.* 沙

一、看圖辨義：第二部分

For question number 5, please look at picture 5.

5. (**A**、**D**) Which TWO of the following are true about the
man? 關於這位男士，下列哪兩項敘述為真？

A. He is in the hospital.
他在醫院。

B. He has cancer. 他得了癌症。

C. He speaks four languages.
他說四種語言。

D. He has a broken leg. 他腳骨折了。

* cancer〔ˈkænsə〕n. 癌症
language〔ˈlæŋgwɪdʒ〕n. 語言
broken〔ˈbrokən〕adj. 骨折的

For question number 6, please look at picture 6.

6. (**B**、**D**) Which TWO of the following are true about the
man? 關於這位男士，下列哪兩項敘述為真？

A. He is sleeping.
他在睡覺。

B. He is in a child's bedroom.
他在一個孩子的臥房裡。

C. He is the Easter Bunny. 他是復活節兔。

D. He is Santa Claus. 他是聖誕老人。

* Easter〔ˈistə〕n. 復活節
bunny〔ˈbʌnɪ〕n. 兔子【文中 bunny 字首須大寫，特指象徵
春天新生的復活節兔】
Santa Claus〔ˈsæntəˌklɔz〕n. 聖誕老人

For question number 7, please look at picture 7.

7. (**A、C**) Which TWO of the following are true about the
picture? 關於這張圖片，下列哪兩項敘述為眞？

    A. The kids are playing chess.
        這些孩子正在下西洋棋。

    B. The kids are playing tennis.
        這些孩子正在打網球。

    C. The boy is wearing glasses. 這男孩正戴著眼鏡。

    D. The girl is wearing glasses. 這女孩正戴著眼鏡。

    * chess〔tʃɛs〕*n.* 西洋棋   tennis〔'tɛnɪs〕*n.* 網球
      glasses〔'glæsɪz〕*n. pl.* 眼鏡

For question number 8, please look at picture 8.

8. (**C、D**) Which TWO of the following are true about the girl?
    關於這位女孩，下列哪兩項敘述為眞？

    A. She is holding a radio.
        她正拿著收音機。

    B. She is standing next to a dog.
        她正站在一隻狗的旁邊。

    C. She is holding an umbrella. 她正拿著一把傘。

    D. She is squating next to a frog.
        她正蹲在一隻青蛙旁邊。

    * radio〔're͵dɪo〕*n.* 收音機   umbrella〔ʌm'brɛlə〕*n.* 雨傘
      squat〔skwɑt〕*v.* 蹲（下）

For question number 9, please look at picture 9.

9. (**A、D**) Which TWO of the following are true about the
horse? 關於這隻馬，下列哪兩項敘述為眞？

A. They are feeding a horse.

他們正在餵馬。

B. It is eating a sandwich.

牠正在吃一個三明治。

C. It has two passengers. 牠有兩名乘客。

D. It has its eyes closed. 牠把牠的眼睛閉上了。

* feed〔fid〕v. 餵　　sandwich〔'sændwɪtʃ〕n. 三明治

passenger〔'pæsṇdʒɚ〕n. 乘客

For question number 10, please look at picture 10.

10. (**B**、**C**) Which TWO of the following are true about the

man? 關於這位男士，下列哪兩項敘述為真？

A. He is at the bank. 他在銀行。

B. He is at a temple. 他在廟裡。

C. He is saying a prayer.

他正在祈禱。

D. He is singing a song. 他正在唱歌。

* temple〔'tɛmpl̩〕n. 廟　　prayer〔prɛr〕n. 祈禱文

二、對答

11. (**C**) What is your favorite season? 你最喜歡的季節是什麼？

A. I think the soup is too salty. 我覺得這湯太鹹了。

B. It's cold outside. 外面很冷。

C. Spring is my favorite time of year.

春天是一年之中我最喜歡的季節。

D. It needs a little more seasoning. 這需要多一點調味料。

* salty〔'sɔltɪ〕adj. 鹹的　　*time of year* 季節 (= *season*)

seasoning〔'sizṇɪŋ〕n. 調味；調味料

12. (**B**) Do you watch a lot of television? 你很常看電視嗎？

    A. I saw it on television. 我在電視上看過這個。

    B. Only on the weekend. 只有在週末的時候。

    C. I'm interested in science. 我對科學很有興趣。

    D. It's physically impossible. 這根本不可能。

    * *be interested in* 對…有興趣
    physically〔'fɪzɪk]ɪ〕*adv.* 根據自然法則地
    physically impossible 根本不可能的

13. (**A**) Are you ready for the test? 你考試準備好了嗎？

    A. I think so. I studied very hard.
        我想是的。我很用功讀書。

    B. You'll have to take the test. 你將必須去考試。

    C. The test is ready. 要準備考試了。

    D. I love it. 我愛它。

    * *be ready for* 準備好做…   *take the test* 參加考試

14. (**C**) Have you ever been fishing? 你釣過魚嗎？

    A. I had fish for dinner. 我晚餐吃魚。

    B. I can't swim. 我不會游泳。

    C. No, I've never been fishing. 不，我沒有釣過魚。

    D. He's fishing for compliments. 他在討人的恭維。

    * fish〔fɪʃ〕*v.* 釣魚；設法獲得
    compliment〔'kɑmpləmənt〕*n.* 稱讚；讚美
    fish for compliments 討人恭維

15. (**D**) What days do you study Chinese? 你哪幾天讀中文？

    A. In March. 在三月。

    B. At six o'clock. 在六點。

C. Next week. 下週。

D. On Mondays and Wednesdays. 每週一和每週三。

＊Chinese〔tʃaɪ'niz〕*n.* 中文

16.（**D**）Is this your first time driving a car? 這是你第一次開車嗎？

　　A. Yes, I have a license. 是的，我有執照。

　　B. Yes, I know the way. 是的，我知道路。

　　C. Yes, I am in control. 是的，由我掌控。

　　D. No, I have been driving for two years.

　　　　不是的，我已經開兩年車了。

　　＊license〔'laɪsn̩s〕*n.* 執照　　***in control*** 掌控；管理

17.（**A**）Where are you going? 你要去哪裡？

　　A. I have a dentist's appointment. 我和牙醫有約。

　　B. Have a good time! 玩得愉快！

　　C. I just got here. 我剛到這裡。

　　D. Nice to meet you. 很高興認識你。

　　＊dentist〔'dɛntɪst〕*n.* 牙醫
　　appointment〔ə'pɔɪntmənt〕*n.* 預約；約診

18.（**B**）Where have you been? 你去哪裡了？

　　A. I've been there before. 我以前去過那裡。

　　B. I was at the library. 我在圖書館。

　　C. Maybe your friend can do it. 或許你的朋友可以做到。

　　D. No, I'm not hungry. 不，我不餓。

19.（**C**）Is something wrong? You look worried.

　　　　哪裡有問題嗎？你看起來很擔心。

　　A. You're always wrong. 你總是出錯。

B. It's Sunday. 今天是週日。

C. I lost my wallet. 我弄丟了我的皮夾。

D. Check in the pantry. 檢查看看食品儲藏室。

* worried〔'wɜɪd〕adj. 擔心的

   wallet〔'wɑlɪt〕n. 皮夾　　check〔tʃɛk〕v. 檢查；確認

   pantry〔'pæntrɪ〕n. 食品儲藏室

20. (**A**) What did you do last night? 你昨晚做了什麼？

A. I went to see a movie with Greg.

   我和葛瑞格去看電影。

B. It was a long night. 那是個漫長的夜晚。

C. I am afraid of the dark. 我怕黑。

D. I'm always the last to know. 我總是最後一個知道的。

* *the dark* 黑暗

(三) 簡短對話

For question 21, you will listen to a short conversation.

M：Are you still watching television in the family room?

   妳還在起居室看電視嗎？

W：No. 沒有。

M：Then turn it off. You're wasting electricity.

   那麼就把電視關掉。妳在浪費電。

W：I didn't turn it on, Dad. Ask Jimmy. He was watching

   a movie. 我沒有打開電視，爸。問吉米。他剛剛在看電影。

  * *family room* 家庭娛樂室；起居室【家人休息放鬆看電視玩遊戲的

   空間】　　*turn off* 關掉（電器）

  electricity〔ɪ,lɛk'trɪsətɪ〕n. 電　　*turn on* 打開（電器）

21. (**A**) Q : Who are these people?　這些人是誰？

　　A. Father and daughter.　父女。

　　B. Husband and wife.　夫妻。

　　C. Brother and sister.　兄妹。

　　D. Aunt and Uncle.　阿姨和叔叔。

For question 22, you will listen to a short conversation.

　M : Wow, you look great, Evelyn.　Have you been working

　　out?　哇，妳看起來很棒，艾芙琳。妳一直有在健身嗎？

　W : Yes, I'm taking an aerobic dance class at my gym.　It's

　　included in the membership fee.

　　是的，我在健身房上有氧舞蹈課程。這包含在會費裡面。

　M : How many times a week do you take the class?

　　妳一週上幾次課？

　W : Four times a week.　Sometimes five if I'm feeling

　　ambitious.　一週四次。有時五次，如果我感到充滿野心的話。

　　* ***work out*** 健身；運動　　aerobic〔ˌeəˈrobɪk〕 *adj.* 有氧的

　　gym〔dʒɪm〕 *n.* 健身房　　include〔ɪnˈklud〕 *v.* 包括

　　membership〔ˈmɛmbɚˌʃɪp〕 *n.* 會員資格

　　fee〔fi〕 *n.* 學費；會費　　time〔taɪm〕 *n.* 次數

　　ambitious〔æmˈbɪʃəs〕 *adj.* 有抱負的；野心勃勃的

22. (**B**) Q : What is true about the woman?　關於女士，何者為真？

　　A. She is ambitious in her career.　她對工作充滿抱負。

　　B. She goes to the gym at least four times a week.

　　　她一週至少上健身房四次。

C. She was thinking about taking an aerobic dance class. 她正考慮上有氧舞蹈的課。

D. She just cancelled her membership at the gym. 她剛取消健身房的會員資格。

＊career〔kəˋrɪr〕n. 職業；工作　　*at least* 至少
think about 考慮　　just〔dʒʌst〕adv. 剛剛
cancel〔ˋkænsl̩〕v. 取消

For question 23, you will listen to a short conversation.

W：What do you feel like having for dinner?
你晚餐想要吃什麼？

M：How about pizza? We haven't been to Shakey's in a while. 披薩如何？我們一陣子沒去吃喜客披薩了。

＊*feel like* 想要　　*How about~?* ～如何？
in a while 一段時間

23. (**C**) Q：What are the speakers talking about?
說話者在討論什麼？

    A. Art. 藝術。　　　　　　B. Clothing. 衣服。
    C. Food. 食物。　　　　　D. Shelter. 住處。

＊art〔ɑrt〕n. 藝術　　clothing〔ˋkloðɪŋ〕n.（總稱）衣服
shelter〔ˋʃɛltə〕n. 住處

For question 24, you will listen to a short conversation.

W：Is it hot out there? 外面很熱嗎？

M：Is it hot? You could fry an egg on the sidewalk.
很熱嗎？你可以在人行道上煎蛋了。

out there 外面　　fry〔fraɪ〕v. 油煎
sidewalk〔'saɪd,wɔk〕n. 人行道

24. (**B**) Q：What does the man mean?　男士的意思是什麼？

A. He's going to make an omelet on the sidewalk.
他即將要在人行道上做一個煎蛋捲。
B. It is very hot outside.　外面很熱。
C. There is heavy rain.　有大雨。
D. The streets are filled with food.　街上充滿了食物。

* omelet〔'ɑmlɪt〕n. 煎蛋捲　　*heavy rain* 大雨
be filled with 充滿了

For questions 25 and 26, you will listen to a short conversation.

W：Oh my gosh! Did you hear? You're not going to believe this, Paul.
喔，我的天呀！你有聽到嗎？你不會相信的，保羅。

M：Believe what, Marsha?　相信什麼，瑪莎？

W：Tracy dumped Chad and now she's dating Richard.
翠西拋棄了查德，現在她和理察在約會。

M：Are you sure about that? I saw Tracy and Chad together last night at the café.
妳確定嗎？我昨晚看到翠西和查德一起在咖啡廳。

W：Well, that's what Rhonda told me, and she's Tracy's best friend.　嗯，那是朗達告訴我的，而她是翠西最好的朋友。

M：I'd be careful about spreading gossip around here, Marsha.　我會當心在這裡散播謠言，瑪莎。

* *my gosh* 我的天呀　　dump〔dʌmp〕v. 丟棄；拋棄
date〔det〕v. 和…約會　　café〔kəˈfe〕n. 咖啡廳
be careful about 對…小心；當心
spread〔sprɛd〕v. 散播　　gossip〔ˈgɑsəp〕n. 流言蜚語；謠言

25. (**C**) Q : Who are the speakers? 說話者是誰？

A. Tracy and Chad. 翠西和查德。

B. Richard and Rhonda. 理察和朗達。

C. Paul and Marsha. 保羅和瑪莎。

D. Rhonda and Tracy. 朗達和翠西。

26. (**A**) Q : What is true about the man?

關於那位男士，何者爲眞？

A. He doesn't trust Marsha's gossip.
他不相信瑪莎的謠言。

B. He is Chad's best friend. 他是查德最好的朋友。

C. He used to date Tracy. 他以前和翠西約會過。

D. He has a crush on Rhonda. 他迷戀朗達。

* *used to V.* 以前～　　*have a crush on sb.* 迷戀某人

For questions 27 and 28, you will listen to a short conversation.

W : Have you seen Mr. Compton? I know he's here but I
can't spot him in the crowd. 你有看到康普頓先生嗎？我
知道他在這裡，但是我無法在人群中看到他。

M : No, I've never even met him. What does he look like?
不，我從來沒有見過他。他外表看起來怎樣？

W : He's a middle-aged man in a black business suit.
他是一位穿著黑色西裝的中年男士。

M : That doesn't help! Every man in the room is wearing a black business suit. Can you be more specific?

那沒有幫助！房間裡的每位男士都是穿著黑色西裝。你可以更明確一點嗎？

W : Well, he's got brown hair and he wears a beard.

嗯，他有棕色頭髮，有蓄鬍。

M : How tall is he? 他多高？

W : Oh, he's about your height. 喔，跟你差不多高。

M : Good luck. You're trying to find a needle in a haystack.

祝你好運。你是在大海撈針。

* spot〔spɑt〕v. 發現；看出　　crowd〔kraʊd〕n. 人群
middle-aged adj. 中年的　**business suit** 西裝
specific〔spɪˋsɪfɪk〕adj. 明確的　**has got** 有（= has）
brown〔braʊn〕adj. 棕色的　　beard〔bɪrd〕n. 鬍子
wear a beard 蓄鬍　　height〔haɪt〕n. 高度；身高
Good luck. 祝你好運。【用於表示不介意某人做的事，因為不會影響
　到你】　　needle〔ˋnidl̩〕n. 針
haystack〔ˋhe͵stæk〕n. 乾草堆
find a needle in a haystack 大海撈針（= look for a needle in
　a haystack）

27. (**C**) Q : What is true about Mr. Compton?

關於康普頓先生，何者為真？

A. He is wearing a brown business suit.

他穿著棕色西裝。

B. He is extremely tall. 他非常高。

C. He is somewhere in the crowd. 他在人群的某個地方。

D. He is balding and wears glasses.
他快要禿頭，而且有戴眼鏡。

* extremely〔ɪk'strimlɪ〕*adv.* 極端地；非常
balding〔'bɔldɪŋ〕*adj.* 逐漸禿頭的

28. (**B**) Q：Where are these people? 這些人在哪裡？
A. At a movie premiere. 在一場電影的首映會。
B. At a business conference. 在一場商務會議上。
C. On Mr. Compton's yacht. 在康普頓先生的遊艇上。
D. In a haystack. 在乾草堆裡。

* premiere〔prɪ'mɪr〕*n.* (電影的) 首映
conference〔'kɑnfərəns〕*n.* 會議   yacht〔jɑt〕*n.* 遊艇

For questions 29 and 30, you will listen to a short conversation.

M：How many lottery tickets did you buy for tonight's big
drawing? 妳今晚的大抽獎買了幾張彩券？

W：None. I didn't get a chance to stop by the mini-mart.
一張都沒有。我沒有機會順道去小商店。

M：Oh no! What time is it? 喔，不！現在幾點了？

W：It's six o'clock. 六點。

M：The cut-off time is six-thirty. I still have time. Where
are my numbers?
截止時間是六點半。我還有時間。我的號碼在哪裡？

W：They're right here in my purse. 就在我的錢包裡。

* ***lottery ticket*** 彩券   drawing〔'drɔɪŋ〕*n.* 抽籤；抽獎
chance〔tʃæns〕*n.* 機會；時機

stop by 順道拜訪；中途順便到
mini-mart *n.* 迷你超市；小商店（= *minimart*）
cut-off time 截止時間　　purse〔 pɜs 〕*n.* 錢包

29.（**B**）Q：What are the speakers talking about?
　　　　　說話者在討論什麼？
　　　A. The mini-mart. 小商店。
　　　B. Lottery tickets. 彩券。
　　　C. Account numbers. 帳號。
　　　D. The woman's purse. 女士的錢包。
　　　* ***account number*** 帳號

30.（**A**）Q：What is true about the woman?
　　　　　關於這位女士，何者為真？
　　　A. She didn't buy the lottery tickets. 她沒有買彩券。
　　　B. She doesn't have the man's numbers.
　　　　她沒有那位男士的號碼。
　　　C. She wasn't hungry. 她不餓。
　　　D. She can't find her purse. 她找不到錢包。

四、短文聽解

Questions 31 and 32 are based on the following report.

　　The music business is in a state of change right now.
Record labels have been forced to modify their business
models in response to evolving consumer demands.
They've had to reinvent their distribution model and start
from scratch. The few remaining record stores are on their

last legs and that's no mystery. Consumers now prefer
downloading their music. They can get their occasional
CD purchase from big-box discounters like ShopMart.
Record stores that fail to adapt to the new realities of music
distribution will continue to go bust no matter what
happens to the economy.

　　音樂界現在正處於轉變的情況。唱片公司被迫改變他們的商
業模式，來因應消費者演變的需求。他們必須徹底改變他們的配
銷模式，並從頭開始。剩餘少數的唱片行還在硬撐，而這是眾所
皆知的事。消費者現在偏好下載音樂。他們偶爾會從大型廉價商
店購買雷射唱片，像是「購物市場」。唱片行若無法適應音樂分
佈的現實狀況，無論經濟狀況如何，都將會持續倒閉。

** ─────────────────────

business〔'bɪznɪs〕n. 行業；事業　　　state〔stet〕n. 狀態；情況
right now 現在　　　*record label* 唱片公司
force〔fors〕v. 強迫　　modify〔'mɑdə,faɪ〕v. 改變；修正
model〔'mɑdḷ〕n. 模型；模式　　*business model* 商業模式
in response to 回應　　evolving〔ɪ'valvɪŋ〕adj. 演變的
consumer〔kən'sumɚ〕n. 消費者
demand〔dɪ'mænd〕n. 需求
reinvent〔,riɪn'vɛnt〕v. 重新發明；徹底改造
distribution〔,dɪstrə'bjuʃən〕n. 分配；分佈；配銷
from scratch 從頭開始　　remaining〔rɪ'menɪŋ〕adj. 剩下的
record store 唱片行　　*on one's last legs* 很疲憊的；垂死的
mystery〔'mɪstərɪ〕n. 秘密；謎　　prefer〔prɪ'fɝ〕v. 偏好
download〔'daʊn,lod〕v. 下載
occasional〔ə'keʒənḷ〕adj. 偶爾的
purchase〔'pɝtʃəs〕n. 購買　　big-box adj. 大型的
discounter〔dɪs'kaʊntɚ〕n. 廉價商店

fail to V. 未能…   adapt〔ə'dæpt〕*v.* 適應；順應 < *to* >
reality〔rɪ'ælətɪ〕*n.* 事實；現實
bust〔bʌst〕*adj.* 破產的 (= *bankrupt*)
economy〔ɪ'kɑnəmɪ〕*n.* 經濟

31. (**A**) What do consumers now prefer to do?
消費者現在偏好做什麼？

     A. Download their music. 下載他們的音樂。

     B. Modify their business models. 改變他們的商業模式。

     C. Respond to demand. 回應需求。

     D. Start from scratch. 重新開始。

     * respond〔rɪ'spɑnd〕*v.* 回應 < *to* >

32. (**C**) What is happening to record stores? 唱片行發生什麼事？

     A. They are solving a mystery. 他在正在解開謎團。

     B. They are downloading music. 他們正在下載音樂。

     C. They are closing. 他們正一一關閉。

     D. They are thriving. 他們的業績蒸蒸日上。

     * solve〔sɑlv〕*v.* 解決   close〔kloz〕*v.* 停止營業
thrive〔θraɪv〕*v.* 繁榮；興盛；發達

Questions 33 and 34 are based on the following report.

Every year around 60 shark attacks are reported worldwide, although death is quite unusual. Despite the relative rarity of shark attacks, the fear of sharks is a common phenomenon, having been fueled by horror fiction and films, such as the Jaws series. Almost all shark experts feel that the danger presented by sharks has been exaggerated. Many have attempted to dispel the myth of sharks being man-eating monsters. Marin County in California, on the coast of the Pacific Ocean, holds the record for the most shark attacks in the world.

　　每年全世界大約有 60 起鯊魚攻擊事件被報導，雖然死亡是相當不尋常的。儘管鯊魚攻擊相當罕見，對鯊魚的恐懼卻是個普遍的現象，這是一直受到恐怖小說和電影的煽動，像是大白鯊系列的電影。幾乎所有鯊魚的專家都認為鯊魚所引起的危險一直被誇大。很多專家試圖去破除鯊魚為吃人怪獸的迷思。美國加州馬林郡，位於太平洋岸，保持最多鯊魚攻擊事件的世界紀錄。

**

around〔ə'raund〕prep. 大約　　shark〔ʃɑrk〕n. 鯊魚
attack〔ə'tæk〕n. 攻擊　　report〔rɪ'port〕v. 報導
worldwide〔'wɝld'waɪd〕adv. 在全世界
quite〔kwaɪt〕adv. 相當；頗
unusual〔ʌn'juʒʊəl〕adj. 不尋常的
despite〔dɪ'spaɪt〕prep. 儘管（= in spite of）
relative〔'rɛlətɪv〕adj. 比較上的；相對的
rarity〔'rɛrətɪ〕n. 稀少；罕見　　fear〔fɪr〕n. 恐懼
common〔'kɑmən〕adj. 普通的；一般的
phenomenon〔fə'nɑmə,nɑn〕n. 現象
fuel〔fjuəl〕v. 煽動；刺激　　horror〔'hɔrɚ〕n. 恐怖
horror fiction 恐怖小說　　film〔fɪlm〕n. 電影
jaw〔dʒɔ〕n. 顎　　**Jaws** n. 【電影】大白鯊
series〔'sɪrɪz〕n. 系列　　expert〔'ɛkspɝt〕n. 專家
present〔prɪ'zɛnt〕v. 呈現
exaggerate〔ɪg'zædʒə,ret〕v. 誇大　　attempt〔ə'tɛmpt〕v. 嘗試
dispel〔dɪ'spɛl〕v. 消除　　myth〔mɪθ〕n. 迷思
man-eating adj. 食人的　　monster〔'mɑnstɚ〕n. 怪物
county〔'kaʊntɪ〕n. 縣；郡

Marin County 馬林郡【美國加利福尼亞州的一個郡】
coast〔kost〕*n.* 海岸；沿岸　　　*the Pacific Ocean* 太平洋
hold the record 保持紀錄

33. (**B**) Why do people fear sharks? 人們為何會害怕鯊魚？
　　A. Sharks can attack in water or on land.
　　　鯊魚會在水裡或陸地上攻擊。
　　B. People are misinformed about the danger presented
　　　by sharks.
　　　關於鯊魚所引起的危險，人們所得到的消息並不正確。
　　C. Jaws 3 was a really good movie.
　　　大白鯊第三集真是一部很棒的電影。
　　D. Death is quite unusual. 死亡是相當不尋常的。
　　* misinform〔͵mɪsɪnˋfɔrm〕*v.* 向（人）誤報；給（人）錯誤消息

34. (**D**) Approximately how many shark attacks are reported
　　every year? 每年大約有幾起鯊魚攻擊事件被報導？
　　A. 30.　　　　　　　　　B. 40.
　　C. 50.　　　　　　　　　D. 60.

Questions 35 and 36 are based on the following report.

　　There is strong evidence that laughter can actually
improve health and help fight disease. When we laugh,
changes occur in many parts of the body, even the arm,
leg and trunk muscles. Fifteen facial muscles contract
and the respiratory system is upset, making you gasp. In
extreme circumstances, the tear ducts are activated and
the face becomes moist and often red. Laughter relaxes

the whole body. A good, hearty laugh relieves physical tension and stress, leaving your muscles relaxed for up to 45 minutes after.

　　有強力的證據顯示，笑實際上可以增進健康，並幫助對抗疾病。當我們笑的時候，身體很多的部位會發生改變，甚至是手臂、腿、和軀幹的肌肉。十五條臉部的肌肉會收縮，而且呼吸系統會受到干擾，讓你喘不過氣。在極端的情況中，會觸動淚腺，而臉會變濕，而且常常會變成紅色。笑會放鬆整個身體。開懷大笑會釋放身體的緊張和壓力之後，使你的肌肉放鬆長達 45 分鐘。

‒‒‒‒‒‒‒‒‒‒‒‒‒‒‒‒‒‒‒

evidence〔'ɛvədəns〕n. 證據　　　laughter〔'læftɚ〕n. 笑

actually〔'æktʃuəlɪ〕adv. 實際上　　improve〔ɪm'pruv〕v. 增進

health〔hɛlθ〕n. 健康　　　fight〔faɪt〕v. 對抗

disease〔dɪ'ziz〕n. 疾病　　　occur〔ə'kɝ〕v. 發生

trunk〔trʌŋk〕n. 軀幹　　　muscle〔'mʌsḷ〕n. 肌肉

facial〔'feʃəl〕adj. 臉部的　　　contract〔kən'trækt〕v. 收縮

respiratory〔rɪ'spaɪrəˌtorɪ〕adj 呼吸的

system〔'sɪstəm〕n. 系統　　　upset〔ʌp'sɛt〕v. 干擾

gasp〔gæsp〕v. 喘氣　　　extreme〔ɪk'strim〕adj. 極端的

circumstances〔'sɝkəmˌstænsɪz〕n. pl. 情況　　　tear〔tɪr〕n. 眼淚

duct〔dʌkt〕n. 導管　　　***tear duct*** 淚腺

activate〔'æktəˌvet〕v. 啟動；觸發　　　moist〔mɔɪst〕v. 濕的

relax〔rɪ'læks〕v. 使放鬆　　　good〔gud〕adj. 充分的

a good laugh 痛快的笑　　　hearty〔'hɑrtɪ〕adj. 衷心的

relieve〔rɪ'liv〕v. 減輕；緩和　　　physical〔'fɪzɪkḷ〕adj. 身體的

tension〔'tɛnʃən〕n. 緊張　　　stress〔strɛs〕n. 壓力

leave〔liv〕v. 使處於（某種狀態）　　　***up to*** 高達

35. (**A**) What happens when we laugh?
　　 我們笑的時候會發生什麼事？

A. Fifteen facial muscles contract.
   十五條臉部肌肉會收縮。
B. The respiratory system is calm. 呼吸系統很平穩。
C. Tear ducts are deactivated. 淚腺會關閉。
D. The face becomes dry and blue. 臉變得又乾又藍。

* calm〔kɑm〕adj. 平靜的   deactivate〔dɪˈæktəˌvet〕v. 關閉

36. (**A**) What happens after we laugh? 我們笑之後會發生什麼事？
   A. Muscles are relaxed for up to 45 minutes.
      肌肉會放鬆長達 45 分鐘。
   B. We are gasping for air. 我們會氣喘吁吁。
   C. The whole body stiffens. 整個身體會很僵硬。
   D. Physical tension is increased. 身體的緊張程度會增加。

* ***gasp for air*** 大口吸氣；氣喘吁吁
   stiffen〔ˈstɪfən〕v. 變僵硬   increase〔ɪnˈkris〕v. 增加

Questions 37 and 38 are based on the following report.

When you can't forgive yourself, it's easy to lose faith in a higher power. Religion can sometimes hinder forgiveness and letting go. There are some religions that have more guilt than others. In Catholicism, for example, there's more responsibility, and there's a lot more of that inherent guilt going around—but you will not see that in Buddhism. One way of coping is to get angry at God. Nevertheless, forgiveness—of others, and ultimately, of yourself—is a big part of many faiths.

當你無法原諒你自己的時候，很容易就喪失對更高力量的信仰。宗教有時候會阻礙原諒和放手。有一些宗教比其他的有更多

罪惡感。舉例來說,在天主教的信仰中有更多的責任,而且也有
更多固有的罪惡感流傳其中——而你在佛教裡面不會看到那樣的
情況。其中一個處理的方是,就是對上帝生氣。然而,原諒——
對他人,而最後是對你自己——是很多信仰的一個重要的部分。

**

forgive〔fə'gɪv〕v. 原諒　　lose〔luz〕v. 失去;喪失
faith〔feθ〕n. 信念;信仰　　*higher power* 更高力量;神
religion〔rɪ'lɪdʒən〕n. 宗教　　hinder〔'hɪndə〕v. 阻礙
forgiveness〔fə'gɪvnɪs〕n. 原諒　　*let go* 放手;釋放
guilt〔gɪlt〕n. 罪惡感;內疚
Catholicism〔kə'θalə,sɪzəm〕n. 天主教
responsibility〔rɪ,spansə'bɪlətɪ〕n. 責任
inherent〔ɪn'hɪrənt〕adj. 固有的　　*go around* 流傳;傳播
Buddhism〔'budɪzəm〕n. 佛教　　cope〔kop〕v. 應付;處理
get angry 生氣　　nevertheless〔,nɛvəðə'lɛs〕adv. 然而
ultimately〔'ʌltəmɪtlɪ〕adv. 最後　　big〔bɪg〕adj. 重要的

37. (**B**) What is Catholicism? 什麼是天主教?
　　A. A higher power. 一個更高的力量。
　　B. A religious faith. 一個宗教信仰。
　　C. A form of Buddhism. 一種佛教的形式。
　　D. A big responsibility. 一個重大的責任。
　　* form〔fɔrm〕n. 形式

38. (**B**) When is it easy to lose faith in a higher power?
　　什麼時候容易喪失對更高力量的信仰?
　　A. When God is angry. 當上帝生氣的時候。
　　B. When you can't forgive yourself.
　　　　當你無法原諒自己的時候。
　　C. When there is guilt going around.
　　　　當罪惡感四處流傳時。

D. When you see it in Buddhism.
當你在佛教裡看到它的時候。

Questions 39 and 40 are based on the following report.

This week is National Men's Health Week, which was created by Congress in 1994 to raise the awareness of the health threats uniquely affecting men. Today I'm going to talk about heart disease. This is the deadliest disease known to man. More than 1 in 3 adult men have some sort of heart disease and more than 390,000 men died of the killer in 2010, according to the American Heart Association. But you're a fit, healthy guy, right? Why would you die of heart disease? Believe it or not, not every victim of the disease is overweight or inactive.

本週是全國男士健康週，這是在 1994 年由國會所創立的，目的是要提升對只會影響男性的健康威脅的意識。今天，我要講的是心臟病。這是人類所知最致命的疾病。三位成人男性中，就有超過一位罹患某種心臟疾病，而且根據美國心臟協會的說法，在 2010 年，有超過三十九萬名的男性死於這致命的疾病。但是你是一位健康的人，是吧？你怎麼會死於心臟病呢？信不信由你，不是每一個心臟病的患者都是過重或是懶散的。

** ————————————————

national〔'næʃənḷ〕*adj.* 國家的；全國的
create〔krɪ'et〕*v.* 創造　　Congress〔'kɑŋgrəs〕*n.* 國會
raise〔rez〕*v.* 提高　　awareness〔ə'wɛrnɪs〕*n.* 意識
threat〔θrɛt〕*n.* 威脅　　uniquely〔ju'niklɪ〕*adv.* 唯獨地
affect〔ə'fɛkt〕*v.* 影響　　***heart disease*** 心臟病

deadly〔'dɛdlɪ〕*adj.* 致命的　　***known to sb.*** 被某人知道
man〔mæn〕*n.* 人類　　adult〔ə'dʌlt〕*adj.* 成年的
some〔sʌm〕*adj.* 某個　　sort〔sɔrt〕*n.* 種類 (= *kind*)
die of 死於　　killer〔'kɪlɚ〕*n.* 殺手；致命的東西
American Heart Association 美國心臟協會
fit〔fɪt〕*adj.* 健康的　　guy〔gaɪ〕*n.* 人；傢伙
believe it or not 信不信由你
victim〔'vɪktɪm〕*n.* 受害者；患者
overweight〔,ovɚ'wet〕*adj.* 過重的
inactive〔ɪn'æktɪv〕*adj.* 不活動的；懶散的

39. (**A**) What is the speaker most likely going to do next?
    說話者接下來最可能做什麼？

    A. Talk about the risk factors of heart disease.
       談論關於心臟病的危險因子。

    B. Check his pulse. 檢查他的脈搏。

    C. Count to ten before getting angry. 在生氣前數到十。

    D. Make fun of an inactive, overweight guy.
       嘲笑一位懶散過重的人。

    * likely〔'laɪklɪ〕*adv.* 可能地　　risk〔rɪsk〕*n.* 危險；風險
      factor〔'fæktɚ〕*n.* 因素　　***risk factor*** 危險因子
      pulse〔pʌls〕*n.* 脈搏　　count〔kaʊnt〕*v.* 數
      make fun of 嘲笑

40. (**B**) How many men have some form of heart disease?
    有多少男士罹患某種心臟病？

    A. All of them. 全部的男士。

    B. More than 1 in 3. 每三個當中超過一個。

    C. Around 400,000. 大約四十萬個。

    D. 1994 to 2010. 1994 到 2010 年。

    * form〔fɔrm〕*n.* 類型；種類

高中英聽測驗模擬試題 ⑨ 詳解

一、看圖辨義：第一部分

For question number 1, please look at picture 1.

1. (**C**) A boy does not like a girl. He is breaking her heart.

　　　一個男孩不喜歡一個女孩。他正在傷她的心。

　　　break one's heart 傷某人的心

For question number 2, please look at picture 2.

2. (**A**) Two boys like the same girl. The girl is holding some flowers. 兩個男孩喜歡同一個女孩。這女孩正拿著一些花。

　　　* hold〔hold〕*v.* 拿著

For question number 3, please look at picture 3.

3. (**A**) A couple is enjoying a meal.　They are in an uncrowded
restaurant.

一對男女正在享用餐點。他們在一間不擁擠的餐廳。

　　* couple〔ˋkʌpḷ〕 *n.* 一對男女；夫妻
　　　uncrowded〔ʌnˋkraʊdɪd〕 *adj.* 不擁擠的

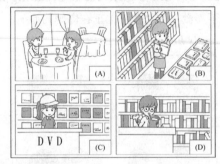

For question number 4, please look at picture 4.

4. (**B**) A woman is standing on a balcony.　A man is kneeling
in front of her.

一位女士正站在陽台上。一位男士在她前面下跪。

　　* balcony〔ˋbælkənɪ〕 *n.* 陽台　　kneel〔nil〕 *v.* 下跪
　　in front of 在⋯前面

一、看圖辨義：第二部分

For question number 5, please look at picture 5.

5. (**B**、**C**) Which TWO of the following are true about the
man? 關於這位男士，下列哪兩項敘述為眞？

A. He is using his smart phone.
他正在用他的智慧型手機。

B. He is reading a newspaper.
他正在讀一份報紙。

C. He is standing between two women.
他正站在兩個女人中間。

D. He is dating the woman on the left.
他正在跟左邊的女人約會。

* smart phone〔'smɑrt͵fon〕*n.* 智慧型手機
date〔det〕*v.* 與…約會   left〔lɛft〕*n.* 左邊

For question number 6, please look at picture 6.

6. (**A**、**B**) Which TWO of the following are true about the girl
in the bathtub?
關於在浴缸裡的女孩，下列哪兩項敘述為眞？

A. She is sleeping. 她正在睡覺。

B. She is listening to music. 她正在聽音樂。

C. She is having lunch.
她正在吃午餐。

D. She is dead. 她死掉了。

* bathtub〔'bæθ͵tʌb〕*n.* 浴缸
have〔hæv〕*v.* 吃

For question number 7, please look at picture 7.

7. (**A**、**C**) Which TWO of the following are true about the girl?
關於這位女孩，下列哪兩項敘述為眞？

A. She is riding a scooter.
她正在騎機車。
B. She is walking her dog.
她正在遛狗。
C. She is wearing a helmet. 她正戴著安全帽。
D. She is thinking of a boy. 她正想起一個男孩。

* scooter〔'skutɚ〕*n.* 機車　***walk a dog*** 遛狗
helmet〔'hɛlmɪt〕*n.* 安全帽　***think of*** 想起；想到

For question number 8, please look at picture 8.

8. (**C**、**D**) Which TWO of the following are true about the
picture? 關於這張圖片，下列哪兩項敘述為眞？

A. The girls are afraid of dogs.
這些女孩怕狗。
B. The girl on the left is allergic
to cats. 左邊的女孩對貓過敏。
C. Both girls are crouching. 兩個女孩正蹲著。
D. Both girls have shopping bags.
兩個女孩都有購物袋。

* allergic〔ə'lɝdʒɪk〕*adj.* 過敏的 *< to >*
crouch〔'krautʃ〕*v.* 蹲伏　***shopping bag*** 購物袋

For question number 9, please look at picture 9.

9. (**A**、**B**) Which TWO of the following are true about the
people in the picture?
關於圖片中的人，下列哪兩項敘述為眞？

A. They are making a toast.
他們在敬酒。

B. They are seated at a table.
他們坐在餐桌旁。

C. They are driving in a car. 他們正在開車。

D. They are talking to the waiter.
他們正在跟服務生講話。

* toast〔tost〕*n.* 吐司；乾杯
make a toast 敬酒【古時常會把烤吐司泡在酒裡一起喝，喝酒時説 a toast 就是乾杯的意思】
be seated 坐（= *sit*）　　waiter〔'wetɚ〕*n.* 服務生

For question number 10, please look at picture 10.

10. (**C、D**) Which TWO of the following are true about the picture? 關於這張圖片，下列哪兩項敘述為眞？

A. The man is on the bus.
這位男士在公車上。

B. It's noon. 現在是中午。

C. It's 3:00 a.m. 現在是上午三點。

D. The man is seated at a desk. 這男士坐在辦公桌前。

* *a.m.* 上午（= *ante meridiem*）

二、對答

11. (**C**) What did you get for your birthday?
你生日得到了什麼？

A. My sister's birthday is tomorrow.
我妹妹的生日是明天。

B. My brother couldn't be here. 我弟弟當時不能來這裡。

C. My father bought me a bicycle.

我爸爸買給我一輛腳踏車。

D. My mother is leaving for work. 我媽媽正要去工作。

* *leave for* 動身前往

12. (**B**) What size T-shirt do you wear? 你穿什麼尺寸的 T 恤？

A. That's a cool T-shirt. 那是一件很酷的 T 恤。

B. I wear a medium. 我穿中號的 T 恤。

C. It's too long. 它太長了。

D. I don't like the color. 我不喜歡這個顏色。

* size〔saɪz〕*n.* 尺寸　　cool〔kul〕*adj.* 酷的
medium〔'midɪəm〕*n.* 中號

13. (**B**) Is Fred coming to your party? 弗瑞德會來你的派對嗎？

A. You've met Fred. 你已經見過弗瑞德了。

B. No, he can't make it. 不，他沒辦法來。

C. I'm having a party. 我在辦派對。

D. You're not invited. 你沒有被邀請。

* *make it* 抵達；能來；能出席　　*have a party* 舉行派對

14. (**A**) Does this bus go to the airport? 這公車有去機場嗎？

A. No, this one goes to the zoo.

沒有，這輛是去動物園。

B. Yes, this is the airport. 有，這就是機場。

C. Pay your fare when you get off the bus.

當你下公車時要付車資。

D. Take a bus to the airport. 搭公車去機場。

* airport〔'ɛr,port〕*n.* 機場　　fare〔fɛr〕*n.* 車資
get off 下（車）

15. (**A**) Do you know where Jane is? 你知道珍在哪裡嗎？

  A. I think she's at work. 我想她在工作。

  B. I've known Jane since grade school.
   我從小學就認識珍了。

  C. Jane is a nice person. 珍是個很好的人。

  D. Did you find Jane? 你找到珍了嗎？

  * ***at work*** 在工作　　grade〔gred〕*n.* 小學；年級
  grade school 小學（ = *elementary school* ）

16. (**D**) Have you read the Harry Potter books?
  你讀了哈利波特了嗎？

  A. Sure, you can use it. 當然，你可以用它。

  B. I've got so many books. 我有很多書。

  C. I'm a slow reader. 我書讀得很慢。

  D. No, I haven't. 不，還沒。

  * ***Harry Potter*** 哈利波特【英國作家 J.·K.·羅琳的奇幻文學系列小說，
  共 7 集】　　***have got*** 有（ = *have* ）

17. (**C**) How's your new job? 你的新工作如何？

  A. I got a job. 我找到一份工作了。

  B. Everyone has to work. 每個人都必須工作。

  C. I like it a lot. 我非常喜歡這新工作。

  D. I'm on my way to work. 我在去上班的途中。

  * ***on one's way to*** 在去⋯的途中

18. (**D**) Glenda is a sweet girl, isn't she?
  格倫達是個貼心的女孩，不是嗎？

  A. She is never late. 她從不遲到。

  B. Have a taste. 要有品味。

  C. Oh, you brought cookies. 噢，你帶餅乾來。

D. Yes, I have to agree. 是的，我不得不同意。

* sweet〔swit〕*adj.* 貼心的；討人喜歡的
taste〔test〕*n.* 品味　　cookie〔'kʊkɪ〕*n.* 餅乾

19.（ **D** ）Can you play a musical instrument? 你會演奏樂器嗎？

A. I've never heard that song before.
　　我之前從來沒有聽過那首歌。

B. I like rock music. 我喜歡搖滾樂。

C. No, I wasn't there. 不，我不在那裡。

D. Yes, I can play the piano. 是，我會彈鋼琴。

* play〔ple〕*v.* 演奏　　musical〔'mjuzɪkḷ〕*adj.* 音樂的
instrument〔'ɪnstrəmənt〕*n.* 器具
musical instrument 樂器　　***rock music*** 搖滾樂

20.（ **A** ）How's the water, kids? 那水怎麼樣啊，孩子們？

A. It's nice and warm, Dad. Come on in!
　　水很好而且很溫暖，爸。快下來水裡吧!

B. I'm not thirsty. 我不渴。

C. We're swimming. 我們正在游泳。

D. That's your problem. 那是你的問題。

* kid〔kɪd〕*n.* 小孩　　***come on in*** 進來呀

三、簡短對話

For question 21, you will listen to a short conversation.

M：How was traffic on your commute this morning?
　　你今天通勤時交通狀況如何？

W：Nothing out of the ordinary. Why?
　　沒有什麼不正常的。為什麼這樣問？

M：Highway 69 was backed up all the way to South Fork.

69 號公路當時一路回堵到南福克。

W：Oh, I live out in Brownsburg, so I'm coming from the other direction.

噢，我住在伯朗斯堡那裡，所以我是從另一個方向來的。

* traffic〔'træfɪk〕n. 交通　　commute〔kə'mjut〕n. 通勤路程
out of the ordinary 不正常的
highway〔'haɪ,we〕n. 公路　　**be backed up** 堵塞
all the way 整個途中；一路上　　out〔aʊt〕adv. 離開城市
direction〔də'rɛkʃən〕n. 方向

21. (**A**) Q：Which of the following statements is true?
下列敘述何者為真？

A. Both the man and the woman drive to work.
這位先生和這位女士兩人都開車上班。

B. The man and the woman live in the same town.
這位男士和這位女士住在同一個城鎮。

C. Only the woman had trouble getting to work this morning. 只有這女士今天早上上班有麻煩。

D. South Fork and Brownsburg are neighboring towns.
南福克與伯朗斯堡是鄰近的城鎮。

* **have trouble + V-ing** 做…有困難；很難～
get to V. 得以～
neighboring〔'nebərɪŋ〕adj. 鄰近的

For question 22, you will listen to a short conversation.

M：How much did you pay for your bicycle?

這台腳踏車你付了多少錢？

W : I paid NT$15,000, but the price has come down since I bought it. 我付了台幣一萬五千元，但自從我買了它之後，價格就開始下降。

M : When did you buy it? 你什麼時候買的？

W : A couple of months ago. It now goes for NT$10,000. If I had known it would be so much cheaper, I would have waited. 幾個月前。現在它要台幣一萬元。如果我早知道它會變得這麼便宜，我就會再等一等。

* **come down** （價格）下降　　couple〔ˋkʌpl〕*n.* 兩個；少量
a couple of 幾個　　**go for** 售價為～

22. (**A**) Q : What does the woman say? 這女士說了什麼？

　　A. She paid too much for her bicycle.
　　　她付了太多錢買腳踏車。

　　B. She could have paid more for her bicycle.
　　　她原本可以為她的腳踏車付更多錢。

　　C. She only buys things when they are on sale.
　　　她只買特價的東西。

　　D. She bought the bicycle too late. 她太晚買腳踏車了。

　　* **on sale** 特價的；打折的

For question 23, you will listen to a short conversation.

W : Why are you breathing so heavily? 你為什麼氣喘吁吁？

M : I had to take the stairs. The elevator is out of order.
　　我得爬樓梯。電梯故障了。

* breathe〔brið〕*v.* 呼吸　　　**breathe heavily** 喘粗氣；氣喘吁吁

stair〔stɛr〕*n.* 樓梯　　***take the stairs*** 爬樓梯
elevator〔'ɛlə,vetɚ〕*n.* 電梯　　***out of order*** 故障的

23. (**C**)　Q：Why did the man have to take the stairs?

為什麼這位男士得爬樓梯？

A. His breathing was heavy. 他氣喘吁吁。
B. The stairs were broken. 樓梯壞了。
C. The elevator isn't working. 電梯沒有在運作。
D. He needed the exercise. 他需要運動。

* broken〔'brokən〕*adj.* 損壞了的　　work〔wɜk〕*v.* 運作
exercise〔'ɛksɚ,saɪz〕*n.* 運動

For question 24, you will listen to a short conversation.

W：Good luck on the CPA exam, Bruce.

祝你會計師考試順利，布魯斯。

M：I'm going to need a lot more than luck, Tina. I need a miracle. 我需要的不只是好運而已，蒂娜，我需要的是奇蹟。

* ***CPA exam*** 會計師考試 (= *certified public accountant exam*)
luck〔lʌk〕*n.* 運氣　　miracle〔'mɪrəkl̩〕*n.* 奇蹟

24. (**C**)　Q：What does the man mean? 這位男士是什麼意思？

A. He is going to ace the exam. 他即將在考試得高分。
B. He enjoys taking exams. 他很喜歡考試。
C. He is not prepared for the exam. 他考試還沒準備好。
D. He doesn't believe in miracles. 他不相信奇蹟。

* ace〔es〕*v.* 在…得高分　　enjoy〔ɪn'dʒɔɪ〕*v.* 喜歡；享受
take a exam 參加考試
prepared〔prɪ'pɛrd〕*adj.* 準備好的 <*for*>
believe〔bə'liv〕*v.* 相信　　***believe in*** 相信有

For questions 25 and 26, you will listen to a short conversation.

W : Honey, I think it's time for a new refrigerator. This one is on its last legs. 親愛的，我想是時候該買台新的冰箱了。這台已經快要不能用了。

M : Yes, and while we're at it, we might as well get a new dishwasher. The old Wash-o-matic has seen better days. 是啊，而且趁這時候，我們不妨也買一台新的洗碗機。這台老舊的「自動洗」已經太舊了。

W : Harper's Appliances is having a sale this month. 哈柏電器行這個月正在打折。

M : Are they? 是嗎？

W : Yes, they're offering 25% off all household appliances plus free delivery and installation. 是啊，他們所有的電器都打七五折，加上免費運送及安裝。

M : Sounds like a winner to me. Let's go down to Harper's this weekend. 聽來很划算。我們這個週末就去哈柏電器行看看吧。

* honey〔ˋhʌnɪ〕n. 親愛的　　refrigerator〔rɪˋfrɪdʒəˏretɚ〕n. 冰箱
on one's **last legs** 快不能用的；垂死的；疲憊的（= *very tired*）
while one is at it 趁著做某事的時候（= *while one is doing it*）；
　順便　　**might as well** 不妨；最好（= *had better*）
get〔gɛt〕v. 買　　**have seen better days** 今非昔比；太舊了
appliance〔əˋplaɪəns〕n. 家電　　sale〔sel〕n. 廉價出售
offer〔ˋɔfɚ〕v. 提供　　*25% off* 七五折
household〔ˋhausˏhold〕adj. 家庭的
household appliance 家電用品　　plus〔plʌs〕prep. 加上

free〔fri〕*adj.* 免費的　　delivery〔dɪ'lɪvərɪ〕*n.* 運送
installation〔ˌɪnstə'leʃən〕*n.* 安裝
winner〔'wɪnɚ〕*n.* 成功者；可能成功的人或事物
go down to 去…

25. (**B**) Q : What do they need? 他們需要什麼？

　　A. New legs. 新的腿。

　　B. New appliances. 新的家電。

　　C. New furniture. 新的家具。

　　D. New sounds. 新的聲音。

　　* furniture〔'fɝnɪtʃɚ〕*n.* 家具

26. (**D**) Q : What is true about Harper's?

　　　　關於哈柏電器行，何者為眞？

　　A. They charge extra for delivery. 他們會額外收運費。

　　B. They don't sell Wash-o-matic dishwashers.

　　　　他們沒賣「自動洗」的洗碗機。

　　C. They are on their last legs. 他們很疲憊。

　　D. They are having a sale this month.

　　　　他們這個月在打折。

　　* charge〔tʃɑrdʒ〕*v.* 收費　　extra〔'ɛkstrə〕*adv.* 額外地；另外

For questions 27 and 28, you will listen to a short conversation.

W : How was the golf outing with Mr. Jenkins?

　　跟詹金斯先生出去打高爾夫球打得怎麼樣？

M : It was OK. I'm not much of a golfer.

　　打得還可以。我稱不上是個好的高爾夫球手。

W : Really? I thought you were a regular Tiger Woods.

　　眞的嗎？我以爲你經常打出老虎伍茲的水準。

M：Hardly! I've played the game maybe half a dozen times in my life. 才不是呢！我這輩子打過的高爾夫可能才六次。

W：Oh, I must have you confused with someone else. 噢，我一定是把你跟其他人搞混了。

M：Anyway, Jenkins seemed to enjoy himself, considering he was the only member of the group who actually knows what he's doing. 不管怎樣，詹金斯似乎玩得很愉快，考慮到他是這群人當中實際上唯一有經驗的。

W：That's all that matters, I guess. 我想那才是最重要的。

M：Yes, if Jenkins is happy, then we're all happy. 是啊，如果能讓詹金斯開心，那麼我們全都很開心。

* golf〔gɔlf〕n. 高爾夫球　　outing〔'aʊtɪŋ〕n. 短途旅遊；遠足
  not much of 稱不上是　　golfer〔'gɔlfə〕n. 打高爾夫的人
  regular〔'rɛgjələ〕adj. 規律的；經常的
  Tiger Woods 老虎伍茲【美國高爾夫球手】
  hardly〔'hɑrdlɪ〕adv. 幾乎不；絕不
  dozen〔'dʌzn̩〕n. 一打；十二個　　*must have p.p.* 當時一定～
  confuse〔kən'fjuz〕v. 使混淆　　*enjoy oneself* 玩得愉快
  considering〔kən'sɪdərɪŋ〕conj. 有鑑於；考慮到
  member〔'mɛmbə〕n. 成員　　actually〔'æktʃʊəlɪ〕adv. 實際上
  know what sb. is doing 有經驗的；經驗老到的
  matter〔'mætə〕v. 重要　　guess〔gɛs〕v. 猜測；猜想

27. (**C**) Q：What is true about the man?
　　關於這位男士，何者正確？

　　A. He is Tiger Woods. 他是老虎伍茲。

　　B. He is easily confused. 他很容易搞糊塗。

C. He is not very good at golf.　他不是很擅長打高爾夫。

D. He is a professional golfer.　他是職業的高爾夫球選手。

* confused〔kən'fjuzd〕*adj.* 困惑的；糊塗的
  be good at 擅長　　professional〔prə'fɛʃənl〕*adj.* 職業的

28. (**A**)　Q：What is true about the woman?

關於這位女士，何者正確？

A. She did not attend the golf outing.

她沒有出去打高爾夫球。

B. She beat Mr. Jenkins in a game of golf.

她在一場高爾夫球賽中打敗了詹金斯先生。

C. She wanted to go golfing but was denied.

她想去打高爾夫球，但被拒絕了。

D. She has been golfing over a dozen times.

她打高爾夫已經超過十二次了。

* attend〔ə'tɛnd〕*v.* 參加　　beat〔bit〕*v.* 打敗
  golf〔gɑlf〕*v.* 打高爾夫球　　deny〔dɪ'naɪ〕*v.* 拒絕；否認
  time〔taɪm〕*n.* 次數

For questions 29 and 30, you will listen to a short conversation.

M：Could I borrow your cell phone?　我可以借你的手機嗎？

W：OK, but what's wrong with yours?

好，但你的手機怎麼了？

M：The battery is dead.　I forgot to charge it last night.

電池沒電了。我昨晚忘了充電。

W：And you don't have a power supply at your desk.

而且你桌上沒有電源供應器。

M：Or an extra battery.　或是額外的電池。

W：Here. Bring it back when you're finished.

　　拿去吧。你用完時再拿來還我。

*　borrow〔'bɑro〕v. 借（入）　　**cell phone** 手機
What's wrong with~? ～怎麼了？　　battery〔'bætərɪ〕n. 電池
dead〔dɛd〕adj.（電器）沒電的　　charge〔tʃɑrdʒ〕v. 充電
supply〔sə'plaɪ〕n. 供應　　**power supply** 電源供應器
extra〔'ɛkstrə〕adj. 額外的
finished〔'fɪnɪʃt〕adj. 完成的；結束的

29.（ **A** ）Q：Where are these people? 這些人在哪裡？

　　A. They are in an office. 他們在一間辦公室裡。

　　B. They are on a tour bus. 他們在一輛遊覽車上。

　　C. They are at the bank. 他們在銀行。

　　D. They are in jail. 他們在監獄裡。

*　tour〔tʊr〕n. 觀光；遊覽　　**tour bus** 遊覽車
　jail〔dʒel〕n. 監獄

30.（ **C** ）Q：What did the man forget to do? 這位男士忘了做什麼？

　　A. Pay for his desk. 付書桌的錢。

　　B. Bring his cell phone to work. 帶手機去上班。

　　C. Recharge the battery of his cell phone.

　　　　把手機電池重新充電。

　　D. Plug in the power supply. 插電源供應器的插頭。

*　recharge〔ri'tʃɑrdʒ〕v. 給～充電　　**plug in** 使～接上插頭

四、短文聽解

Questions 31 and 32 are based on the following report.

　　How do you keep your clothes bright, fresh, and in
just-purchased condition? The key to clean clothing is

what you do before loading the washer. A little bit of TLC before washing can go a long way when you're doing the laundry. Here are some helpful tips. Soaking clothes overnight in a tub of water really helps loosen dirt and grime and can be especially effective when your clothes have that dingy-all-over look. For stubborn food stains, such as coffee, soy sauce, or mustard, blot the troubled area with foam shaving cream and allow it to sit for half an hour. Then simply wash it in warm water.

　　要如何使你的衣服保持色彩鮮豔及如剛買的狀態？乾淨的衣服的關鍵，就在於你放衣服進洗衣機之前所做的事。當你在洗衣時，洗衣前的一點點悉心呵護是大有幫助的。以下就是一些有用的訣竅。用一缸水把衣服浸泡一整晚，真的有助於鬆脫污泥和污垢，而且當你的衣服是看起來整個髒兮兮的時候，特別有效。對於頑強的食物污漬，像是咖啡、醬油或芥末，塗泡沫刮鬍膏在惱人的地方，然後讓它靜置半小時。之後只要在溫水裡清洗即可。

** ————————————

clothes〔kloz〕*n. pl.* 衣服　　bright〔braɪt〕*adj.* 明亮的；明豔的
fresh〔frɛʃ〕*adj.* 新鮮的；鮮明的　　purchase〔'pɝtʃəs〕*v.* 購買
just-purchased　*adj.* 剛買的；新買的
condition〔kən'dɪʃən〕*n.* 情況　　key〔ki〕*n.* 關鍵
clothing〔'kloðɪŋ〕*n.* 衣服　　load〔lod〕*v.* 裝載
washer〔'wɑʃɚ〕*n.* 洗衣機
TLC 悉心呵護（= *tender loving care*）
go a long way 大有幫助　　laundry〔'lɔndrɪ〕*n.* 待洗的衣物
do the laundry 洗衣服　　tip〔tɪp〕*n.* 訣竅
soak〔sok〕*v.* 浸泡　　overnight〔'ovɚ'naɪt〕*adv.* 一整夜
tub〔tʌb〕*n.* 浴缸　　loosen〔'lusn̩〕*v.* 使鬆脫

dirt〔 dɝt 〕n. 污泥　　grime〔 graɪm 〕n. 污垢
effective〔 ɪ'fɛktɪv 〕adj. 有效的　　dingy〔 'dɪndʒɪ 〕adj. 骯髒的
dingy-all-over adj. 到處髒兮兮的
stubborn〔 'stʌbən 〕adj. 頑強的　　stain〔 sten 〕n. 污漬
soy〔 sɔɪ 〕n. 黃豆；醬油　　sauce〔 sɔs 〕n. 醬
soy sauce 醬油　　mustard〔 'mʌstəd 〕n. 芥末
blot〔 blɑt 〕v. 塗抹　　troubled〔 'trʌbḷd 〕adj. 惱人的
area〔 'ɛrɪə 〕n. 區域；地方　　foam〔 fom 〕n. 泡沫
shave〔 ʃev 〕v. 刮（鬍子）　　cream〔 krim 〕n. 乳霜；乳膏
shaving cream 刮鬍膏　　allow〔 ə'lau 〕v. 容許；讓
sit〔 sɪt 〕v. 靜置　　simply〔 'sɪmplɪ 〕adv. 簡單地；只

31. (**B**) What is the key to clean clothing?
　　　乾淨的衣服的關鍵是什麼？
　　A. Cool temperatures. 較涼的溫度。
　　B. What you do before loading the washer.
　　　在你把衣服放進洗衣機之前所做的事。
　　C. Adding soy sauce to the mix. 加醬油到混合物裡。
　　D. A little bit of SOS. 一點點求救信號。

　　* cool〔 kul 〕adj. 涼爽的　　temperature〔 'tɛmpərətʃə 〕n. 溫度
　　mix〔 mɪks 〕n. 混合物　　**a little bit** 一點點
　　SOS 求救信號

32. (**B**) What may help remove stubborn food stains?
　　　什麼東西能夠幫助除掉頑強的食物污漬？
　　A. Dirt and grime. 污泥與污垢。
　　B. Foam shaving cream. 泡沫刮鬍膏。
　　C. Treating the stain with mustard. 用芥末來處理污漬。
　　D. Leaving the stains overnight. 把污漬擱置一整晚。

　　* remove〔 rɪ'muv 〕v. 除掉　　treat〔 trit 〕v. 處理

Questions 33 and 34 are based on the following report.

Heart disease isn't just a man's disease—it's also a major women's health threat. To reduce your risk, take charge of your heart health by making healthier lifestyle choices. For example: Don't smoke. If you smoke or use other tobacco products, ask your doctor to help you quit. Eat a healthy diet: put down the French fries. Choose vegetables, fruits, whole grains, high-fiber foods and lean sources of protein, such as fish. Limit foods high in saturated fat and sodium. Include physical activity in your daily routine. Choose sports or other activities you enjoy, from brisk walking to ballroom dancing.

心臟病不只是男人會得的疾病——它也是女人健康的一大威脅。要減少你的風險，就要選擇健康的生活方式，來掌控你的心臟健康。例如：別抽菸。如果你抽菸或使用其他的菸草產品，就要請醫生幫助你戒除。要健康的飲食：放下薯條吧。選擇蔬菜、水果、全麥食品、高纖食品及無脂肪的蛋白質來源，例如魚。限制富含飽和脂肪及高鈉的食物。將運動納入每天的例行公事中。選擇你喜歡的運動或其他的活動，從健走到跳交際舞等都可以。

** ————————————————————

disease〔dɪˋziz〕*n.* 疾病　　major〔ˋmedʒɚ〕*adj.* 主要的
health〔hɛlθ〕*n.* 健康　　threat〔θrɛt〕*n.* 威脅
reduce〔rɪˋdjus〕*v.* 減少　　risk〔rɪsk〕*n.* 風險
take charge of 掌管　　healthy〔ˋhɛlθɪ〕*adj.* 健康的
lifestyle〔ˋlaɪf͵staɪl〕*n.* 生活方式　　tobacco〔təˋbæko〕*n.* 菸草
product〔ˋprɑdəkt〕*n.* 產品　　quit〔kwɪt〕*v.* 戒除
diet〔ˋdaɪət〕*n.* 飲食；節食　　***put down*** 放下

French fries 炸薯條   whole〔hol〕*adj.* 全部的
grain〔gren〕*n.* 穀物   **whole grains** 全麥食品
fiber〔'faɪbɚ〕*n.* 纖維   high-fiber *adj.* 高纖的
lean〔lin〕*adj.* 無脂肪的   source〔sɔrs〕*n.* 來源
protein〔'protiɪn〕*n.* 蛋白質   limit〔'lɪmɪt〕*v.* 限制
be high in 富含~   saturated〔'sætʃə,retɪd〕*adj.* 飽合的
fat〔fæt〕*n.* 脂肪   sodium〔'sodɪəm〕*n.* 鈉
include〔ɪn'klud〕*v.* 包括；納入
physical〔'fɪzɪk!〕*adj.* 身體的   activity〔æk'tɪvətɪ〕*n.* 活動
daily〔'delɪ〕*adj.* 每天的   routine〔ru'tin〕*n.* 例行公事
brisk〔brɪsk〕*adj.* 輕快的   **brisk walking** 健走
ballroom〔'bɔl,rum〕*n.* 舞廳   **ballroom dancing** 交際舞

33. (**D**) How can women reduce their risk for heart disease?
   女士們要如何減少她們罹患心臟疾病的風險？

   A. By using tobacco products. 藉由使用菸草產品。

   B. By eating foods high in saturated fat.
      藉由吃富含飽合脂肪的食物。

   C. By asking the doctor to help them quit their diets.
      藉由詢問醫生來幫助她們停止節食。

   D. By making healthier lifestyle choices.
      藉由選擇更健康的生活方式。

   * diet〔'daɪət〕*n.* 節食

34. (**D**) Which of the following is not a part of a healthy diet?
   下列何者不是健康的飲食？

   A. Whole grains. 全麥食品。

   B. Fruits. 水果。

   C. Lean sources of protein. 無脂肪的蛋白質來源。

   D. French fries. 薯條。

Questions 35 and 36 are based on the following report.

Interested in pursuing a career in the health care industry? Now might be a good time to start preparing. As an industry, health care is projected to create about 3.2 million jobs from 2008-2018, according to the U.S. Department of Labor. Medical and health services managers, who plan, direct, coordinate, and supervise the delivery of health care, can enjoy the best of both worlds. Employment of medical and health services managers will grow by 16 percent from 2008-2018.

對從事醫療照顧產業有興趣嗎？現在可能是開始準備的好時機。依據美國勞工部的說法，醫療照顧業從 2008 到 2018 年，預估能夠創造三百二十萬個工作機會。醫療保健服務的經理負責規畫、指揮、協調、和監督健康照顧的提供，能夠享有兩全其美的生活。從 2008 到 2018 年，醫療保健服務經理的工作將會成長百分之十六。

** ─────────────────

be interested in 對…有興趣　　pursue〔pɚˋsu〕*v.* 追求；從事
career〔kəˋrɪr〕*n.* 職業；生涯　　health〔hɛlθ〕*n.* 健康
care〔kɛr〕*n.* 照顧　　industry〔ˋɪndəstrɪ〕*n.* 產業
project〔prəˋdʒɛkt〕*v.* 預估　　create〔krɪˋet〕*v.* 創造
department〔dɪˋpɑrtmənt〕*n.* 部門
labor〔ˋlebɚ〕*n.* 勞動；勞工　　medical〔ˋmɛdɪkl̩〕*adj.* 醫療的
service〔ˋsɝvɪs〕*n.* 服務　　manager〔ˋmænɪdʒɚ〕*n.* 經理
plan〔plæn〕*v.* 規畫　　direct〔dəˋrɛkt〕*v.* 指揮
coordinate〔koˋɔrdn̩͵et〕*v.* 協調
supervise〔ˋsupɚ͵vaɪz〕*v.* 監督
delivery〔dɪˋlɪvərɪ〕*n.* 遞送；提供

world〔wɜld〕n. 世界；領域
enjoy the best of both worlds 享有最好的精神和物質生活；
兩全其美　　employment〔ɪmˈpɔɪmənt〕n. 僱用；工作
by〔baɪ〕prep. 相差…

35. (**C**) Who is this report for? 這份報告是要給誰看的？

 A. People seeking medical treatment. 尋求醫療的人。

 B. Doctors and nurses. 醫生和護士。

 C. People interested in a career in health care.
  對醫療照顧業有興趣的人。

 D. People who work for the U.S. Department of Labor.
  在美國勞工部工作的人。

 * seek〔sik〕v. 尋求　　treatment〔ˈtritmənt〕n. 治療

36. (**B**) How many jobs are projected to be created in health
 care from 2008 to 2018?
 從 2008 到 2018 年，預估會創造多少醫療照顧方面的工作機會？

 A. 16 percent. 百分之十六。

 B. 3.2 million. 三百二十萬個。

 C. Health services managers. 保健服務經理。

 D. Now might be a good time to start.
  現在可能是開始的好時機。

Questions 37 and 38 are based on the following report.

  A leather jacket worn by U.S. singer Michael Jackson
in his renowned "Thriller" video has sold at an auction in
California for $1.8 million. Jackson wore the jacket in the
1983 video, in a scene with a troupe of zombies who rise
from their graves and break into a dance routine. It was

bought by a Texas commodities trader who said he planned to use it to raise money for children's charities. The sale was organized by Julien's Auction in Beverly Hills. Some of the proceeds will go to an animal preserve in California where Michael Jackson's two Bengal tigers, Thriller and Sabu, are living.

美國歌手麥可·傑克森在他知名的專輯《戰慄》影片中所穿的皮夾克，已經在加州的一場拍賣會中，賣了一百八十萬美金。傑克森在 1983 年的音樂影片中，穿了這件外套，是在他跟一群從墳墓中復活，並突然開始跳舞的殭屍在一起的場景。一位德州期貨交易員買走這件外套，他說他計畫要用它來為兒童慈善團體募款。這個拍賣是由在比佛利山莊的朱利安拍賣行所籌劃。它的部分收益會捐給位於加州的動物保護區，那裡是麥克·傑克森的兩隻孟加拉虎，戰慄與薩布，居住的地方。

** ─────────────────────

leather〔'lɛðɚ〕*adj.* 皮製的
renowned〔rɪ'naʊnd〕*adj.* 有名的
thriller〔'θrɪlɚ〕*n.* 令人驚悚的事物或人【文中所指《Thriller》，名列金氏世界紀錄歷年最暢銷專輯，其中譯名稱為《戰慄》】
video〔'vɪdɪ,o〕*n.* 影片　　auction〔'ɔkʃən〕*n.* 拍賣；拍賣行
scene〔sin〕*n.* 場景　　troupe〔trup〕*n.* 一隊；一團
zombie〔'zɑmbɪ〕*n.* 殭屍　　rise〔raɪz〕*v.* 上升；復活
grave〔grev〕*n.* 墳墓　　***break into*** 突然開始
routine〔ru'tin〕*n.* 例行公事；慣例　　***dance routine*** 一套舞蹈
Texas〔'hɛlpfəl〕*n.* 德州【為美國土地面積最大的州】
commodity〔kə'mɑdətɪ〕*n.* 商品；期貨
trader〔'tredɚ〕*n.* 交易員　　***commodities trader*** 期貨交易員
raise〔rez〕*v.* 募（款）　　charity〔'tʃærətɪ〕*n.* 慈善機構
organize〔'ɔrgə,naɪz〕*v.* 組織；籌劃

Beverly Hills (ˈbɛvəlɪ ˈhɪlz) n. 比佛利山莊【美國洛杉磯附近小城，因許多有名明星居住而聞名】

proceeds (ˈprosidz) n. pl. 收益　**go to** 被給予

preserve (prɪˈzɜv) n. 保護區

California (ˌkæləˈfɔrnjə) n. 加州【位於美國】

Bengal (bɛŋˈgɔl) n. 孟加拉【位於印度】

37. (**D**) What was sold at an auction? 什麼東西在拍賣會中售出？

 A. A 1983 video. 一個 1983 年的影片。

 B. Texas commodities. 德州商品。

 C. Michael Jackson's two Bengal tigers.
  麥可・傑克森的兩隻孟加拉虎。

 D. Michael Jackson's leather jacket.
  麥可・傑克森的皮夾克。

38. (**A**) Why is the item so special? 這個物品爲什麼這麼特別？

 A. It was worn in a famous scene from the "Thriller"
  video. 它是在《戰慄》影片中的知名場景裡被穿過的。

 B. It was bought by Julien's Auction.
  它是被朱利安拍賣行買走的。

 C. It gets sold in Beverly Hills. 它是比佛利山莊被賣掉的。

 D. It does a dance routine. 它跳了一段舞蹈。

 * item (ˈaɪtəm) n. 物品

Questions 39 and 40 are based on the following report.

 Sometimes when a country loses a military conflict, they are forced to make war reparations. War reparations are payments intended to cover damage or injury during a war. Generally, the term refers to money or goods changing hands, rather than land or property transfers. One criticism of war reparations is that after years of war, the populace of the losing side is likely already impoverished, and the imposition of war reparations therefore may drive the people into deeper poverty, both fueling long-term resentment of the victor and making the actual payments unlikely.

有時候當一個國家在一場軍事衝突輸了，他們會被迫要支付戰爭賠款。戰爭賠款是要用來支付戰爭期間的損失或傷害。通常，這個名詞是指轉手的金錢或商品，而不是土地或房產的轉移。有個對戰爭賠款的批評，是認為多年征戰後，輸掉戰爭的那一方的老百姓很可能早已陷入貧困，因此戰爭賠款的徵收，可能會使人們更加貧窮，不僅會加深對勝利者長期的怨恨，而且也會讓實際的付款不太可能發生。

** ——————————————

lose〔luz〕v. 輸掉　　military〔'mɪləˌtɛrɪ〕adj. 軍事的
conflict〔'kɑnflɪkt〕n. 衝突
force〔fors〕v. 強迫　　war〔wɔr〕n. 戰爭
reparations〔ˌrɛpə'reʃənz〕n. pl. 賠款【戰敗國付給戰勝國的賠償】
payment〔'pemənt〕n. 款項　　intend〔ɪn'tɛnd〕v. 打算
cover〔'kʌvɚ〕v. 支付　　damage〔'dæmɪdʒ〕n. 損害
injury〔'ɪndʒərɪ〕n. 傷害　　generally〔'dʒɛnərəlɪ〕adv. 通常
term〔tɝm〕n. 名詞；用語　　*refer to* 是指
goods〔gʊdz〕n. pl. 商品　　*change hands* 轉手；歸另一人所有
property〔'prɑpɚtɪ〕n. 財產；地產
transfer〔'trænsfɝ〕轉移　　criticism〔'krɪtəˌsɪzəm〕n. 批評
populace〔'pɑpjəlɪs〕n. 老百姓；民眾
impoverished〔ɪm'pɑvərɪʃt〕adj. 窮困的
imposition〔ˌɪmpə'zɪʃən〕n. 徵收

drive〔draɪv〕v. 驅使　　deep〔dip〕adj. 嚴重的
poverty〔'pɑvətɪ〕n. 貧窮　　fuel〔'fjuəl〕v. 加燃料；激起
long-term adj. 長期的　　resentment〔rɪ'zɛntmənt〕n. 怨恨
victor〔'vɪktɚ〕n. 勝利者　　actual〔'æktʃuəl〕adj. 實際的
unlikely〔ʌn'laɪklɪ〕adj. 不太可能的

39. (**C**) What are war reparations?　戰爭賠款是什麼？

A. Money used to pay for more weapons.
用來買武器的錢。

B. Funds distributed among poor people.
分發給窮人的資金。

C. Payments intended to cover damage or injury during
a war.　打算用來支付戰爭期間的損害或傷害的款項。

D. Bribes taken from corrupt officials.
從貪污的官員拿來的賄賂。

* weapon〔'wɛpən〕n. 武器　　funds〔fʌndz〕n. pl. 資金
distribute〔dɪ'strɪbjut〕v. 分發
bribe〔braɪb〕n. 賄賂　　corrupt〔kə'rʌpt〕adj. 貪污的
official〔ə'fɪʃəl〕n. 官員

40. (**C**) Who pays for the war reparations?　由誰支付戰爭賠款？

A. The winning side.　贏的一方。

B. The side that started the conflict.　發動衝突的一方。

C. The losing side.　輸的一方。

D. Both sides.　雙方。

* winning〔'wɪnɪŋ〕adj. 獲勝的
losing〔'luzɪŋ〕adj. 失敗的

高中英聽測驗模擬試題⑩詳解
(參考試卷)

一、看圖辨義：第一部分

For question number 1, please look at picture 1.

1. (**A**) A young man has just finished playing basketball. He is buying a cola from a vending machine.

一個年輕人剛打完籃球。他正從自動販賣機買一瓶可樂。

* *vending machine* 自動販賣機

For question number 2, please look at picture 2.

2. (**B**) A father is holding his little boy, while the nurse is giving him a shot.

一位父親抱著他的小兒子，當時護士小姐正在給他的孩子打針。

* hold〔hold〕v. 抱著　　*give sb. a shot* 給某人注射

For question number 3, please look at picture 3.

3. (**A**) Two male students are getting into a fight with each other. A woman is trying to stop them.

   兩個男學生正在打架。一個女人正試圖阻止他們。

   　　* ***get into*** 參與；開始　　fight〔faɪt〕*n.* 打架
   　　each other 彼此；互相

For question number 4, please look at picture 4.

4. (**D**) Today is Friday, April 15th, and it's now 4:30 p.m.

   今天是四月十五日星期五，時間是下午四點三十分。

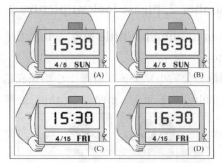

一、看圖辨義：第二部分

For question number 5, please look at picture 5.

5.（ **B、D** ）Which TWO of the following are true about the man in the picture? 關於圖片中的男士，下列哪兩項敘述為眞？

    A. He's having a job interview.
       他正在進行工作面試。

    B. He's worried about an upcoming test.
       他在擔心一場即將到來的考試。

    C. He's enjoying talking to a customer.
       他正跟一位顧客談得很愉快。

    D. He's working as a clerk in a store.
       他正在一家商店擔任店員。

    * interview〔'ɪntə‚vju〕*n.* 面試　　***be worried about*** 擔心
    upcoming〔'ʌp‚kʌmɪŋ〕*adj.* 即將來臨的
    customer〔'kʌstəmə〕*n.* 顧客　　***work as*** 擔任
    clerk〔klɝk〕*n.* 店員

For question number 6, please look at picture 6.

6.（ **B、C** ）Which TWO are true about the banned items?
    關於被禁止的物品，下列哪兩項敘述為眞？

    A. All American high schools ban comic books.
       全美國的高中都禁止漫畫書。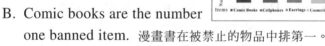

    B. Comic books are the number one banned item. 漫畫書在被禁止的物品中排第一。

    C. More schools ban cellphones than earrings.
       禁止手機的學校比禁止耳環的學校還多。

D. More than fifty percent of American high schools ban cosmetics.

有超過百分之五十的美國高中禁止化妝品。

* banned〔bænd〕 *adj.* 被禁止的
item〔'aɪtəm〕 *n.* 項目；物品
cellphone〔'sɛl,fon〕 *n.* 手機
earring〔'ɪr,rɪŋ〕 *n.* 耳環
cosmetics〔kɑz'mɛtɪks〕 *n. pl.* 化妝品

For question number 7, please look at picture 7.

7.（**A、C**）Which TWO of the following are true about the woman in the picture? 關於圖片中的女士，下列哪兩項敘述為眞？

A. She's pressing an elevator button.
她正在按電梯的按鈕。

B. She's admiring herself in a mirror.
她正在欣賞鏡中的自己。

C. She's standing all by herself. 她正獨自站著。

D. She's wearing a skirt. 她正穿著一件裙子。

* press〔prɛs〕 *v.* 按；壓　　elevator〔'ɛlə,vetə〕 *n.* 電梯
button〔'bʌtn̩〕 *n.* 按鈕　　admire〔əd'maɪr〕 *v.* 欣賞
mirror〔'mɪrə〕 *n.* 鏡子　　*by oneself* 某人自己；獨自

For question number 8, please look at picture 8.

8.（**A、D**）Which TWO of the following are true about the summer program?

關於暑期課程，下列哪兩項敘述為眞？

A. It was held at Korea University. 在韓國大學舉辦。

B. It lasted more than two months.

此課程持續超過兩個月。

C. It included 1,400 courses.

此課程包含一千四百門課。

D. It invited 60 world famous professors.

此課程邀請六十國有名的教授。

* program〔ˈprogræm〕n. 課程
　hold〔hold〕v. 舉行　　last〔læst〕v. 持續
　course〔kors〕n. 課程
　professor〔prəˈfɛsɚ〕n. 教授

For question number 9, please look at picture 9.

9. (**A、D**) Which TWO of the following are true about the departures? 關於離境班機，下列哪兩項敘述為眞？

A. The flight to New York departs at 14:50.

飛往紐約的班機於 14:50 出發。

B. The flight to Hong Kong departs at 15:10. 飛往香港的班機於 15:10 出發。

C. The flight to Madrid departs from Gate 24.

飛往馬德里的班機於 24 號登機門出發。

D. The flight to Amsterdam departs from Gate 15.

飛往的阿姆斯特丹班的機於 15 號登機門出發。

* departure〔dɪˈpartʃɚ〕n. 出發；離開
　flight〔flaɪt〕n. 班機　　depart〔dɪˈpart〕v. 出發
　gate〔get〕n. 登機門
　Madrid〔məˈdrɪd〕n. 馬德里【西班牙首都】
　Amsterdam〔ˌæmstɚˈdæm〕n. 阿姆斯特丹【荷蘭首都】

For question number 10, please look at picture 10.

10. (**A、B**) Which TWO of the following have the least
influence on teens' money management?

下面哪兩項對青少年的金錢管理的影響最小？

A. Media. 媒體。
B. Friends. 朋友。
C. Teachers. 老師。
D. Parents. 父母。

> Where teens learn to manage money
>
> Parents 93%
> Own experiences 90%
> Teachers 59%
> Friends 42%
> Media 37%

* least〔list〕*adj.* 最小的；最少的
influence〔ˈɪnfluəns〕*n.* 影響；作用
teens〔tinz〕*n. pl.* 青少年 (= *teenagers*)
management〔ˈmænɪdʒmənt〕*n.* 管理
media〔ˈmidɪə〕*n. pl.* 媒體

二、對答

11. (**A**) How did your English test go last week?

你上禮拜的英文考試考得如何？

A. I got a 90. 我得到 90 分。
B. I surely will. 我確信我會。
C. Math is my favorite subject. 數學是我最喜歡的科目。
D. The math test was on Monday. 數學考試是在禮拜一。

* go〔go〕*v.* 進展

12. (**B**) You look so cool in that jacket. Where did you get it?

你穿那件夾克看起來很酷。你在哪裡買的？

A. Sorry. I don't get it. 對不起。我不懂你的意思。
B. Thank you. I got it at a garage sale.

謝謝你。我在一個車庫拍賣買到的。

C. OK. I will stay away from the window.

好的。我會遠離那扇窗。

D. Jack is in his room getting ready to go to bed.

傑克在他的房間準備好要上床睡覺。

get it 聽懂；了解

garage sale （在車庫中進行的）舊貨出售；車庫拍賣

stay away from 遠離

13. (**A**) Why did you close the window? 你爲什麼要關窗？

A. It's cold in here. 這裡很冷。

B. I forgot to open it. 我忘記去關了。

C. We are close friends. 我們是很親密的朋友。

D. She didn't know why. 她不知道爲什麼。

* close〔klos〕*adj.* 親密的

14. (**A**) Sue and I are going to the movies. Would you like to join us? 蘇和我正要去看電影。你想加入我們嗎？

A. Thanks, but I'm afraid I can't.

謝謝，但我恐怕不行。

B. Oh, yes. I enjoyed it a lot. 喔，是的。我很享受。

C. Yes. I can't agree with you more.

是的。我非常同意你的說法。

D. Why not? I have a lot of homework to do.

爲什麼不？我有很多功課要做。

go to the movies 去看電影

I can't agree with you more. 我非常同意你的說法。

15. (**A**) I think I'm getting to like English, day by day.

我覺得我開始一天一天地喜歡上英文了。

A. Me too. 我也是。

B. Never mind. 沒關係。

C. I like to get up early. 我喜歡早起。

D. What day is today? 今天是星期幾？

* *get to V*. 開始~　　*day by day* 一天一天地；逐日
never mind 沒關係　　*get up* 起床

16. (**B**) Excuse me, can I ask you some questions about your summer program?

不好意思，可以請問你一些關於暑期課程的問題嗎？

A. No. Not at all. 不。一點也不。

B. Sure. How may I help you?

當然可以。我要如何幫你？

C. Sorry. What's going on here?

對不起。這裡發生什麼事？

D. Okay. I have a question for you.

好的。我有一個問題要問你。

* program〔'progræm〕*n.* 課程　　*not at all* 一點也不
go on 發生

17. (**C**) You look so sweaty. Have you been playing basketball?

你看起來滿身是汗。你去打籃球了嗎？

A. Yes, I must get some sleep. 是的，我一定要睡一會兒。

B. Well, I have to do my homework.

嗯，我必須做我的功課。

C. Yeah, I need to take a quick shower.

是的，我需要快速沖個澡。

D. Right, I'm going to play basketball.

對，我正要去打籃球。

* sweaty〔'swɛtɪ〕*adj.* 滿身是汗的　　*take a shower* 沖澡

18. (**C**) I saw Jenny holding a sign in front of the school.
　　　我看到珍妮拿著一張標語在學校前面。

　　　A. Yes. Jenny says the signature is fake.
　　　　是的。珍妮說那個簽名是假的。

　　　B. There are always posters on the wall.
　　　　總是有海報在牆上。

　　　C. Right. She was protesting the tuition increase.
　　　　對。她正在抗議學費調漲。

　　　D. Jenny is holding Bob's hand.　珍妮正握著鮑伯的手。

　　　* sign〔saɪn〕*n.* 標誌；告示　　signature〔'sɪɡnətʃɚ〕*n.* 簽名
　　　fake〔fek〕*adj.* 假的　　poster〔'postɚ〕*n.* 海報
　　　protest〔prə'tɛst〕*v.* 抗議　　tuition〔tu'ɪʃən〕*n.* 學費
　　　increase〔'ɪnkris〕*n.* 增加　　hold〔hold〕*v.* 握著

19. (**A**) What topic will Professor Brown speak on tonight?
　　　布朗教授今天晚上要講的主題是什麼？

　　　A. He'll focus on British literature.
　　　　他會聚焦在英國文學上。

　　　B. He's the best speaker on our campus.
　　　　他是我們校園裡最會演講的人。

　　　C. His presentation was completely off topic.
　　　　他的演講完全偏離主題。

　　　D. He's the spokesperson for the university.
　　　　他是大學的發言人。

　　　* *focus on* 集中於
　　　British〔'brɪtɪʃ〕*adj.* 英國的　　literature〔'lɪtərətʃɚ〕*n.* 文學
　　　campus〔'kæmpəs〕*n.* 校園　　*on campus* 在校園裡
　　　presentation〔,prɛzn̩'teʃən〕*n.* 演講；上台報告
　　　completely〔kəm'plitlɪ〕*adv.* 完全地　　off〔ɔf〕*prep.* 脫離
　　　spokesperson〔'spoks,pɝsn̩〕*n.* 發言人

20. (**C**) The course is very demanding. It requires one term
paper, one take-home exam, and two oral presentations.
這門課的要求很高。需要一份期中報告、一份帶回家的考試，
及兩次口頭報告。

   A. How about taking a trip abroad?
那去國外旅行如何？

   B. Meet the demands of your clients.
要達到你客戶的要求。

   C. Just plan ahead and manage your time well.
只要事先計畫和管理好你的時間。

   D. Listen carefully to others' presentations.
要仔細聽他人的報告。

  * demanding〔dɪˋmændɪŋ〕*adj.* 要求高的
require〔rɪˋkwaɪr〕*v.* 需要　　*term paper* 學期報告
oral〔ˋɔrəl〕*adj.* 口頭的　　abroad〔əˋbrɔd〕*adv.* 到國外
meet〔mit〕*v.* 符合　　demand〔dɪˋmænd〕*n.* 要求
client〔ˋklaɪənt〕*n.* 客戶　　ahead〔əˋhɛd〕*adv.* 事先
manage〔ˋmænɪdʒ〕*v.* 管理

三、簡短對話

For question 21, you will listen to a short conversation.

  M：Janice, would you like to go to a movie with me this
weekend?
珍妮斯，你這個週末想跟我一起去看電影嗎？

  W：Yeah, I'd love to. I'm busy most of the day on
Saturday, but Saturday night is fine. 好啊，我很樂意。
我星期六白天大部分時間都很忙，但星期六晚上可以。

M：Great.　How about we meet at the west exit of the train
　　station at eight o'clock?　We can walk down to the
　　cinema from there.　太棒了。那我們約八點整在火車站的
　　西邊出口碰面，如何？我們可以從那邊走到電影院。

W：Sure, that sounds great!　Bye, Bob.
　　當然好，聽起來很棒！再見，鮑伯。

　　How about…? 如何…？　　exit〔ˈɛgzɪt , ˈɛksɪt〕*n.* 出口
　　walk down to 走去…　　cinema〔ˈsɪnəmə〕*n.* 電影院

21.（ **D** ）Q：Where will Janice and Bob meet?
　　　　　　珍妮斯和鮑伯會在哪裡見面？
　　　　　　A. 8:00 PM.　晚上八點。
　　　　　　B. Sunday night.　星期六晚上。
　　　　　　C. In the cinema.　在電影院裡。
　　　　　　D. At the train station.　在火車站。

For question 22, you will listen to a short conversation.

M：Who is your role model, Mary?　誰是你的楷模，瑪莉？

W：Ms. Wang, of course.　She's a real polyglot.
　　當然是王小姐。她真的是個精通數國語言的人。

M：A polyglot, what do you mean?
　　一個精通數國語言的人，你是什麼意思？

W：Well, you know, she's a native speaker of Mandarin
　　Chinese.　But she speaks French, German, Spanish,
　　Polish, and Russian, equally fluently.
　　嗯，你知道的啊，她的母語是中文。但她還會說與中文同樣
　　流利的法文、德文、西班牙文、波蘭文，和俄文。

* **role model**　榜樣；模範
polyglot〔'palɪ,glat〕*n.* 精通數國語言的人
native speaker　說母語的人　　***Mandarin Chinese***　標準中文
French〔frɛntʃ〕*n.* 法文　　German〔'dʒʒmən〕*n.* 德文
Spanish〔'spænɪʃ〕*n.* 西班牙文　　Polish〔'palɪʃ〕*n.* 波蘭文
Russian〔'rʌʃən〕*n.* 俄文　　equally〔'ikwəlɪ〕*adv.* 同樣地
fluently〔'fluəntlɪ〕*adv.* 流利地

22. (**B**) Q : Which of the following descriptions is true about
　　　 Ms. Wang?　下列關於王小姐的敘述何者為眞？

　　A. She works as a fashion model. 她是個時裝模特兒。

　　B. She is fluent in several languages.
　　　她好幾種語言都很流利。

　　C. She is a native speaker of Japanese.
　　　她的母語是日文。

　　D. She enjoys traveling around the world.
　　　她喜歡環遊世界。

　　* fashion〔'fæʃən〕*n.* 流行；時尚；時裝
　　 fluent〔'fluənt〕*adj.* 流利的

For question 23, you will listen to a short conversation.

M : Holly, how do you like the soup?
　　荷莉，妳覺得這湯如何？

W : It tastes like something's missing.
　　這湯嚐起來好像少了些什麼。

M : But I followed every step in the recipe.　What could
　　have gone wrong?
　　可是我是照著食譜的每個步驟。會是哪裡出了錯呢？

W : It's actually not that bad, considering this is the first time you made it. A little bit of salt and pepper will add some flavor. 這湯其實不差，以你第一次做來說。加一點點鹽和胡椒能增加一些味道。

* soup〔sup〕*n.* 湯　　taste〔test〕*v.* 嚐起來
missing〔'mɪsɪŋ〕*adj.* 缺少的　　follow〔'falo〕*v.* 遵循
step〔stɛp〕*n.* 步驟　　recipe〔'rɛsəpɪ〕*n.* 食譜
go wrong 出錯　　actually〔'æktʃʊəlɪ〕*adv.* 實際上
considering〔kən'sɪdərɪŋ〕*prep.* 就…而論；考慮到
salt〔sɔlt〕*n.* 鹽　　pepper〔'pɛpɚ〕*n.* 胡椒
add〔æd〕*v.* 增加　　flavor〔'flevɚ〕*n.* 味道

23. (**D**) Q : Which of the following statements is true about this conversation? 下列關於這段對話的敘述何者為真？

　　A. The man made the soup without using a cookbook.
　　　　這位男士做湯時沒有參考食譜。
　　B. The man missed several important steps in the recipe. 這位男士錯過了食譜裡的一些重要的步驟。
　　C. The woman enjoyed the soup to her heart's content.
　　　　這位女士盡情地享受這道湯。
　　D. The woman didn't think the soup was salty enough.
　　　　這位女士覺得湯不夠鹹。

* cookbook〔'kʊk,bʊk〕*n.* 食譜　　miss〔mɪs〕*v.* 錯過
to one's heart's content 盡情地　　salty〔'sɔltɪ〕*adj.* 鹹的

For question 24, you will listen to a short conversation.

W : Good morning, class. Let's continue our discussion on the issue of global warming. Does everyone have the handout I gave you last week?

早安，同學們。我們繼續我們在全球暖化議題上的討論吧。
大家都有我上禮拜給的講義嗎？

W：Yes, Ms. Norman. 是，諾曼小姐。

M：Hmm, I forgot to bring mine. Maybe I could share
yours, Joan?

嗯，我忘記帶我的講義。也許我可以和妳一起用妳的，瓊？

W：No problem, Larry. 沒問題，賴瑞。

* class〔klæs〕*n.* 全班同學　　issue〔ˈɪʃju〕*n.* 議題
  global warming 全球暖化　　handout〔ˈhænd‚aut〕*n.* 講義
  share〔ʃɛr〕*v.* 分享

24. (**C**)　Q：What can be inferred from the conversation?
　　　　　由這段對話可推論出什麼？

　　A. Larry is Joan's teacher. 賴瑞是瓊的老師。

　　B. Larry and Joan are in a PE class.
　　　　賴瑞和瓊在上體育課。

　　C. Larry doesn't have the handout with him.
　　　　賴瑞沒有帶講義。

　　D. Larry didn't get the handout from Ms. Norman.
　　　　賴瑞沒有從諾曼小姐那裡拿到講義。

* infer〔ɪnˈfɝ〕*v.* 推論　　***PE*** 體育（= *physical education*）

For questions 25 and 26, you will listen to a short conversation.

W：Your dog is really cute, and well-behaved. When did
you start training him?

你的狗真可愛，而且好有規矩。你是什麼時候開始訓練牠的？

M：When he was still a puppy. 從牠還是小狗的時候。

W : That's really early. 那還真是早。

M : Well, it's never too early to train your dog. Training sessions are really important.

嗯，訓練你的狗永遠不嫌早。訓練課程真的很重要。

W : How long should the training sessions last?

訓練課程應該要持續多久呢？

M : Try to keep them short, consistent, and fun. You can start with easy commands, so that your dog can learn them easily. He also gets a sense of achievement.

試著讓訓練課程短、前後一致，而且有趣。你可以從簡單的命令開始，這樣一來妳的狗就可以簡單地學習指令。牠也可以得到成就感。

W : Right. That's important. Should I give him lots of rewards? 對。成就感很重要。我應該給牠很多的獎賞嗎？

M : Definitely. Make sure he knows he is doing a great job, and in the end, he will enjoy the training sessions.

絕對要。確保牠知道自己所做得很棒，而且到最後牠將會喜歡訓練課程。

W : Anything else I should know? 還有其他我該知道的事嗎？

M : Be patient and realistic. It takes time for your puppy to get used to your commands. But you will find the training sessions very rewarding afterwards.

要有耐心，並且很實際。妳的小狗適應妳的指令需要一些時間。但之後妳會發現訓練課程是非常值得的。

* well-behaved〔ˋwɛl bɪˋhevd〕*adj.* 守規矩的
puppy〔ˋpʌpɪ〕*n.* 小狗　　session〔ˋsɛʃən〕*n.* 上課時間
consistent〔kənˋsɪstənt〕*adj.* 前後一致的；連貫的
fun〔fʌn〕*adj.* 有趣的　　command〔kəˋmænd〕*n.* 命令
so that 以便於　　sense〔sɛns〕*n.* 感覺
achievement〔əˋtʃivmənt〕*n.* 成就
a sense of achievement 成就感　　reward〔rɪˋwɔrd〕*n.* 獎賞
definitely〔ˋdɛfənɪtlɪ〕*adv.* 確定地；一定　　*make sure* 確定
do a great job 做得好　　*in the end* 最後
patient〔ˋpeʃənt〕*adj.* 有耐心的
realistic〔͵riəˋlɪstɪk〕*adj.* 實際的　　take〔tek〕*v.* 需要；花費
get used to 習慣於
rewarding〔rɪˋwɔrdɪŋ〕*adj.* 有益的；有報酬的
afterwards〔ˋæftəwədz〕*adv.* 之後

25.（ **B** ）Q：What is this conversation about?
　　　　　這段對話是關於什麼？
　　A. How to feed your dog. 如何餵你的狗。
　　B. How to train your dog. 如何訓練你的狗。
　　C. How to reward your dog. 如何獎勵你的狗。
　　D. How to get to know your dog. 如何了解你的狗。
　* get to V. 得以～

26.（ **D** ）Q：According to the conversation, which of the
　　　　　following is true? 根據這段對話，下列何者為眞？
　　A. It's not good to train your dog too early.
　　　太早訓練你的狗不好。
　　B. Avoid giving too many rewards to your dog.
　　　避免給你的狗太多獎賞。
　　C. It's very important to be strict with your dog.
　　　嚴格對待你的狗是很重要的。

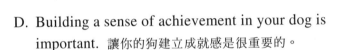

D. Building a sense of achievement in your dog is important. 讓你的狗建立成就感是很重要的。

* strict〔strɪkt〕*adj.* 嚴格的

For questions 27 and 28, you will listen to a short conversation.

W：Hi, Stewart. I'm back. Where are you?
嗨，史都華。我回來了。你在哪哩？

M：Hi, there. I'm in the kitchen, Sophie. I hope you're hungry. 嗨。我在廚房裡，蘇菲。我希望你肚子餓了。

W：I'm absolutely starving. I'm freezing, too. Do you know how cold it is outside?
我餓壞了。我也覺得好冷。你知道外面有多冷嗎？

M：No idea. I've been working at home all day, and haven't been out. 不知道。我一整天都在家裡忙著，而且都沒有出門。

W：My fingers feel like they are about to drop off. It must be -15, at least. Gosh, I really hate February. So, what's for dinner?
我的手指冷到好像要掉下來了。一定最少有零下十五度。天啊，我真的很討厭二月。所以，我們晚餐吃什麼？

M：I fixed us some spaghetti. That should warm you up.
我為我們弄了些義大利麵。應該能讓妳暖和起來。

W：Oh, great. That's exactly what I need right now. Is it ready or do I have time for a quick shower first?
喔，太棒了。這正是我現在所需要的。已經好了嗎？或者我還有時間先快速沖個澡？

M：It'll be on the table in a moment. 晚餐立刻上桌。

W：I hoped you say that. 我就希望你這麼說。

> * **Hi, there**. 嗨，你好。
> absolutely〔ˈæbsəˌlutlɪ〕*adv.* 絕對地；非常地
> starving〔ˈstɑrvɪŋ〕*adj.* 飢餓的　　freezing〔ˈfrizɪŋ〕*adj.* 極冷的
> (**have**) **no idea** 不知道　　**be about to V**. 即將～；正要～
> **drop off** 掉下來　　**at least** 至少
> gosh〔gɑʃ〕*interj.* 天啊；哎呀　　hate〔het〕*v.* 討厭
> fix〔fɪks〕*v.* 準備（飯菜）　　spaghetti〔spəˈgɛtɪ〕*n.* 義大利麵
> **warm up** 使溫暖　　**in a moment** 立刻；馬上
> exactly〔ɪgˈzæktlɪ〕*adv.* 正是

27. (**B**) Q：What's the weather like outside?
　　　　　　　外面的天氣如何？
　　　　A. It's fifty degrees. 溫度是 50 度。
　　　　B. It's extremely cold. 非常冷。
　　　　C. It has warmed up a bit. 已經有點回暖了。
　　　　D. It's raining cats and dogs. 雨下得很大。
　　　　* degree〔ˈdɪgri〕*n.* 度　　extremely〔ɪkˈstrimlɪ〕*adv.* 非常地
　　　　a bit 有點　　**rain cats and dogs** 下傾盆大雨

28. (**A**) Q：When is the couple going to eat their dinner?
　　　　　　　這對男女什麼時候要吃晚餐？
　　　　A. Right away. 馬上。
　　　　B. In half an hour. 再過半小時。
　　　　C. After the woman's shower. 在女士淋浴完之後。
　　　　D. When they have warmed up. 當他們暖和起來時。
　　　　* couple〔ˈkʌpl̩〕*n.* 一對男女

For questions 29 and 30, you will listen to a short conversation.

W : Chris, did you go to Professor Johnson's lecture Tuesday night?
克里斯，你星期二晚上有去聽強森教授的演講嗎？

M : I wish I could have, but I've been busy with this project. So, what was the lecture about? 我希望我有去，但我在忙這個計劃。所以，演講內容是關於什麼？

W : Mismanagement of water resources. 水資源的不當管理。

M : Sounds interesting. 聽起來很有趣。

W : Yeah, he said water shortage is probably the most serious environmental problem we face, apart from climate change. The earth has all the water it needs to supply the six billion people who live on it with clean, safe drinking water. But millions of people are going to die because of water shortages. 是呀，他說水源短缺大概是除了氣候變遷之外，我們所面臨的最嚴重的環境問題。地球擁有的水，足以供給住在其上的六十億人口乾淨、安全的飲用水。但數以百萬計的人卻會因為水源短缺而死亡。

M : And that is because water resources are mismanaged? 而那是因為水資源管理不當？

W : Precisely. So, what's your project about, Chris? 沒錯。所以，你的計劃是關於什麼，克里斯？

M : Packaging and recycling. The report is due tomorrow. 包裝和資源回收。報告明天要交。

* lecture〔'lɛktʃə〕*n.* 演講　　***be busy with*** 忙於
  project〔'prɑdʒɛkt〕*n.* 計劃
  mismanagement〔mɪs'mænɪdʒmənt〕*n.* 管理不善
  resource〔rɪ'sors〕*n.* 資源
  yeah〔jɛ〕*adv.* 是的（= *yes*）
  shortage〔'ʃɔrtɪdʒ〕*n.* 缺乏
  environmental〔ɪn,vaɪrən'mɛntḷ〕*adj.* 環境的；環境（保護）的
  face〔fes〕*v.* 面臨　　***apart from*** 除了⋯之外
  climate〔'klaɪmɪt〕*n.* 氣候
  supply〔sə'plaɪ〕*v.* 供給
  billion〔'bɪljən〕*n.* 十億
  precisely〔prɪ'saɪslɪ〕*adv.* 對；確實如此
  packaging〔'pækɪdʒɪŋ〕*n.* 包裝
  recycling〔ri'saɪklɪŋ〕*n.*（資源、垃圾）回收利用
  due〔dju〕*adj.* 到期的

29.（**C**）Q：What was the topic of Professor Johnson's lecture?
　　　　強森教授的演講主題是什麼？

　　　A. Oil shortages. 石油短缺。

　　　B. Climate change. 氣候變化。

　　　C. Water resources. 水資源。

　　　D. Business management. 企業管理。

30.（**A**）Q：Which of the following statements is true about
　　　　Chris? 下列關於克里斯的敘述何者為真？

　　　A. He missed an interesting talk Tuesday night.
　　　　他錯過星期二晚上一場有趣的演講。

　　　B. He is busy with his research on climate change.
　　　　他忙著他氣候變遷的研究。

　　　C. He just finished a report on population increases.
　　　　他剛完成一份關於人口增加的報告。

D. He enjoyed attending Professor Johnson's lecture.
他喜歡參加強森教授的演講。

* talk〔tɔk〕*n.* 談話；演講　　research〔'risɝtʃ〕*n.* 研究
population〔͵pɑpjə'leʃən〕*n.* 人口　　attend〔ə'tɛnd〕*v.* 參加

四、短文聽解

Questions 31 and 32 are based on the following report.

Ichihara City in Japan recently opened what is called the Biggest Public Toilet in the World. The toilet, located in front of a railway station, is boxed in glass and sits in the middle of a garden of flowers and plants. For privacy, there's a two-meter high fence surrounding the garden. According to a local government official, it is hoped that the unusual toilet will become a tourist attraction. At the moment, it is only for women, but according to the official, it may be open to everyone in the future. The toilet was designed by Soh Fujimoto, who recently rose to international fame with his winning design for the new Taiwan Tower to be built in Taichung. The architect says that public toilets are both public and private, so designing them can be a very motivating challenge.

日本的市原市，最近開設了所謂「全世界最大的公共廁所」。此廁所位於火車站前，被包裝在玻璃箱裡，坐落在有花卉和植物的花園中。為了保護隱私，周圍還有一道兩公尺高的圍牆環繞著花園。據一位當地政府官員表示，希望這非比尋常的廁所將會成為旅遊景點。目前，該廁所只開放給女性使用，但根據官員的說

法，未來也可能開放給所有人。這個廁所是由藤本草所設計的，他最近因爲台中台灣塔的這項設計而得獎，因而國際知名度迅速攀升。這位建築師說，公廁是既公共又私密，因此設計這些廁所是一項非常激勵人心的挑戰。

**

Ichihara City　市原市　　recently〔'risɳtlɪ〕adv. 最近
open〔'opən〕v. 開設；開放　adj. 開放的
what is called　所謂的　　toilet〔'tɔɪlɪt〕n. 廁所
be located in　位於　　railway station　火車站
box〔bɑks〕v. 把…裝箱　　sit in　坐落於；位於
in the middle of　在…當中　　privacy〔'praɪvəsɪ〕n. 隱私
fence〔fɛns〕n. 柵欄；籬笆；圍牆
surround〔sə'raʊnd〕v. 圍繞　　local〔'lokḷ〕adj. 當地的
official〔ə'fɪʃəl〕n. 官員　　tourist attraction　觀光勝地
at the moment　現在；目前　　design〔dɪ'zaɪn〕v. n. 設計
Soh Fujimoto　藤本草　　rise〔raɪz〕v. 上升；晉升；地位提高
international〔,ɪntə'næʃənḷ〕adj. 國際性的
fame〔fem〕n. 名聲　　winning〔'wɪnɪŋ〕adj. 獲勝的
tower〔'taʊɚ〕n. 塔　　architect〔'ɑrkə,tɛkt〕n. 建築師
public〔'pʌblɪk〕adj. 公共的
private〔'praɪvɪt〕adj. 非公開的；祕密的
motivating〔'motə,vetɪŋ〕adj. 激勵人心的
challenge〔'tʃælɪndʒ〕n. 挑戰

31. (**C**) In the future, what may happen to the toilet described in the report?　在未來，這份報導中所描述的廁所會發生什麼事？

 A. It may become even bigger. 它可能會變得更大。

 B. It may be moved to Taichung. 它可能會遷移到台中。

 C. It may be open to both men and women.
  它可能會開放給男人和女人使用。

 D. It may be surrounded by a twenty-meter-high fence.
  它可能會被一道二十公尺高的圍牆所環繞。

32. (**B**) Who is Sou Fujimoto? 藤本草是誰？
　　A. A gardener. 一位園丁。
　　B. An architect. 一位建築師。
　　C. A town planner. 一位城鎮規劃人。
　　D. A government official. 一位政府官員。
　　* gardener〔'gɑrdnɚ〕*n.* 園丁
　　　planner〔'plænɚ〕*n.* 計畫者；設計者

Questions 33 and 34 are based on the following report.

　I traveled to the United States from London in the summer of 1977. It was my first trip to America, and it was also the first time I had been overseas. Actually, it was the first time I had ever taken a vacation by myself. Flying was particularly expensive in those days. I stayed with my aunt's family in Philadelphia for five weeks, and got to know my cousin, Robert. He and I would hang out at the local mall, and spend all of our time and money on Asteroids. At the time, it was the latest and greatest in computer game technology, and we thought it was awesome. Now of course, it looks incredibly primitive today.

　在 1977 年的夏天，我從倫敦到美國旅行。那是我第一次到美國，並且也是我第一次到海外。其實，那甚至是我第一次獨自度假。搭飛機在那個時候特別貴。我住在費城的姑姑家五個星期，並認識了我的表弟，羅伯特。我和他常去當地的購物中心，把我們所有的時間和金錢花在小行星上。當時，小行星是最新，也是最偉大的電腦遊戲科技，而且我們認為它是真的很棒。當然，現在它看起來令人難以置信的原始。

** ————————————————

> ***travel to*** 前往　　overseas (ˈovəˈsiz) *adv.* 到海外
> actually (ˈæktʃuəlɪ) *adv.* 實際上　***take a vacation*** 度假
> ***by oneself*** 某人自己；獨自　　flying (ˈflaɪɪŋ) *n.* 飛行；搭飛機
> particularly (pəˈtɪkjələlɪ) *adv.* 特別
> ***in those days*** 在那時候　　stay (ste) *n.* 暫住
> Philadelphia (ˌfɪləˈdɛlfjə) *n.* 費城【位於美國賓州，爲美國第五大城】
> ***get to V.*** 得以～　　cousin (ˈkʌzn̩) *n.* 表（堂）兄弟姊妹
> ***hang out*** 常去某處；閒逛　　mall (mɔl) *n.* 購物中心
> asteroid (ˈæstəˌrɔɪd) *n.* 小行星　　latest (ˈletɪst) *adj.* 最新的
> technology (tɛkˈnɑlədʒɪ) *n.* 技術；工藝
> awesome (ˈɔsəm) *adj.* 很棒的
> incredibly (ɪnˈkrɛdəblɪ) *adv.* 令人難以置信地
> primitive (ˈprɪmətɪv) *adj.* 原始的；舊式的

33. (**A**) What did the speaker do for the first time in 1977?
　　　說話者在 1977 年第一次做了什麼？

　　A. Fly to a foreign country. 搭飛機到外國。

　　B. Meet his British cousin. 見到他的英國表弟。

　　C. Work part-time at a local mall.
　　　在當地購物中心打工。

　　D. Take a vacation with his parents.
　　　與他的雙親一起度假。

　　*****for the first time*** 生平第一次
　　　part-time (ˌpɑrtˈtaɪm) *adv.* 兼差地

34. (**A**) What did the two cousins spend all their money on?
　　　兩個表兄弟把他們的錢都花在哪裡？

　　A. A computer game. 一個電玩遊戲。

　　B. Traveling in America. 在美國旅遊。

　　C. The latest cellphones. 最新型的手機。

D. Looking for primitives. 尋找原始人。

* cellphone (ˈsɛlˌfon) *n.* 手機
primitive (ˈprɪmətɪv) *n.* 原始人

Questions 35 and 36 are based on the following report.

What should you expect and how should you behave
if you have to attend a business meeting in the U.S.A.?
First, arrive on time. Punctuality is very important to
Americans, especially in the Northeast and Midwest.
If you are late, Americans will think you are unreliable.
Second, expect very little friendly conversation before
getting down to business. Time is important to
Americans, and business is done without delay. Third,
although meetings may appear relaxed, they are taken
seriously. Americans tend to be informal and friendly,
but they are still serious. Fourth, if you make a
presentation, it should be direct and to the point. Also,
use statistics. Americans are impressed by hard data
and evidence. Finally, focus on getting a contract signed,
rather than building a relationship. A relationship may
develop later, but the contract comes first.

假如你要前往美國參加一場商務會議，你應該預想什麼且該
如何表現？首先，準時抵達。守時是對美國人很重要，特別是在
東北部和中西部地區。如果你遲到了，美國人會認為你是不可靠
的。其次，要預想在辦正事之前，友好的交談是不多見的。對美
國人來說，時間是非常重要的，而且生意完成不拖延。第三，雖

然會議可能會看來好像很輕鬆，但他們仍認真地看待會議。美國人傾向於不拘禮節的和友好的，但他們仍然是嚴肅的。第四，如果你做一份簡報，簡報應該是直接且一針見血的。此外，使用統計數據。美國人是對實際數據和證據印象深刻的。最後，聚焦在獲得合約的簽訂，而不是建立關係。關係可能以後會發展，但合約是第一位。

**

expect〔ɪkˈspɛkt〕v. 預期
behave〔bɪˈhev〕v. 行為舉止；表現　　attend〔əˈtɛnd〕v. 參加
on time 準時　　punctuality〔ˌpʌŋktʃʊˈælətɪ〕n. 守時；準時
Northeast〔ˈnɔrθˌist〕n. 美國東北部
Midwest〔ˈmɪdˌwɛst〕n. 美國中西部
unreliable〔ˌʌnrɪˈlaɪəbḷ〕adj. 不可信任的
get down to 開始做某事；認真處理某事
delay〔dɪˈle〕n. 延遲　　**without delay** 立刻；馬上
appear〔əˈpɪr〕v. 看來好像　　relaxed〔rɪˈlækst〕adj. 放鬆的
be taken seriously 被認真看待　　**tend to** 易於；傾向於
informal〔ɪnˈfɔrml̩〕adj. 不正式的
presentation〔ˌprɪzɛnˈteʃən〕n. 上台報告；簡報
to the point 切中要點　　statistics〔stəˈtɪstɪks〕n. pl. 統計數字
impressed〔ɪmˈprɛst〕adj. 印象深刻的
hard〔hɑrd〕adj. 可靠的　　data〔ˈdetə〕n. pl. 資料
evidence〔ˈɛvədəns〕n. 證據　　**focus on** 專注於
contract〔ˈkɑntrækt〕n. 契約　　sign〔saɪn〕v. 簽署
rather than 而不是　　build〔bɪld〕v. 建立
develop〔dɪˈvɛləp〕v. 發展　　**come first** 首先要考慮到的

35. (**C**) Which of the following would be a mistake at a business meeting in the U.S.A.?
下列何者在美國的商務會議會是個錯誤？

A. To arrive on time. 準時抵達。

B. To take the meeting seriously. 認真看待會議。

C. To chat for a while before starting.

會議開始前先聊一下天。

D. To use hard data in a presentation.

簡報中運用可靠的資料。

* chat〔tʃæt〕v. 聊天

36. (**C**) Which of the following is the most essential to American businesspeople?

下列哪一項對美國商務人士是最不可或缺的？

A. Preparing a long speech. 準備長篇的演講。

B. Wearing casual clothing. 穿著休閒服飾。

C. Getting a contract signed. 得到合約簽訂。

D. Quickly building a relationship. 快速地建立關係。

* essential〔ɪ'sɛnʃəl〕adj. 必要的；不可或缺的

Questions 37 and 38 are based on the following report.

　　The Children's Museum of Phoenix is a wonderful place of imagination, creativity, and just fun. Designed for children ages zero to ten, this is not your typical museum. Here, we want you to touch *everything.* And with over 48,000 square feet of space, there's plenty to touch. The museum offers more than 300 play experiences. In addition, we offer different types of classes and programs, from music and yoga, to math and science, and our special arts and crafts room is a young artist's dream come true. You can find us in the

heart of downtown Phoenix on the southeast corner of
7th Street. The Children's Museum of Phoenix is a
proud receiver of many awards, including being named
one of the best children's museums in the United States.

　　鳳凰城兒童博物館是一個有想像力、創造力、樂趣的奇妙
地方。這是專為 0 到 10 歲的孩子們所設計的，不是典型的博物
館。在這裡，我們希望你能摸到「所有的事物」。有超過 48,000
平方英尺的空間，讓你能接觸到很多東西。博物館提供超過
300 種遊戲的體驗。此外，我們還提供不同類型的課程，從音
樂和瑜伽，到數學與科學，而且我們的特殊工藝室，是讓小小
藝術家夢想成真的地方。你可以在鳳凰城市中心的第七街東南
角找到我們。鳳凰城兒童博物館得到許多令人驕傲的獎項，包
括被評為美國最好的兒童的博物館之一。

** ─────────────────

　　wonderful〔'wʌndəfəl〕adj. 奇妙的；很棒的
　　imagination〔ɪˌmædʒə'neʃən〕n. 想像力
　　creativity〔ˌkrie'tɪvətɪ〕n. 創造力
　　typical〔'tɪpɪk!〕adj. 典型的　　square〔skwɛr〕adj. 平方的
　　space〔spes〕n. 空間　　plenty〔'plɛntɪ〕n. 很多東西
　　experience〔ɪk'spɪrɪəns〕n. 體驗；經驗
　　in addition 此外　　program〔'progræm〕n. 課程
　　yoga〔'jogə〕n. 瑜珈　　craft〔kræft〕n. 工藝
　　a dream come true 夢想成真
　　downtown〔'daʊnˌtaʊn〕adj. 市中心的
　　southern〔ˌsaʊθ'ist〕adj. 東南方的
　　receiver〔rɪ'sivə〕n. 接受者　　award〔ə'wɔrd〕n. 獎項
　　name〔nem〕v. 把⋯叫做

37. (**D**) What is special about this museum?
　　　此博物館有什麼特別之處？

A. The admission is free. 入館是免費的。
B. It has a souvenir store. 它有紀念品商店。
C. It's popular among teenagers.
　　它在青少年間很受歡迎。
D. Visitors are allowed to touch the exhibits.
　　參觀者可以觸碰館內的展覽品。

* admission〔əd'mɪʃən〕n. 入場　　free〔fri〕adj. 免費的
　souvenir〔'suvə,nɪr〕n. 紀念品
　teenager〔'tin,edʒɚ〕n. 青少年　　exhibit〔ɪg'zɪbɪt〕n. 展覽品

38. (**A**) Who is most likely the target audience of this talk?
　　誰是這段話的目標聽眾？
　　A. Parents of young children. 有幼童的父母。
　　B. Supporters of the museum. 博物館的支持者。
　　C. Senior high school teachers. 高中教師。
　　D. Artists of the City of Phoenix. 鳳凰城的藝術家。

　　* target〔'tɑrgɪt〕n. 目標　　young〔jʌŋ〕adj. 年幼的
　　supporter〔sə'pɔrtɚ〕n. 支持者

Questions 39 and 40 are based on the following report.

　　Few people doubt that online learning can help
teachers be more effective, and make classes more
interesting. What are the trends in online learning?
One is to replace traditional textbooks with more
engaging and interactive ways of learning. Another is
to use the Internet to find great lectures and effective
course materials. And a third trend is the use of social
networks to help teachers and students communicate

and work together. Of course, no one knows exactly
what education will be like in the future, but current
trends make it almost certain that online learning will
play an increasingly important role. In fact, a recent
U.S. Department of Education study showed that
blended learning, which is a combination of online
learning and classroom teaching, improved student
grades by 14 percent.

　　很少有人懷疑線上學習可以幫助老師更能打動人心，而且
使課程更有趣。線上學習的趨勢是什麼？第一個是以更有吸引
力和互動性的學習方式，取代傳統的課本。另一個趨勢是使用
網路來找到很棒的課程和有效的教材。第三個趨勢則是利用社
群網絡來幫助老師和學生溝通，並且共同努力。當然，沒有人
確切知道未來的教育會變得如何，但目前的趨勢使我們幾乎可
以確定，線上學習將扮演一個越來越重要的角色。事實上，最
近一項美國教育部的研究表示，線上學習與課堂教學結合的混
合式學習，能提高學生的成績達 14%。

doubt〔daʊt〕v. 懷疑　　online〔'ɑn,laɪn〕adj. 線上的
effective〔ɪ'fɛktɪv〕adj. 有效的；給人深刻印象的
trend〔trɛnd〕n. 趨勢　　replace〔rɪ'ples〕v. 取代
traditional〔trə'dɪʃənḷ〕adj. 傳統的
textbook〔'tɛkst,bʊk〕n. 教科書
engaging〔ɪn'gedʒɪŋ〕adj. 有魅力的
interactive〔,ɪntə'æktɪv〕adj. 相互作用的；互動的
material〔mə'tɪrɪəl〕n. 材料；資料
social〔'soʃəl〕adj. 社會的；社交的
network〔'nɛt,wɜk〕n. 網路
communicate〔kə'mjunə,ket〕v. 傳達

work together 合作　　exactly〔ɪg'zæktlɪ〕*adv.* 確切地
current〔'kɜənt〕*adj.* 目前的　　certain〔'sɜtn̩〕*adj.* 確定的
increasingly〔ɪn'krisɪŋlɪ〕*adv.* 越來越
department〔dɪ'pɑrtmənt〕*n.* 部門；部
blended〔'blɛndɪd〕*adj.* 混合的
combination〔,kɑmbə'neʃən〕*n.* 組合；結合（體）
improve〔ɪm'pruv〕*v.* 改善；增進　　grade〔gred〕*n.* 成績

39.（**C**）According to the report, which of the following is **NOT**
a trend in online learning?
根據這份報告，下列何者不是線上學習的趨勢？
A. Using social networks to help communication.
運用社群網路以幫助溝通。
B. Replacing textbooks with other ways of learning.
用其他學習的方式取代教科書。
C. Replacing interactive learning with classroom
teaching. 用課堂教學取代互動式學習。
D. Using the Internet to find lectures and course
materials. 運用網路找演講和課程教材。

40.（**D**）What is "blended learning"? 什麼是「混合式教學」？
A. Effective and interesting online teaching.
有效且有趣的線上教學。
B. Combining different kinds of news media.
結合各種不同的新聞媒體。
C. A blending of all the resources of the Internet.
混合各種網路上的資源。
D. A mix of online learning and classroom teaching.
混合線上學習學和課堂教學。
* combine〔kəm'baɪn〕*v.* 結合　　mix〔mɪks〕*n.* 混合

高中英語聽力測驗詳解 ①

主　　　編 / 李 冠 勳

發 行 所 / 學習出版有限公司　　☎ (02) 2704-5525

郵 撥 帳 號 / 05127272 學習出版社帳戶

登 記 證 / 局版台業 2179 號

印 刷 所 / 裕強彩色印刷有限公司

台 北 門 市 / 台北市許昌街 10 號 2 F　　☎ (02) 2331-4060

台灣總經銷 / 紅螞蟻圖書有限公司　　☎ (02) 2795-3656

美國總經銷 / Evergreen Book Store　　☎ (818) 2813622

本公司網址　www.learnbook.com.tw

電 子 郵 件　learnbook@learnbook.com.tw

書 + MP3 一片售價：新台幣二百八十元正

2014 年 10 月 1 日初版

4713269380948